Basic Fly Tying

CHARLIE CRAVEN'S

Basic Fly Tying

CHARLIE CRAVEN

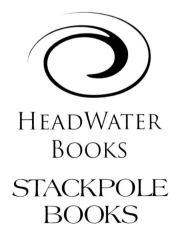

HEADWATER
BOOKS

STACKPOLE
BOOKS

Published by
HEADWATER BOOKS
531 Harding Street
New Cumberland, PA 17070
www.headwaterbooks.com

STACKPOLE BOOKS
5067 Ritter Road
Mechanicsburg, PA 17055
www.stackpolebooks.com

Printed in China

First edition

10 9 8 7 6 5 4 3 2 1

ISBN: 978-0-9793460-2-6

Cover design by Caroline Stover
Cover photographs by Charlie Craven

Library of Congress Control Number: 2008922044

For my wife Kris and our three great kids,
Charlie, Julie, and Jack. I love you all.

Contents

Acknowledgments

I have been fortunate in my life to meet and work with so many fine people who have freely given their time and experience to help me get to where I am today. I am truly in awe of their generosity.

Thanks to my parents, Dick and Cece Craven, for always encouraging me. Only with your support and advice could I have come this far.

Thanks to my oldest and dearest friend Ross Bartholomay for being a sturdy sounding board and providing a voice of reason and unending support over the years, and to Matt Prowse, my newest, dearest friend, for many great days on the water, the gift of hilarity, and rowing me down the river more than I deserve.

Thanks to Van Rollo and Erik Johnson. Without your help and support I would not be what I am today, and for this I will never thank you enough. Thanks to Umpqua Feather Merchants for support, encouragement, and the avenue to market my flies to the masses. Thanks to Michael White for always being there with a young gun's perspective. I am fortunate to call you my friend.

Much appreciation goes out to my good friend John Barr for having the faith in my photography skills to let me shoot the pictures for his book, the years of advice and guidance, and for always saying what needs to be said. Thanks to Greg Garcia, for all the feedback, politely telling me when to rein it in, and all that you do for Charlie's Fly Box. Many thanks to Jay Nichols of Headwater Books for hours of editing, unending encouragement, and having the guts to give me the opportunity to write this book.

And finally, thanks to my wonderful wife, Kris, and my three great kids, Charlie, Julie, and Jack. You make my life complete and keep me grounded. Without you, none of this matters. Having your support and love makes me lucky to be living my dream—stroking my ego doesn't hurt either.

Introduction

JAY NICHOLS PHOTO

This is the part where the author gets to go on and on about his years of experience, tells you why you should listen to his advice above all others, and gets to toot his horn for as long as he can capture your attention. Here, the reader can get a good idea of the overall tone of the upcoming book, and perhaps decide just how much attention to pay to the techniques and advice forthcoming.

That being said, I am going to come right out and say that I am just an average guy of average intelligence who just so happens to have tied a whole bundle of flies

in my life. I have been a commercial fly tier for nearly thirty years now, and in that time have tied flies for almost every species of gamefish in nearly every location in the world, though I mostly tie trout flies for the Rocky Mountain region of the United States.

I started tying flies with a kit given to me by my parents when I was about eight years old. It was of little consequence that I knew nothing about tying flies and only had a small pamphlet explaining how to go about it. I dove right in, and I tied every one of those pretty little bits of fluff contained in the kit to hooks, producing some

Fly tying is not rocket science. Tie enough flies with perfection as a goal, and your technique will improve. (You'll also fill your boxes in the meantime.)

Commercial tiers have developed tricks for speed, quality, and consistency in fly patterns.

of what were, in hindsight, the ugliest flies ever created. Many of my flies were tied inside out and backward, as I generally would start at the front of the hook and work to the rear. These abominations caught the local sunfish just fine, and I thought perhaps that I was truly gifted. Little did I realize that fly tying would later play a big part in my life. I still remember rushing home from school each day to sit down and tie as much as I could. I was enthralled with every bit of fur and feathers from the kit and even took to harvesting some of my own materials from our backyard songbirds. (Never leave an eight-year-old unattended with a BB gun.)

My tying improved dramatically after I mowed our neighbor's lawn for five weeks to save enough money to buy a copy of Jack Dennis' *Western Trout Fly Tying Manual Volume 1.* Up until this book, I had no formal instruction, and I had yet to see anyone else tie a fly. Dennis' book really got my juices flowing and kept me at the bench until all hours of the night. I fell in love with tying and even remember my mom actually "grounding" me from tying flies at one point as a punishment for some forgotten sin. (It probably had something to do with that BB gun.)

From those days forward, I tied every evening and all day on weekends. Eventually, I became good enough to land small jobs tying flies for friends and family, which then led to tying commercially for a fly distributor in Thornton, Colorado. Monte Andres ran a little company

called The Rocky Mountain Fisherman and bought flies from local tiers and then distributed them to local outdoor shops and gas stations. He ran an ad in the newspaper looking for tiers, and my father pointed out to me that perhaps I could make this into a real job and even save up enough money to buy my first car. I was about twelve years old at the time, and the prospect of being paid to tie flies was like someone offering to pay me to play in the yard.

I got the job with Monte, and that was the beginning of my commercial fly tying career. Since then, I have tied flies for most of the Denver-area shops, building lifelong relationships with some of the best tiers and fishermen in Colorado. I have to take this chance to thank those patient folks for putting up with a young kid and all his questions over the years. Folks like George and Dot Mayer, Tim Heng, Roy Palm, Terry and Lori Nicholson, Bill Schappel, and Ken Walters offered me opportunities to tie flies for their shops and helped me so much along the way. I owe much to these fine folks and feel fortunate to have known them for as long as I have.

When I was in middle school, I began teaching basic beginning fly-tying classes for a local fishing and hunting store. I later taught classes for some of the finer shops in the Denver area, which may have taught me more about fly tying than I have taught my students.

Tying and teaching eventually led to guiding trout fishermen on the South Platte River, a job that I enjoyed to no end. Alas, I finally learned to do the math and realized that guiding was no way to raise a family. I gave it up to run a fly shop in Boulder, Colorado, but I quickly knew that working for someone else just wasn't for me.

In late 2004, with the help of friends and family, I was able to open a fly shop of my own. Charlie's Fly Box is located in Arvada, Colorado, not far from where I now live. It had been a lifelong dream to first make my passion my avocation, and secondly, to do it under my own roof. The shop has been a huge success, and I look forward to going to work every day. I am so lucky to be graced with the opportunity to do what I love and have made many friends in the process. So, there's my life story in a nutshell. Here's what it means to you.

Having been a commercial tier for most of my life, I have developed (and borrowed) quite a few nifty little tricks to facilitate quicker, easier, and more efficient fly tying. From a commercial standpoint, time is money because the more flies you can tie in a given period of time, the more money you make. Many of these tips used for speed and efficiency can help the recreational tier—tying a fly in six steps instead of nine makes every-one more productive and efficient. To the commercial tier this means more money in less time, while for the hobbyist this makes for more flies in the box. And we all know there is no such thing as too many flies.

What I hope to convey in this book is the idea that anyone can learn to tie flies well, given a modicum of manual dexterity, the willingness to learn, and the ability to reason. Much of fly tying is merely a compilation of skills learned one at a time. Developing these skills takes time and practice but is not beyond the capability of anyone with at least an average level of intelligence and dexterity. There is very little magic involved in lashing fur and feathers to a hook, but reading some books would make it seem as though one needs a Wizardology degree to even get started. Fly tying is not that hard.

I first began writing what has become this book over fifteen years ago. It started as a set of handwritten notes to copy and hand out in my fly-tying classes. It always bothered me that students had to concentrate on writing notes during class instead of watching and learning. I later added simple line drawings to help things along, and finally, with the advent of digital cameras,

Fly tying is not that hard. With determination and practice, you'll be tying great looking flies in no time.

Tie flies by the dozen or at least the half dozen so you can refine your proportions on tough flies like Humpies (above).

started adding photos to the directions. It was a long road to figure out how to work the camera well enough to produce good pictures, and I still don't consider myself a "photographer." Photography is hard; fly tying is easy.

My basic philosophy of fly tying is that there are few problems or issues that can't be solved by familiarity with a material, practice, and persistence. Becoming familiar with a material comes from using it, noting how it reacts when tied to a hook, and understanding its properties. Practice is what you do to gain this familiarity and persistence is what keeps you from giving up on it all when it doesn't work well the first time.

Problem solving is also a huge part of tying flies, and when students ask me how to do this or that, I often respond by asking, "How do *you* think you should do it?" I love to see new tiers think their way through something and figure it out on their own. Most of my own tying skills were developed in this manner, as I had no one to ask in most cases. I will show you all sorts of tips and

tricks and techniques in this book, all proven to work well and resulting in wonderful flies, but all I can do here is show you how I tie the flies. It is up to you to learn how *you* tie them. If a material or technique isn't working the way you think it should, ask yourself, "What can I do to fix this?" If thread torque is pushing a material around the far side of the hook shank when you try to tie it down, it won't do any good to make fifty more turns over it. You'll need to outsmart that thread torque. Undoubtedly, you are smarter than a lowly spool of thread.

On another note, I've always hated dry textbook-style writing and have done my best to inject a bit of levity into this book. I believe a little humor here and there helps to break things up and helps us remember that these are just flies, not nuclear reactors. If you tie a bad one, cut the materials from the hook and start over. Even better, give it away to someone who doesn't tie their own flies yet. Chances are they'll think it's great and will heap praise on you to all their friends. Remember, you are doing this for fun.

Practice these flies to learn basic techniques that you can use to tie many other patterns.

In closing, and as a thank you for reading this far, I will now give you the secret to tying beautiful fish-catching flies with efficiency: Practice, practice, practice.

It is now your job to go through this book, tying the flies in the order they are presented and mastering the techniques as you go. I have built this book and my fly-tying classes on this cumulative and comprehensive approach, feeding various techniques and materials to you in the form of effective, fish-catching flies. Few patterns truly branch out from traditional techniques. Practice these flies to learn basic techniques that you can use to tie many other patterns. When you are faced with a fly that at first looks challenging or complex, such as a Stimulator or Copper John, you will have the confidence to analyze it and break it into a series of techniques and steps that will be familiar to you after working through this book.

You will need to tie several dozens of each of these flies to get even a rudimentary understanding of what you are doing. Buy your hooks by the hundred and

don't complain about using them up. Tie lots and lots of flies. This is how you learn to tie flies. You have to actually sit down and do it. It's even better if you sit down and do it every day. Leave your vise and tools out where you can get to them easily and make a point of tying at least a few flies every day. If you bury your tools and materials away in a box or drawer, it takes that much more effort to drag them out and practice.

Tie flies by the dozen or at least the half dozen. Tying one fly at a time only assures that you will forget what you did wrong on that fly by the next time you sit down to tie. Tying multiple flies at a sitting allows you to make minor adjustments to the amount of hair or dubbing, how much thread tension you're applying, and the proportions of the fly while they are still fresh in your mind.

If tails, wings, or other body proportions are off when you tie them in, fix them immediately. I know this sounds obvious, but you'd be surprised how many times a student brings me an otherwise perfect fly, and I say,

You will need to tie several dozens of each of these flies to get even a rudimentary understanding of what you are doing.

"The tail is a little long," and they reply, "Yeah, I noticed that when I tied it in." *Then why didn't you fix it?* I think. The whip-finish does not magically fix any errors you've made in the tying process, so be sure that *you* do.

Don't ever give up on a technique as "just too hard." If you give up and admit defeat, you assure that you will never learn that technique. Stick with it and persevere to conquer the task at hand. Tiers that say things like "I don't tie dry flies because I'm not very good at it" aren't realizing the reason they are not good at it is because they don't practice enough.

Please also promise that you will never utter the terrible phrase, "The fish don't care." I most often hear this from someone who ties ugly flies as a way of justifying their incompetence. Truthfully, the fish don't care in most instances, but they're pea-brained water dwellers, so we can't exactly go around asking them for approval. If you're going to do something, do it right. Don't justify poor technique and ugly flies with the comment "It will still catch fish." Of course it will catch fish—so do worms and cheese. If it was just about catching fish you'd be reading a book on purse seining or long lining. Strive for excellent flies and great technique and do not settle for less. When I take a fly out of my vise, I nearly always say, "I can do better." And on every fly I tie, I honestly try to do that.

CHAPTER 1

How to Use This Book

I have put this book together in the same order that I teach these flies in my fly-tying classes. The techniques build on each other, adding and expanding on new techniques with each fly. To fully grasp the techniques and flies used in this book, start at the beginning and tie the flies in the order they are presented. We will start with some simple patterns, the Brassie and Black Beauty, which may tempt you to skip ahead to some of the more eye-catching flies later in the book. Resist. The first few flies presented here lay the groundwork for many of the methods used later in the text. Once I have explained a technique on a pattern, I will typically just refer back to the fly that it was introduced in, rather than explaining every step of every fly. It is up to you to col-

lect all these tips and tidbits as you go. Stacking the hair for a Stimulator tail is exactly the same as stacking the hair for the wing of the Elk Hair Caddis, so I feel it is redundant to photograph and explain these steps several times over. The methods used to attach various materials are outlined both in the Attachment Techniques chapter and on the first fly that uses them.

It has been my experience that presenting the flies and techniques this way prevents students from becoming overwhelmed with choices, ideas, and notions. Take baby steps to start, paying close attention to the directions, as they all come more into play as you progress through the book.

The techniques for the flies in this book (above) build on each other, adding and expanding on new techniques with each fly.

1

RIGHT- OR LEFT-HANDED TYING

If you look closely while flipping through this book, you may note that I tie left-handed. I started tying this way when I was a kid because the cheap vise I had was tightened down with a wing nut that just happened to be on the left side of the vise. It seemed to me that the knob should face me, so I set the vise up with the jaws facing to my left. Everything about this has worked out fine for me so far, but that is not the reason I am bringing this up here.

Teaching fly-tying classes over the years, I've noticed that if you are naturally right-handed it is often easier to learn to tie with your *left* hand, and vice versa. That is, a naturally right-handed tier would wrap the thread with his left hand, with the jaws of the vise pointing to his left. This method leaves your weaker hand the single task of wrapping and controlling the thread and lets you transfer some of the more delicate and precise work to your dominant hand. The dominant hand can, in this case, freely work the scissors and place materials on the hook. After watching people try to tie using the conventional method and struggle to place wings on the hook using their weak hand, it occurred to me that it could be a lot easier if I started folks off tying the way I do. The use of the dominant hand to do the technical work just made more sense to me. It was actually kind of enlightening when I figured out that it is indeed tough to do so many fly tying tasks because you are doing them with your weak hand. Granted, fly tiers need to be at least a little bit ambidextrous anyway, but transferring some of this more specific work to the dominant hand has proven to be a valuable practice.

Other advantages of off-handed tying are:

Hand-to-hand wraps are now made predominantly with your strong hand, allowing better control over the placement and spacing of materials.

Your strong hand is now at the rear of the hook, making it easier to access the materials and letting you use the hook shank and the vise to help brace your hand for better positioning.

With your strong hand at the rear of the hook, tilting wire and hackle wraps slightly back toward the bend to butt them together becomes easier. Wraps made with the thread hand tend to spiral forward a bit, often spacing the turns too much.

Wrapping the thread with your left hand will untwist the thread so it lies flat along the hook, forming a smooth underbody. Right-handed tying results in a tightly-corded thread that requires constant untwisting to keep it flat.

The scissors are used in the dominant hand, again, from the rear side of the hook. Making tapered cuts from the generally more slender back end of the fly is easier and more precise than the same cut from the front.

With the bobbin and scissors hand separated, there is no risk of breaking your thread and sending the scissor tips back into your face. Carrying the scissors in your hand is part of efficient tying; stabbing your eye out is not.

I introduced this idea into my classes about twelve years ago and have had few people who gave it an honest try disagree with me. The only caveat is that if you have tied in the conventional manner for any length of time it can be very hard to make the switch. Of course, I'm not saying that you can't become a great tier by tying right-handed, but I think you can become a great tier faster by tying left-handed.

While I admit that I have justified most of this technique with after-the-fact arguments, right-handed tiers generally do the same thing. No one likes change, and I am absolutely not suggesting that you switch from right- to left-handed tying in midstream. As I said before, making the switch can be nearly impossible if you have already developed the habits and techniques inherent in right-handed tying. If you are just beginning your tying career, however, I believe that left-handed tying is easier, more efficient and intuitive, and will result in better flies.

All this being said, after a cage match with my publisher, we agreed to flip all the photos to adhere to the conventional right-handed tying method. I guess even I have to bow down to The Man sometimes.

THE LINGO

Note: For hook terminology, see chapter 3, page 17.

Tail: Extends from the hook bend, imitates the tail of the bug and helps the heaviest part of the hook (the bend) on dry flies float.

Ribbing: Wire, tinsel, or other material spiral-wrapped through the body or abdomen to reinforce or add segmentation and flash.

Abdomen: Commonly referred to as the body of the fly, this is the rear portion of the fly (usually 50 to 75 percent of the total hook length).

Wing case: Quill section of turkey, duck, or goose feather or synthetics like Thin Skin or Swiss Straw pulled over the thorax to imitate the wing buds of the natural.

Thorax: Front section of the fly body, sometimes covered by a wing case. Usually the front 25 to 50 percent of the total hook length.

Wings: Hair, feather, or synthetic material tied in on the front portion (exactly where varies with the pattern) of the hook to imitate the wings of the natural insect; generally classified as upright for mayflies or down for caddis and stoneflies.

Hackle collar: Hackle feather or feathers wrapped in the thorax area of a dry fly or nymph, forming a bushy collar.

Palmering: To rib or spiral-wrap a hackle feather through the abdomen or thorax of a fly. Applies to dry flies such as Stimulators, nymphs, and some streamers such as Woolly Buggers.

Forward: Toward the hook eye, as in "wrap forward to the 50 percent point."

Back (or backward): Toward the hook bend.

Thread hand: The hand you wrap the thread with. If you are tying right-handed, you will wrap the thread with your right hand; if you tie left-handed, like I do, you will wrap the thread with your left hand.

Material hand: The other hand that you place and wrap materials with. For right-handed tiers, that is your left hand; for left-handed tiers, your right.

Travel/spiral wraps: Thread wraps with wide spaces between them used to travel from one point on the hook to another, not necessarily binding anything down. Spiral wraps are like the stripe on a barber pole.

Concentric wraps: Thread or other material wrapped so they are abutting each other. No spaces should show between them and the wraps should at least touch each other on the edges and possibly even overlap (in the case of thread).

Posting: Wrapping thread around the base of a wing to gather the material into a single clump. See Parachute Blue-Winged Olive, chapter 20.

Helicopter: To break off wire by rotating it in a circular motion.

Pinch wrap: Using the fingers of your material hand to hold and pinch a material in place while simultaneously pinching a loop of thread. The pinch wrap allows you to counteract thread torque and place materials on the top of the hook with ease.

Dubbing: Used as a noun, dubbing refers to natural or synthetic fur, or even a mix of the two, that is twisted around the tying thread and then used to build bodies on flies. Used as a verb, the word means the actual act of twisting the fur onto the thread.

Thread torque: The propensity of the thread tension to push or pull materials around the shank as you try to bind them down.

X-wraps: X-wraps divide a clump of material into two separate bunches by crossing from front to back and then back to front or vice versa. I use X-wraps in place of the more common figure-eight wraps, as the X-wraps don't influence the other clump of material as figure-eight wraps do.

Butt ends: The butt ends of hair or a feather are the ends that were previously attached to the hide or stem. Butts are typically thicker and more ragged than the tips.

Tip ends: Tip ends are the natural tips of the hair or feather fibers being tied in. The tip ends of these fibers typically taper to a point.

CHAPTER 2

Tools

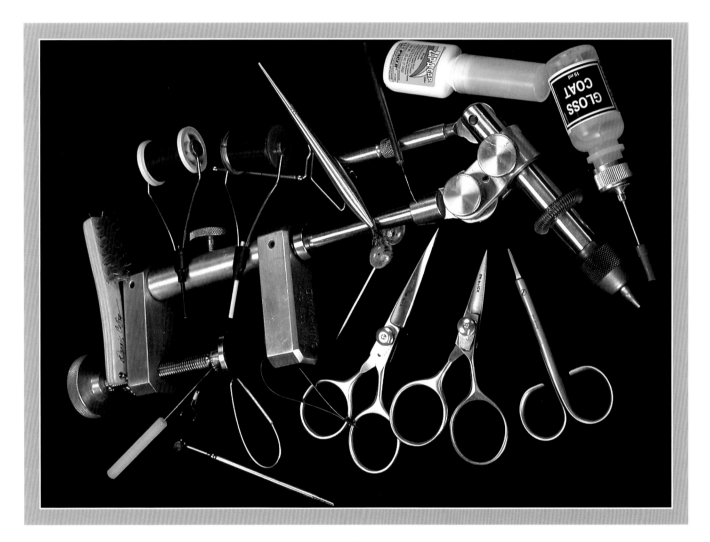

Okay, so you've decided to take up fly tying. You realize that you need some tools, so you roll down to the local fly shop and take stock of what they have to offer. This is where things can get a little hairy—vises run upward of $300, bobbins run up to $80, there are a mind-boggling array of scissors and several varieties of whip-finishing tools, and the curmudgeon in the back of the shop is telling you to just skip them altogether and tie your whip-finishes by hand. It's a lot to digest.

Keep one thing in mind at this point—you get what you pay for. I hate to see folks come into class with a cheap tool kit, because it tells me two things: They are going to have to go through a lot of unnecessary frustration because the tools just don't work, and they are going to end up buying better stuff before the class is over. I see this happen all the time both with tying tools and rods and reels. While many low-priced tools and kits are available, they tend to be of poor quality. Top-quality tools will make a difference in the quality of your flies.

A selection of quality tools makes your tying faster, easier, and more efficient, and it will save you money in the long run.

Buying the best you can afford will make your tying easier, less stressful, and save you money in the long run. You won't have to buy the tools twice—once the cheap way and once the right way.

Based on my own experience, I offer the following recommendations and explanations of each tool that I routinely use. I rarely use a tool where good technique will suffice. Give these a chance but don't feel obligated to use them, as you are the best judge of what will work for you. Incidentally, I have not been paid to recommend any of the tools listed below. They are my recommendations based on years of use and functionality; I do not make any of them or receive any compensation for their use here.

VISE

The vise is the most important tying tool. Yes, I am well aware that you can tie flies without a vise, but that feat is more of a parlor trick than a practical answer to tying. A vise needs to do two things: It should hold the hook tightly enough to prevent it from slipping while you tie, and it should be sturdy enough to not move while you're tying. Your vise should be able to hold a variety of hook sizes securely. You may think you'll never tie large saltwater, bass, or pike flies, but you will. When you get into tying, it takes on a life of its own. Soon you'll be booking trips to Belize or planning a weekend trip for northern pike. Save yourself the trouble and get a vise that will do it all the first time around.

The first option to consider is whether you want a model with a pedestal base or a C-clamp. The pedestal base is handy for traveling where you never know what kind of surface will be available to tie on. It's also nice if you don't have a designated fly-tying area. You can put a pedestal base down on the kitchen table, tie some flies, and then easily put it away. The down side to pedestal bases is that they are seldom heavy enough for serious thread tension, such as when tying large deer-hair bass flies or even winging Humpies and Wulffs. I can tip most pedestal bases over when I really crank down on the thread.

C-clamps are more secure. It drives me nuts to have my vise move around while I tie, and the C-clamp eliminates any movement from the vise itself. I can also adjust the head height of the vise (something you can't do, or can't do much of, with a pedestal base version) so that it is exactly where I want it. The only downsides to the C-clamp are the clamp may not be large enough to fit over the edge of your tying table, be it at home or traveling, and your significant other may have a problem with you clamping your vise onto the dining room table.

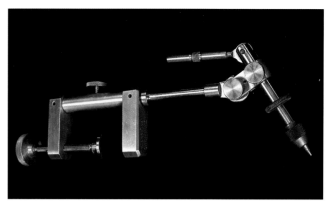

Dyna-King Professional, C-clamp vise.

Some vises have interchangeable jaws. Generally, the jaws that come in the vise are sufficient for most tying, but midge and magnum jaws are available for tying extra small or extra large flies.

Another option available in a vise is rotary or standard. Rotary vise jaws allow the hook to be positioned so the shank rotates in a single plane, allowing you to hold onto the materials and rotate the hook, rather than wrap the material around the hook as with a standard vise. This can be helpful when wrapping hackles and ribbing materials as it lets you see the material more clearly and control it better. I find rotary vises to be more trouble than they are worth. While they can be really cool to watch someone tie with, I find that you can spend more time learning to use the vise than learning to tie flies. Everything they do can be done just as well with your fingers, and you already know how to use them. I also find that the angle of the jaws on a rotary vise is such that there is no place to rest and stabilize your hand when tying in wings and the like. I don't believe in using a tool to do the work when it adds to the work.

The jaws on standard-style vises are at a slight, and sometimes adjustable, angle. I prefer these because the vise collar is positioned conveniently as a rest to lend stability to the material hand, the hook bend is more exposed, and the hook is more available for material application. Many standard vises also offer a rotary mode, where the jaws will turn in a 360-degree circle, albeit, with the hook shank out of line and wobbly. I use this rotary function often to check the far side of the fly or reposition the fly so that gravity works to my advantage. I never use it to wrap material.

Now, for my personal recommendation. I have used a C-clamp Dyna-King Pro for the past twenty years and find it to be flawless in its hook holding, sturdiness, and versatility. The jaws on all Dyna-King vises have two notches to hold large hooks and a serrated tip for smaller hooks. The Pro has an adjustable head angle and rotary function, so you can turn the fly in the vise to view the other side. The vise is stainless steel and aluminum and is a solid piece of machinery made for heavy use. If you are going to get serious about tying, get one of these. I say "serious" because this vise carries a price tag of around $300. This is a pretty penny for something to hold a fish hook, but you'll never need to buy another. If you're not quite so serious, Dyna-King makes a whole series of vises that have essentially identical jaws and hook-holding features with varying degrees of adjustment that start at around $135. The Voyager II and Kingfisher are both excellent vises in a more reasonable price range.

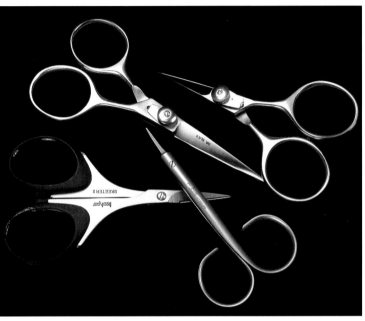

Use different scissors for different jobs. Clockwise from bottom left: Kershaw Skeeter Scissors, Dr. Slick 5-inch Razor Scissors, Dr. Slick 4-inch Razor Scissors, and Rubis Micro-Tip Scissors.

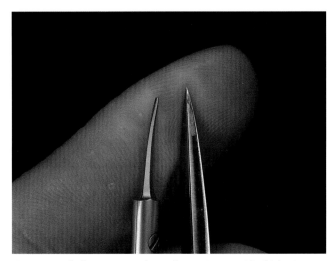

Scissors with fine tips cut closer than scissors with thick tips. Check the width of the blades from the side as shown here to determine the blades' thickness.

SCISSORS

The next most important tool is a good pair of scissors. I use different types of scissors for different applications. I like a pair with long blades for cutting heavy materials like deer and elk hair or for cutting long strips of Thin Skin or wing material sheeting. I use a short, fine-tip pair for small flies and fine work, and I use scissors with curved blades for trimming materials into a curved shape. I also keep an old or cheap pair of scissors on hand for trimming wire and heavy materials so I don't dull my good ones.

I recommend the 4- and 5-inch Dr. Slick Razor Scissors, the Rubis Micro-Tip Scissors, and the Kershaw Skeeter Scissor. Wiss-Clip style sewing scissors drive me bananas and have tips and handles that are too wide and clunky for my tastes. I use the Dr. Slick scissors as my main, general-use scissors. Cutting hair, hackle feathers, synthetics, and the like are no problem for these wickedly sharp scissors, and their tips are fine enough to make precise clean cuts in most instances.

For fine work such as clipping hackle fibers and stems, trimming individual fibers, and making precise cuts on flies of all sizes, I use Rubis Micro-Tip Scissors. Scissors cut at the center of the tips' width. If your scissor blades are thick, it is much harder to make a clean, flush cut on any material without exaggerated difficulty. Fine, narrow-tip scissors cut thread tags much closer. Material stubs and wing measurements will be much more accurately placed when clipped with fine-tip scissors as well.

I use the Skeeter Scissors as heavy-duty cutters for large, coarse materials like chenille, yarn, and stiff synthetics like Super Hair and fine wire. Having a heavy-duty pair of scissors handy keeps you from using your good scissors to cut this hard stuff, which makes the good scissors last longer.

To trim wire from the spool, use an old pair of scissors, wire cutters, or fingernail clippers to keep the tips of your good scissors in shape for more precise cutting jobs. Never use good scissors to cut wire. When working with wire on a fly, don't use scissors to cut it. Twist the tag end of heavier-gauge wire around like a helicopter propeller; snap off fine wire with a sharp tug.

For the past several years I have shaved the outside edge of the tips on my fine-tip scissors with a small file to make them thinner. Because blade thickness determines how close to the hook shank you can cut (the cutting edges on a pair of scissors are on the inside of the blades), thinning them makes for much closer and more precise cuts. Be careful not to file the cutting edges and not to make the blades too thin.

Never put your scissors down while you tie! Keeping the scissors in your hand is quicker and more efficient.

Most tying scissors have serrated blades, which prevent hair and other materials from sliding out of the tips as you close them. I prefer scissors with micro-serrations to the ones with coarse serrations, which can leave ragged edges on the material. Micro-serrations keep materials from slipping without leaving rough edges.

All of these scissors have either adjustable finger holes or large finger holes that make it much easier to hold the scissors in your hand while you tie. Why put them down only to have to pick them up again three seconds later? Learn to tie with your scissors in your hand; it makes things easier and more efficient. I put one loop around my ring finger and my thumb in the other, withdrawing my thumb when needed.

When trimming material, such as hackle feathers, chenille, or thread tags, pull it above the hook while the working thread hangs below, and trim it flush with the shank. This removes the material from the vicinity of the thread and prevents you from accidentally cutting the thread. When trimming materials or thread, use the very tips of your scissors and brace your hand against the vise to assure you make a clean, precise cut.

BOBBIN

In Europe they call these bobbin holders, while here in America we just call them bobbins. No matter what you call it, this tool holds and keeps tension on the spool of thread while you tie. You really only need one bobbin to tie flies, but you will end up with several. The last time I counted, I had about twenty-five. You never really go out and buy three or four bobbins at once. They're one of those things you save for an unexcused trip to the fly shop on a rainy day and pick one up here and there. Having several bobbins threaded and at the ready makes

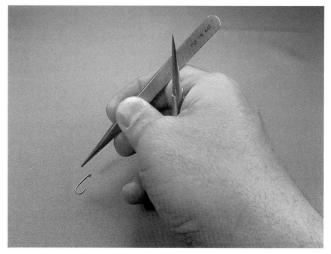

Keeping the scissors looped onto your ring finger allows you to palm them and use the rest of your hand as needed.

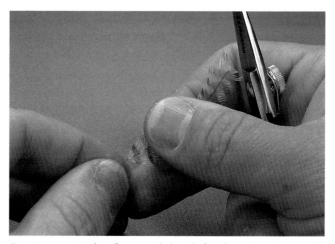

Leaving your index finger and thumb free from the scissors will let you do fine work without putting the scissors down.

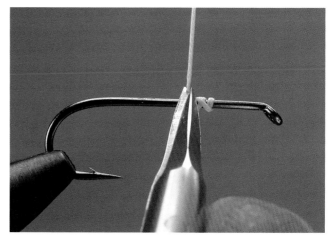

To trim a material close to the hook shank, lay the scissor blades in around the material and push them toward the hook shank while you simultaneously pull out on the material. Pushing and pulling like this assures a closer cut and less stub end.

From left to right: Tiemco ergonomic bobbin, Tiemco large-tube ceramic bobbin, Tiemco standard-tube ceramic bobbin, C&F Midge Bobbin, and Matarelli Bobbin. There are several good bobbins on the market, but I prefer the Tiemco models above all others.

tying easier because you don't have to search for a new color or size of thread and mount it in the bobbin for each new fly you tie.

Avoid cheap bobbins with cheap metal tubes. Every wrap you make with the thread around the hook runs the thread around the inside of the bobbin tube. Eventually, this wears a metal tube down until it becomes sharp. A sharp bobbin tube cuts or frays the thread, which is extremely frustrating. The Matarelli Bobbin is an excep-

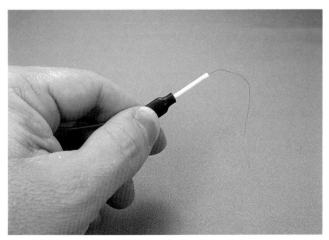

How you hold the bobbin—by the yoke (where the tube and the legs meet), by the tube, or just by one of the legs—is a matter of personal preference. I like to control thread tension by feathering the spool with my fingers of my thread hand.

tion. It is well made and has been durable in my experience. Another pet peeve I have is the cheapo knock-off ceramic insert bobbins that have a small ring of ceramic or, worse yet, plastic at the tip of the tube. These inserts make the bobbins harder to thread without another tool called a bobbin threader. A bobbin needs a tube made entirely of ceramic material because the thread passes all the way through this tube and touches both ends. An insert at the tip end only helps prevent fraying at the tip.

Brass feet are much smoother than plastic feet and allow the thread spool to rotate smoothly and add weight to the bobbin. The weight not only helps hold materials in place, but it prevents the bobbin from spinning out of control when you twist or untwist your thread. Plastic feet often have mill marks on them that catch the spool and prevent it from feeding the thread out smoothly. I use Tiemco bobbins. They have ceramic tubes and brass feet that fit into the thread spool. The ceramic will never wear out and the brass feet feed thread out more smoothly than plastic ones. These bobbins are available in standard tube diameters (for most applications) and heavy (larger) tube diameters for heavier threads and flosses as well as with offset legs that position the thread so it feeds directly into the tube. Tiemco also makes an ergonomic bobbin with an offset yoke to more comfortably fit into your hand. I use both the Standard Tiemco Ceramic and Heavy Tiemco Ceramic

Bobbins for most of my tying. I find the Ergonomic and Offset Bobbins a bit cumbersome, and because they are not symmetrical, they won't spin freely when you twist or untwist the thread.

The legs of a brand new bobbin will typically be pretty tight. To adjust the tension, pull the legs apart a little at a time to lighten the tension or push them together to increase it. The right amount of tension is a personal preference and varies with thread size, but it should be tight enough to keep the thread from coming off the spool under the force of gravity and loose enough to feed out when you apply a reasonable amount of tension.

To thread the bobbin, cut the end of the thread cleanly, place the end in the bottom of the bobbin tube, put the front end of the bobbin in your mouth, and suck the thread through the tube. It is much simpler than it sounds. If you're just starting out tying, your bobbin will be all clean and shiny. Once you've tied for awhile, you may one day discover that you can no longer suck the thread through the tube. What has happened is the wax has rubbed off the thread and clogged the inside of the bobbin tube or you got a little too generous with your dubbing and let some of it get down in the tube.

To clean the bobbin tube, run both ends of a piece of heavy monofilament (3X diameter) up through the tube from the bottom, leaving the loop exposed. Slip an inch-long half strand of polypropylene yarn into the loop and pull it up through the bobbin tube, pulling firmly on the two loose ends that extend from the top of the bobbin. The yarn will just barely fit through the tube, and you'll have to pull hard and steady, but when the yarn comes out the other end, all the gunk that was in the tube will be pulled out along with it.

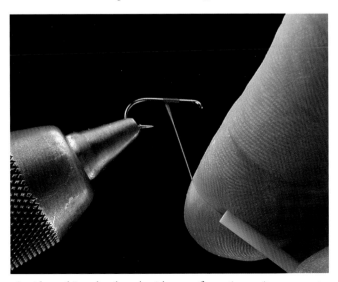

Avoid touching the thread with your fingertips as it comes out of the bobbin tube because this can fray the thread.

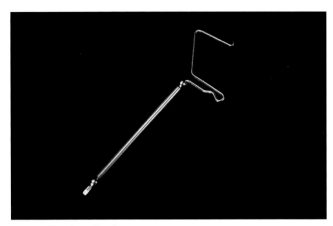

Matarelli whip-finisher.

WHIP-FINISHER

A whip-finisher ties the knot at the end of the fly, which is essentially a nail knot (like you tie your leader to your fly line with). I prefer to use a tool to tie the whip-finish rather than tie it by hand because the tool is always smooth (unlike your fingers) and ties the knot exactly where you want it. There is only one kind of whip-finisher to buy, and that is a Matarelli. This tool is hand-made and polished so it spins freely and doesn't snag your thread. The Matarelli isn't exactly cheap (about $20), but it's the only one you will ever need.

At the risk of drawing the ire of hundreds of old-timers, I must say that I find hand-tied whip-finishes to be typically looser and not as precisely placed as ones tied with a tool. The problem is that fingers have rough spots all over them, and even if you have the softest hands on the block, you still have textured fingerprints that cause the thread to roll and twist off your fingertips. This twist prevents the thread wraps from seating tightly and cinching down securely.

HACKLE PLIERS

Hackle pliers make it easier to hold on to short feathers, biots, and other short or small materials as you wrap them around the hook. Look for fine, smooth tips and a reasonable amount of tension. Many styles are too hard to open comfortably. Avoid so-called midge hackle pliers. You wouldn't use a smaller paintbrush to paint a small house, so why use a smaller pair of pliers on a smaller feather? The pliers are supposed to make it easier to wrap the hackle because they extend out from your fingers and give you better control.

J. Dorin Tear Drop pliers work well. The way the jaws close allows them to grab more surface area of the feather and hold it better. Hackle Tweezers, designed by Robert Jorgenson, have micro-fine tips, grip feathers more securely than anything I have ever used, and are lightweight and precise. Their fine tips make them great

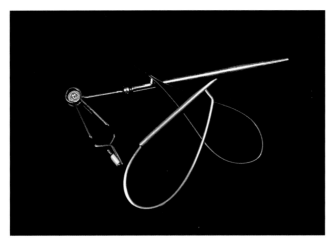

Clockwise from center: Jorgenson Hackle Tweezers, Tiemco Rotary Hackle Pliers, J. Dorin Teardrop Pliers.

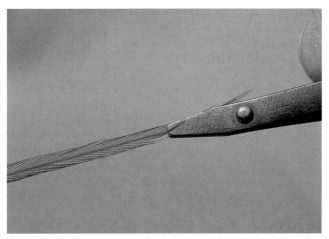

When gripping a feather with your hackle pliers, grab the feather in-line with its stem. If you grab the feather tip at a right angle to the stem, you'll likely break the tip as you wrap. Go ahead and grab as much of the feather tip as you can in the jaws of your pliers. Quality hackle feathers are plenty long, so there is no need to try to grab a tiny bit of the feather.

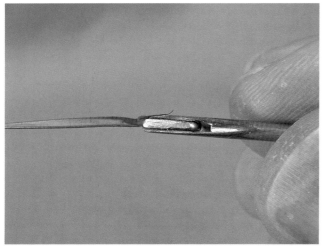

Robert Jorgenson's Hackle Tweezers are great for small hackle feathers and biots. Their fine tips grasp small feathers well.

Use an identical hook to measure proportions.

for smaller hackle feathers and for wrapping biots. I have yet to have them slip off a feather. For parachute patterns, I consider Tiemco Rotary Hackle Pliers a must. This tool has pliers mounted on a swivel handle that allows you to wrap parachute hackles with one hand and make smooth, concentric turns.

To measure tails, wings, or other proportions relative to the hook shank, use your hackle pliers to hold another hook (same size and style) against the materials on the fly you are tying until you can reliably eyeball the proportions on your own.

DUBBING NEEDLE/BODKIN

A bodkin is basically a needle with a handle and is useful for a variety of applications from applying head cement to separating wing fibers. You can purchase these or make one from a hatpin and a wooden dowel. Both Tiemco and Dr. Slick make a nice version with a brass handle that has flat sides so it won't roll off the table.

A bodkin can be as simple or as fancy as you like.

They also have half-hitch tools built into their ends, which could come in handy, although I rarely use a half-hitch anymore.

DUBBING BRUSH

Dubbing brushes come in a variety of styles ranging from simple wire bore-cleaning brushes available at your local sporting goods store to more specific tools used to isolate and pick out dubbing by the strand. I use brushes to make dubbing appear looser, rather than simply applying the dubbing loosely in the first place. Using a dubbing brush gives me more control over the degree of "bugginess" I create, and I can apply that bugginess to only certain parts of the fly more easily. One of my favorite dubbing brushes is the Collier Dubbing Brush made by Dennis Collier, in Longmont, Colorado. Dennis uses these brushes to create some of the most flowing, breathing, and lifelike flies I have ever seen, and I have quickly become a convert. The Tiemco Dubbing Brush is also a favorite, as its smaller brush allows me control over what I am picking out. John Barr makes a dubbing picker that is like a little, barbed needle, and I find it useful on small flies. A strip of Velcro works well for roughing up soft dubbing on flies like scuds and soft-hackles. Cut a shank-length-wide strip from the hook side of the hook-and-loop material and run this back and forth along the fly as if you were polishing a shoe.

HAIR STACKER

A hair stacker helps even the tips of deer, elk, moose, or calf hair. It makes the hair easier to control by making it all the same length and gives the finished fly a cleaner appearance. Clean all the underfur and short hairs out of these types of hair before stacking or you'll never get it stacked.

A hair stacker is a simply made tool, but knowing what the tool needs to do and how that is achieved will help you pick the right one. Many are low-end aluminum or plastic. Look for a quality stacker made of brass or stainless steel/chrome. A good stacker will not have any mill marks where it was machined. These grooves along the inside of the tube catch the hair and prevent it from sliding down the tube.

Make sure that the stacker has a shelf built into the base to hold the tube portion of the tool up off the bottom of the base. This shelf allows the hair to protrude from the end of the stacker when you separate the two pieces. No shelf and the hair stays in the tube, making it impossible to remove cleanly. A cork or neoprene pad on the bottom of the stacker makes for quieter work, something your significant other will never thank you for but here's your chance to cut the complaining off at the pass.

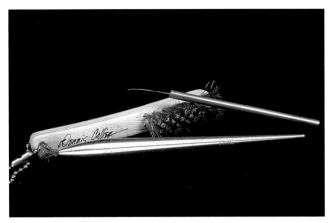

Dubbing brushes help create soft, lifelike flies.

Most good quality stackers come with this, but if yours didn't, retrofit it by cutting a piece from a cork sheet or old mouse pad and gluing it in place.

Some recommend spraying the inside of the stacker with an anti-static spray to keep the hair from sticking, and I can confidently say that this is complete rubbish. The hair is what has the static charge, and you can eliminate most of this static just by pinching it in your fingertips. Furthermore, spraying anything in your stacker only compounds the problem. If anything, I sometimes see brand new stackers with a little grease, oil, or machining residue left in the base, which can cause some problems getting the hair out of the stacker, but this can all be cleaned out with a cotton swab and maybe a little alcohol. I love the Tiemco Classic stacker in sizes small and medium and use them as my workhorses, but I have also used Edgin stackers with great success.

I own three sizes of stackers and use them all, but I think you could get away with one in the medium size.

Hair stackers are essential for evening tips of hair and hackle. They come in all sizes, each having a specific purpose. For starters, a medium-size stacker should suffice.

Whiting Hackle Gauge.

Hold the hackle gauge in your hand rather than placing it on the stem of your vise.

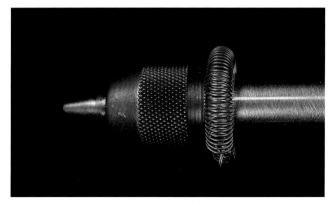

Material springs are inexpensive and useful. Most vises come with them.

Better yet, get a medium and a small and you'll be set for a while. The smaller stacker works great for small, tail-size clumps of hair and wings for smaller flies, while the medium-size stacker works great for most wing applications. If you place a smaller or shorter bunch of hair into a large stacker, the hair falls in at an angle and won't end up square with the bottom of the stacker, possibly resulting in uneven tips. A small stacker has a smaller inside diameter, which makes the hair stand more upright and even inside the tube. I use a large Edgin stacker for big spun-deer-hair bass bugs, but you probably won't need this specialized tool right off the bat.

OTHER USEFUL TOOLS
Hackle Gauge
A hackle gauge (Whiting brand shown) measures the hackle feather in relation to the hook gap size before you pluck the feather from the hide. I find it easier to use if you have the gauge in your hand rather than attached to the post on your vise, which is where they are made to fit. This tool can keep you from wasting a lot of feathers, but they are made with a single standard hook style in mind (though I'm not exactly sure which style it is). This can throw off your hackle size if you are wrapping the feather over a dubbed body or tying on a hook that doesn't match the gauge's calibration. After sizing with the gauge, I like to measure my hackle feathers against the gap of the hook I'm tying on to assure that they are the right size.

Material Spring
A material spring wraps around the shaft of the vise behind the head and holds materials out of the way while you tie. For instance, on the Hare's Ear you can place the ribbing material in the spring while you dub the abdomen. Your vise probably came with one, and if it didn't, make sure you get one. Your vise may require a different style of spring than shown here; many rotary vises require either a much smaller spring or specialized mounting. Check with your vise manufacturer to find out if they offer such items.

Bone Comb
This is a small comb made from steer horn, which does not create static and makes a great tool for cleaning the underfur from deer and elk hair. I prefer the comb to my fingers, particularly for hair that has an unusually large amount of underfur or for particularly big chunks of hair. The comb can really reach in and pull out the underfur, and often all the short hairs along with it.

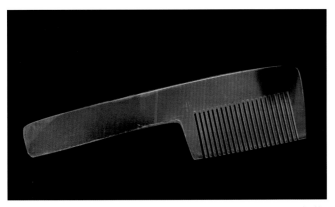

A bone comb is useful for removing underfur from deer and elk hair.

Double-Edge Razor Blades

Double-edge razor blades are much sharper than regular single-edge blades and many times sharper than your best scissors. They are perfect for trimming deer-hair bodies on flies like the Goddard Caddis. I find it easiest to push the blade through the hair in smooth, long strokes. Always cut away from you, just like when Grandpa taught you to whittle. You can bend the blades to make smooth, curved cuts. They are also ideal for stripping the materials from the hooks on flies that didn't go so well.

You must be very careful when working with double-edge blades. I typically break them in half lengthwise, so I only have to worry about one side cutting me at a time. You can cut them in half with an old pair of scissors or tin-snips, but I usually just carefully fold them in half and snap them in two.

De-Barb Pliers

Tiemco makes de-barb pliers with a wire cutter in the back edge of the jaws that I find useful. The front of the jaws are smooth to pinch the smallest barbs flat. You can

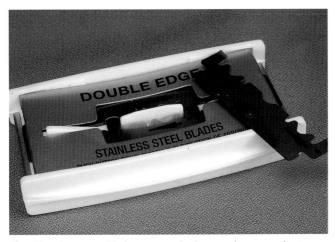

Double-edge razor blades are much sharper than your best scissors and are perfect for shaping deer hair.

Tiemco De-Barb Pliers—get one pair for your bench and one for your vest.

use a pair of hemostats for the same purpose, but then you'll also need a pair of wire cutters for cutting heavy wire, such as medium Ultra Wire when tying #12 Copper Johns. Two tools in one is always a good idea.

HEAD CEMENT AND GLUES

I occasionally use head cement to strengthen or stiffen some materials like turkey, peacock, and duck and goose quills. I also use head cement to help stiffen thread posts on parachute and hair-wing flies. On thread heads, I tend to use head cement as a cosmetic finish more often than I use it to strengthen a fly. If your fly is tied tightly and you've tied a good whip-finish, head cement doesn't add much to the overall durability.

Spilling a bottle of glue on a gold-grade dry-fly neck will challenge the best vocabulary. I usually wait until I'm done tying and have put all my materials away before I break out the cement. Plastic applicator bottles make it much easier to apply the head cement, and they just won't spill. If you can't get these small applicator bottles, apply your head cement with your bodkin. To apply head cement to a fly, dip the tip of your bodkin into the cement and pick up a small droplet. Place the droplet on the thread head and be sure to get it all the way around, top and bottom. I prefer thin head cement.

If you use Dave's Flexament, thin it to 50 percent Flexament cement and 50 percent Flexament thinner.

Gloss Coat and Zap-A-Gap can help strengthen delicate materials.

BTs Dubbing Wax. Dubbing wax should not be applied to the thread. Instead, apply it to the tips of your fingers before twisting the dubbing onto the thread.

Dave's is awfully goopy straight from the bottle, but it is great for undercoating bodies made of herl and the like because it soaks all the way to the hook shank. Always use the appropriate thinner for each type of head cement. Using the wrong thinner can make your previously thick head cement into what resembles a wad of used chewing gum. I also like Wapsi's Gloss Coat for most uses, as it dries shiny and hard and is more like a glue than a finish. Gloss Coat is easily thinned with Wapsi's Fluorescent Thinner, although it comes very thin straight from the bottle.

Zap-A-Gap is cyanoacrylate "super" glue with gap-filling properties. I use it to reinforce peacock herl and other delicate materials. Use it sparingly; it will dry faster and won't bleed through the materials. Excessive amounts will "gas off" onto the outside of the fly, creating a white, fuzzy haze. For this reason, let any fly with glue on it sit out for a few hours to dry before putting it in a fly box. It's also a good idea to wait a few moments after wrapping material over the wet glue to allow it to dry. I have heard that you can keep a bottle of Zap-A-Gap from drying out for many years by keeping it sealed and in the freezer, but I rarely have this problem. Be sure to wipe the tip of the bottle clean and place the cap back on after each use and you should be fine.

DUBBING WAX

I have dry hands and find that dubbing slips through my fingers pretty easily, so a light coating of tacky wax on my fingers helps me gain a bit of traction on the fibers as I twist them on the thread. You might not need it. The idea of putting dubbing wax onto your thread is a bit outdated, but it is still useful when touch dubbing or creating dubbing loops, which I don't cover in this book. Put the lightest coat of wax onto the thumb and

forefinger of your dubbing hand if you didn't come pre-waxed at birth, and that will be plenty. A tube of wax should last you a lifetime and then be passed on to your children, which ought to give you an idea of how much to use at a time. For years now I have used Overton's Wonder Wax, which is still the best stuff I have ever used. Since it's no longer available, that makes it tough on you. The closest wax I have found is BT's Dubbing Wax (tacky formula).

TYING AREA
Chairs

Many years ago I went out and bought the most expensive adjustable office chair I could find and would buy three more today if I could find them again. Your chair is nearly as important as your vise. A good tying chair should have an adjustable height, a supportive seat and seatback, and arm rests. Stools and hard wooden chairs are an invitation for a sore back and neck. I realize that comfort while tying is a subjective term and everyone is different, so rather than go on about what I like, I will only suggest that you go out and try several chairs to find one that suits you.

Lighting and Magnification

You have a variety of different options available for lighting and magnification. The rage lately has been the natural daylight lamps that purportedly give off light similar to natural sunlight, the idea being that these lamps make it easier to accurately match colors to the natural and show true shades better than standard fluorescent and incandescent bulbs. I hate 'em. I prefer a lamp that gives a more concentrated beam of light that I can shine directly on my work and lights up the work area so I don't have any shadows around or on my work.

My preferred lamp has both an incandescent and fluorescent bulb and does exactly what I have described above. Besides, the lamp you have at home doesn't change the color of the dubbing you bought at the fly shop, so a daylight lamp seems a bit too little too late. Look for a lamp, or better yet, two lamps, with long, jointed arms that allow you to mount them out of the way. The long arms can then be extended to bring the light in directly over the top of your vise, illuminating your work and eliminating shadows.

Vise Backgrounds

Many tiers like to use a sheet of blue or gray poster board or other material as a background when tying. I have tied for too many years with a plain brown, wood-grained desktop as my background and have yet to find a reason to change. If your eyes have a few years on them or perhaps your vision isn't what it could be, you may need to look into different background colors and materials. My only requirements for a background are that it produces no glare and there is nothing lying behind where I am working—a three-dimensional item placed behind my work wreaks havoc with my depth of field. Though I don't use magnifiers, reading glasses that you can look over the top of seem to be the most popular, rather than the clamp-mounted or free-standing magnifying glasses listed in all the catalogs.

Travel Bags and Storage

An entire room in my house is devoted to my habit. While I understand that most tiers don't or can't have this option, I can only speak from my experience as far as storing and organizing your materials. I arrange my tying stuff (and my fly boxes) with a controlled chaos, and while I usually know where everything is, my material and fly selection has grown so large that I have to do all I can just to keep up. I don't really organize; I contain.

I think I may own one of every commercially available fly-tying bag ever made. While they all work wonderfully, I have yet to settle on one "best" option. I rarely carry my tying material along on fishing trips anymore unless it is an extended trip to a faraway destination. I do, however, often need to carry materials to various tying demos and shows. For this purpose I most often use a hard plastic storage bin, with the materials for each pattern laid out neatly in gallon-size plastic bags. This keeps me organized during the demo and prevents the audience from having to wait while I dig through a bunch of small bags and dividers to find each material.

Several companies like Fishpond, William Joseph, and Dart make fly-tying carry-all bags, and for the most part they do exactly what they are supposed to. With features like vise pockets, mesh envelopes, and heavy plastic baggies to help store and organize your goodies, these bags can be a boon to the beginning tier or minimalist.

CHAPTER 3

Hooks and Thread

Tiemco 100s, #8 through #24.

An entire book can be (and has been) written on hooks. Rather than try to give a comprehensive rundown of every possibility, I present this brief synopsis to give you an idea of how and why the sizes and styles vary. Hook sizes are technically based on the gap of the hook, which is the distance from the hook point to the shank. They are labeled in a numbered system, from size 1 through size 32, with the number getting larger as the hook gets smaller, thus a size 20 is smaller than a size 10. On the large end of the spectrum, the "ought" system is used to denote what are essentially negative numbers, i.e. 1/0 (0), 2/0 (00), 3/0 (000), and 3/0 is bigger than 1/0.

Dry fly hooks are made of lighter wire, while nymph and streamer hooks are made of heavier wire. Obviously, the heavier wire helps these flies sink and adds some strength, which is important to keep them from bending open when stuck in a big fish or, more likely, river bottom. The hook eye may be in-line with the shank (called straight or ring eye), turned up, or turned down. Most nymph hooks have turned-down eyes, while dry fly hooks can be any of the above. I prefer straight-eye hooks for smaller flies, as the eye doesn't encroach on the hook gap. The exception to this is small parachute flies, where turned-down eyes remain clear of the hackle, which makes it easier to thread the tippet.

PARTS OF THE HOOK

Eye: The loop at the front of the hook that your tippet goes through. The eye can be turned up, down, or straight.

Index point: A term I developed to help beginning tiers leave enough room to whip-finish the fly. Beginners commonly tie everything on the fly right smack up to the eye, leaving no room to tie off the materials and whip-finish the fly. Leaving the index point (one eye length) behind the eye bare during the entire tying process helps cure this problem. As you progress as a tier, you can creep into this area a bit and even cut it by two thirds, as long as you have enough space to tie off the last few parts of the fly without crowding the hook eye. Experience will help with this, but until then, leave a whole eye length—you are bound to creep into it anyway.

Shank: The (usually) straight portion of the hook between the eye and the bend. Some hooks have curved or humped shanks with little or no straight section. In these cases there is some degree of interpretation involved in where the shank ends and the bend begins. If you work too far down the bend of these curved hooks, you can inadvertently shorten the effective throat of the hook, so I use halfway down the curve of the shank for a starting point. If you tie materials all the way down to the barb, it won't matter how many fish eat because you won't hook any of them.

Point: The sharp end of the hook.

Bend: The point at which the hook shank starts to curve down. On a standard (non-curved) shank hook, the thread from the bobbin will hang about even with the point on the barb when it is wrapped to the bend. This is where most tails will be tied in so they extend straight back from the bend in the same plane as the hook shank. The back end of the hook, where the wire bends down to the point, is also referred to as the bend. So there are two uses of this word in relation to hooks: the point where the straight portion of the shank ends and the curve of the hook where it bends down from there.

Throat: The distance from the point to the bend.

Gap: The distance between the hook point and the shank. A larger gap is generally conducive to better fish hooking and holding capability, although a very wide

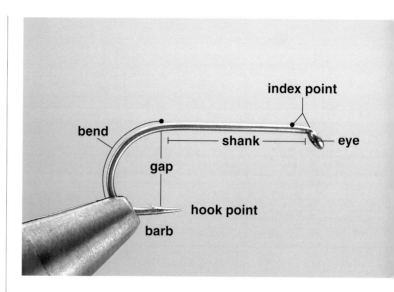

gap can hook fish deeply and damage their tongue or brain. For our purposes, we will assume that a standard hook has a gap equal to half the shank-length. I say "assume" because there is no such thing as a standard hook anymore.

Barb: The barb is the little sticker behind the hook point meant to help hold the fish on the hook and keep it from shaking loose. While the barb does indeed help hold onto the fish, removing barbed hooks cause much more damage to the fish, and perhaps to your own hide if you accidentally hook yourself.

Spear: The distance from the barb to the hook point.

Hooks can also be labeled 1XL (long) or 1XS (short) or 2X wide and so on. A 1X-long or 1XL hook is one eye-length longer than twice the gap of a standard hook. A 1X short or 1XS hook has a shank one eye-length shorter than a standard hook. 2X wide means that the hook gap is the equivalent gap of a hook two sizes bigger. Where this gets confusing is the differentiation, or lack thereof, between a hook with a 1X-short shank and a hook with a 1X-wide gap. Basing these measurements on the hook gap, as we learned above, means that these two hooks are identical. This can be confusing to even experienced tiers. Don't be dismayed; it really all makes sense eventually—breathe in through the nose, out through the mouth.

PINCHING BARBS

Barbless hooks, or hooks with flattened barbs, are easier to remove from fish, penetrate better, and are safer to be around in general. I get a lot more use out of a fly when I don't have to use hemostats to remove it from the fish. I don't know if I've ever had one come apart from the

HOOKS USED IN THIS BOOK

I have compiled a list of the hooks in this book and the applications for which they are best suited. I use Tiemco hooks almost exclusively. They are the best I have found. Daiichi, Gamakatsu, and a variety of other companies also produce excellent hooks. Feel free to expand on this list as your needs dictate.

Tiemco 100 (down-eye, fine wire, dry-fly hook). Though this is a dry-fly hook, I also use these and the 100SP-BL for many small nymphs. (See Brassie steps for a discussion of dry-fly hooks used for nymphs, pages 45–46.)

Tiemco 100SP-BL (down eye, barbless Tiemco Super Point, 1X-heavy dry-fly hook, 1.5X-wide gap). This hook is becoming one of my favorites. It comes out of the box barbless, and the spade-shaped Super Point is wicked sharp. One of the best things about this true barbless hook is the back of the slightly tapered hook point prevents a dropper from slipping off the hook point. True barbless needle-point hooks are smooth along the bend, and the dropper knot sometimes slides off while you are casting. The slightly heavier gauge wire used in this hook makes it great for many small nymphs and heavier dressed dry flies, but it is only available down to a size 20.

Tiemco 101 (Ring- or straight-eye dry-fly hook). On small flies, the ring eye preserves the gap.

Tiemco 2312 (Ring-eye, 2XL). For Stimulators and other large-bodied dry flies, I use this hook instead of the Tiemco 200R. The 2312 has a wider gap and is slightly shorter than the 200R. I find the larger gap hooks and holds fish better, particularly in smaller sizes.

Delicate dry flies, such as this Blue-Winged Olive, are right at home on the Tiemco 100.

Ring-eye hooks like the TMC 101 work well for small dry flies and nymphs like the RS2 (above) or Rusty Spinner.

The Tiemco 100SP-BL is a versatile hook, with dry fly proportions and a heavier gauge wire.

Larger dry patterns such as Stimulators (above) that imitate longer bugs like stonefly adults and hoppers are matched well with longer hooks like the TMC 2312 and 5212.

Tiemco 5262 (2X heavy, 2X long, down-eye nymph and streamer hook). The relationship of gap to shank length is a perfect chassis for stonefly patterns and other large nymphs.

Tiemco 2488 and 2488H (3X-wide gap, 2X short). This is a huge gap on a short hook, which makes for a small fly with great hooking capacity. The 2488H is a heavy wire version for patterns fished deeper or for bigger fish.

Tiemco 2487 or 2457. These hooks have a curved shank reminiscent of many insect larvae and pupae. The 2487 is fine wire; the 2457 is heavier wire. Both of these have down eyes that encroach on the hook gap in small sizes. I use these down to a size 18 and switch to the 2488 or 2488H for smaller flies.

Heavy wire, long-shank hooks like Tiemco 5262s lend themselves well to beadhead flies like Copper Johns (above) and Prince Nymphs.

Many midge larvae and mayfly nymphs have a slight curve to their bodies. Hooks like the Tiemco 2487 and 2488 mimic this shape well.

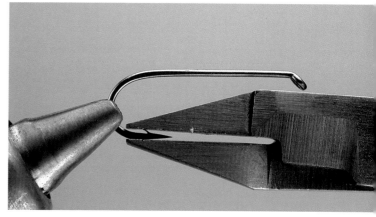

Whether you do it at the vise or onstream, pinch down your hook barbs.

fish's teeth, but the hemos really tear them up fast. Barbless hooks can be twisted out with your fingertips without taking the fish out of the water. I also pinch the barbs down on my hooks to save my own skin. You'll agree with me after an errant cast buries one in the back of your head.

While conventional wisdom says to pinch the barbs flat before you tie the fly in case you happen to accidentally break off the hook point, I wait until I have tied the fly to my tippet. Leaving the barb intact in the interim helps the fly stay firmly anchored in the foam of my fly box, saves me the additional step in the tying procedure, and leaves the point on the barb as a reference point during the tying process.

Many tiers use the jaws of their vise to flatten the barb, which I do occasionally, but you risk wearing a pocket in the jaws. You can also use a pair of hemostats or De-Barb Pliers to mash the barbs, which is what I most commonly do. While most advocate bringing the tips of the pliers directly in from the hook point to pinch the barb, I confess I usually pinch the barb down with the pliers at a right angle to the hook point and have never noticed any difference in the results. I think cheaper hooks do have more of a propensity to break when pinched at a right angle, and perhaps that is why so many tiers support the in-line technique.

THREAD

Fly-tying thread is different from regular sewing thread (although several popular midge patterns, like the Yong Special, call for regular sewing thread). Typically made of nylon or polyester, tying threads are multi-stranded and sometimes bonded. Bonded threads have strands fused together into a cord and can be harder to flatten than flat, ribbon-style threads. Bonded threads tend to spread less on the hook shank and also tend to bite into soft materials, which secures them better.

MOUNTING THE HOOK IN THE VISE

Place the hook in the vise so the shank is parallel to the floor, and the jaws are gripping only enough hook to hold it securely. The bottom corner of the hook bend should be in the top corner of the vise jaws. Adjust the vise jaws properly to hold the hook. As a rule of thumb, I readjust the jaws if I go up two hook sizes or more. Be sure all other adjustments are firmly tightened so the vise doesn't wobble. Make sure the jaws are far enough from the table top to allow you to wrap a long loop of dubbing or thread around the hook.

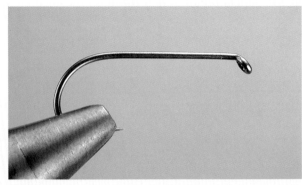

Wrong.

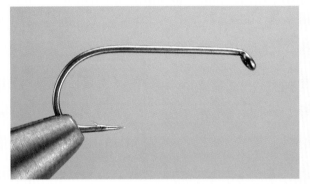

Proper way to insert a hook into the vise jaws.

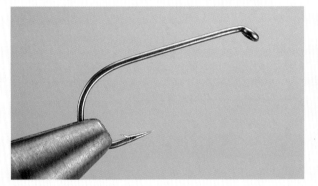

Wrong.

Flat threads create super-smooth tapered underbodies and are the right choice on any thread-bodied fly (like the Black Beauty and the Copper John, which has a thread underbody) or when you are concerned with a smooth taper. The disadvantage of flat threads is that they spread across the hook shank and can be harder to control. I often spin or counterspin the thread to flatten or twist it to my liking and needs. As I tie left-handed, I tend to unwind the factory thread twist and flatten the thread as I wrap it on the shank. If I need to cord the thread up, I spin the bobbin to roll the thread back into a rope. Round thread, or flat thread that has been twisted, tends to bite into materials like hair and hackle stems better than flattened thread. Flattened thread makes smoother tapers and creates fewer ridges in thread-bodied flies or flies that require a smooth thread underbody.

Thread sizes are historically denoted using a zero or "ought" as a measurement. The more zeros or "oughts" you have, the smaller the thread. 6/0 (000000) is smaller than 3/0. Larger threads are typically stronger and are used when you need extreme thread tension, such a spinning deer hair or where thread bulk is needed such as on many saltwater and Alaska-style flies. As a rule of thumb, I use the smallest thread I can deem appropriate. Smaller thread creates less bulk on the hook and allows sufficient turns of thread to bind the materials adequately while allowing you better control over tapers and underbodies. There are times, however, when a larger thread will be better for the task at hand. Tying #16 dry flies with 3/0 monocord would be an exercise in frustration because the thread would create too much bulk, but switch to a #4 Woolly Bugger, and the 3/0 is just about right. All thread sizes and styles are good for something—it's just that none are good for everything.

Recently, many thread manufacturers have either switched to or added the denier size/weight to their thread spool labels. Denier is the thread industry's standard of measurement and denotes the weight, in grams, of 9,000 meters of thread. This number is easier to work with than the outdated ought system. Previously a manufacturer made one size of thread and called it 3/0, then

The thread you choose can make or break your fly patterns. Tying thread comes in a huge range of colors and sizes, but you only need to start with a few different types and colors.

a size a bit smaller and called that 6/0. The problem started when other companies got into the fly-tying thread game and didn't start with the same baseline. So Company B's 6/0 thread was much stronger than Company A's 6/0 but was also much bigger in diameter. It would be like one company making tippet with a 5X label that tested at ten-pound-test, with a corresponding large diameter, while all the other companies stayed with the standard diameter measurement and their 5X only tested at five-pound-test. Different scale.

Denier (den-ear) tells you only the weight of the thread overall, and when presented in this form, many conventional threads have a few surprises wrapped around their spools. Danville 6/0 thread, which has been the standard tying thread for about as long as I have been alive, has a denier rating of 70. UTC 70-denier Ultra Thread is, you guessed it, 70 denier as well. But these two threads have very different tying characteristics. Danville thread has a bit more twist and slightly less stretch, while the Ultra Thread is much shinier and has a good bit of stretch. They are both great threads and both are useful. You could even say these threads are interchangeable and you wouldn't be wrong—just not as picky as I am.

Uni-Thread's popular 8/0 thread actually has a denier of 72, slightly heavier than either the Danville 6/0 or the 70-denier Ultra Thread. The catch is that the Uni-Thread is bonded into a tight cord, making it seem much smaller on the hook. Uni-Thread is made of polyester versus the Danville and Ultra Thread's nylon, so there is less stretch and the colors are drab and toned down.

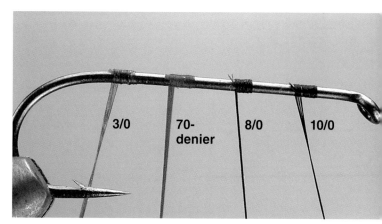

From right to left: flat 10/0, bonded 8/0, flat 70-denier, and flattened 3/0 monocord. Note the cord-like structure of the 8/0 thread in relation to the other flattened threads.

TYPES OF THREAD

This is by no means a list of every thread size available, but it does include most of the threads that are stocked in fly shops and have a practical application.

Kevlar
UTC 280-denier Ultra Thread (280 denier, flat)
UTC 210-denier Ultra Thread (210 denier, flat)
Danville Flat Waxed Nylon (210 denier, flat)
Danville Flymaster Plus (210 denier, flat)
UTC 140-denier Ultra Thread (140 denier, flat)
3/0 Danville monocord (140 denier, slightly twisted)
6/0 Uni-Thread (140 denier, bonded)
6/0 Danville (70 denier, slightly twisted)
UTC 70-denier Ultra Thread (70 denier, flat)
8/0 Uni-Thread (72 denier, bonded)
14/0 Gordon Griffiths (70 denier, slightly twisted)
UTC GSP 50 (50 denier, flat)
10/0 Gudebrod (45 denier, flat)

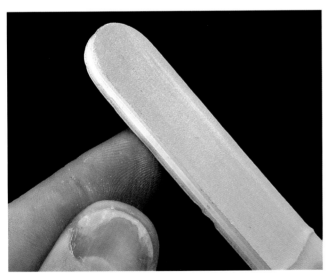

Smooth any rough spots on your fingers that can catch your tying thread.

Ideally, thread manufacturers would label both the denier weight of the thread and the thread configuration—flat, bonded, and lightly twisted—and do away with the ought system. This information would give tiers a much better idea of what we are buying and make thread selection much easier. Until this happens, tiers are left to buy and try each thread.

Thread color should match the dubbing or, at least, the overall shade of the fly. Thin dubbing applications are much easier to achieve with matching thread colors because the thread does not contrast with or show through the dubbing. A good selection of thread colors will make your flies much cleaner looking, like you put some forethought into them, and make for a much more appealing pattern. I use black, white, tan, brown, olive, gray, and pale yellow the most, because those are the colors so many bugs come in. Pick up the thread sizes and colors you need for the flies in this book, and add to it as you tie more patterns.

Most tying thread comes waxed. Contrary to popular belief, this is not to aid in the application of dubbing but to help keep the thread from fraying and adhere the thread to itself as it's wrapped. You'll notice when you break your thread it doesn't unwind from the hook like a tightly wound rubber band. This is because the wax on the thread keeps it stuck to the previous layer. Good thinkin', eh?

Flosses are multi-stranded materials like thread, but they are typically much heavier in weight to more adequately cover the hook shank and build smooth, seamless bodies. Flosses are generally made of rayon, polyester, or silk and are flat when taken directly from the spool. Floss is useful for building underbodies and forming ribs and bodies on larger flies. Floss is typically available in four-strand, two-strand, and single-strand versions. I think single strand is easier to work with than the others. Multi-strand floss is very difficult to work with and spreads tremendously when wrapped. Though separating a single strand from the multiple strands is easy to do, wasting the extra strands sticks in my craw.

WORKING WITH THREAD

Keep your hands and fingers clean when you tie. Even the slightest amount of oil or dirt can discolor your thread and dubbing. Smooth any rough spots on your fingers and nails with an emery board, pumice stone, or fine sandpaper to keep them from catching on the thread as you tie.

Thread wraps and all other materials wraps are *always* made going over the top of the hook away from you. Wraps made in a counter-wrap direction are seldom

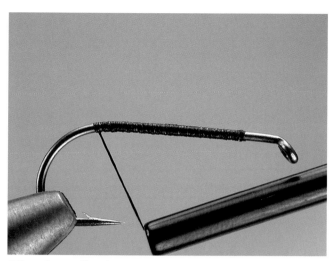

Wrap diagonally when you are at the bend to avoid the hook point.

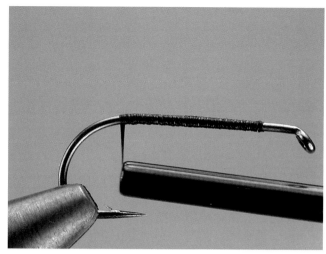

By keeping the thread short, you can wrap around the hook on the inside of the hook gap.

as tight as conventional wraps and generally don't add much reinforcement, which is why I am not a fan of counter-wrapped ribs. Instead, I just change the angle of my wraps to get the desired look and reinforce the materials. Another problem with counter-wrapping a material is that the tying thread is going the opposite direction, and when you try to tie something off that is going in the opposite direction of the thread, the thread will loosen the material wraps by pulling them in the other direction. Conversely, when you tie a material off with thread wraps that are going the same direction as the material being tied off, the thread will tighten those wraps as it pulls over the tag end of that material.

Keep thread or materials under constant tension when you wrap them. The hook shank should flex as you wrap, even when using fine threads. The exception to this is when making soft loops or pinch wraps initially attaching a material to the hook, but these wraps should be backed up with a few tight wraps to firmly anchor the materials. Tie your flies tightly. They must be durable. Ugly flies still catch fish, but if they fall apart when they touch the water, they are of no use to anyone.

When you break your thread, and you invariably will as you learn to tie with maximum tension, start the thread right back over the broken end, then trim all the tag ends. If the thread or materials start to unwind, place your hackle pliers on the loose end to hold it in place until you can get the bobbin rethreaded and reattach the thread.

When you are working near the hook bend, wrap thread or materials diagonally to avoid the hook point. Much of the time, I keep my working thread short from the tip of the bobbin tube to the hook shank, allowing me to wrap the thread around the hook on the inside of

the hook gap. Tiemco bobbins have small tubes that fit inside the gap of even a #20 hook.

When tying a material off, you have to switch hands with the material and thread hand. That is, hold the material in your thread hand above the hook and make the thread wraps to tie it off with your material hand. This assures that the thread crosses the material and firmly secures it to the hook.

When beginning to wrap a material, always be sure that the thread is hanging at the tie-off point in front of the material. Your thread should always be in the way of the material you are wrapping. If the thread is behind the material as you wrap it, there is no way to tie the material off.

Make every wrap of thread with a purpose. Thread wraps can be used to build bulk and tapers, travel from

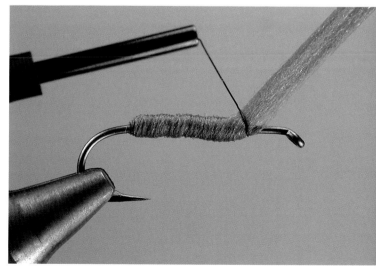

When tying off materials, you have to switch your thread and material hands.

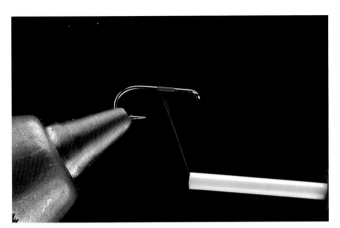

Always turn the smallest circle of thread possible. Small circles (one-inch diameter or less) are more efficient than large ones and allow you much better control over thread placement.

one place on the hook to another, or tie materials down. If a material takes two turns of thread to secure, don't make three. Make sure that every wrap has a purpose and there are no additional unnecessary turns of thread on your flies. Most materials can be solidly anchored with two well-placed tight wraps of thread.

Thread heads on flies should generally be small and unobtrusive. A few tight turns of thread to cover any material butts and form a foundation for the whip-finish are all that are necessary. Often I'll use the actual whip-finish to build the head of the fly to help keep it small. Larger heads are okay on larger flies as long as they're in proportion. The index point is reserved for the thread head. A clean thread head is really a product of good planning as you tie the fly. Be a good planner.

CHAPTER 4

Attachment Techniques

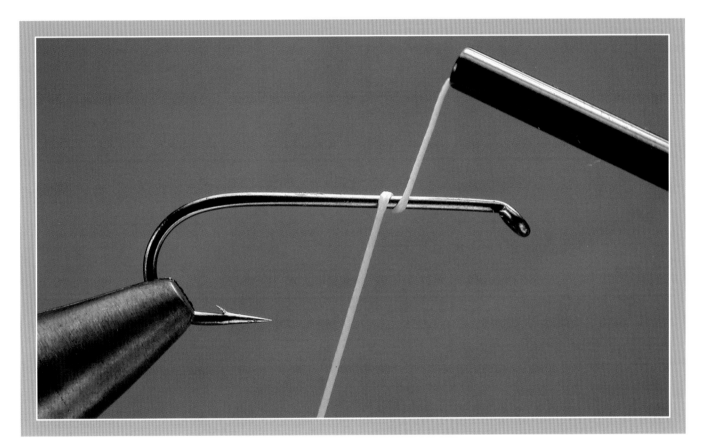

STARTING THE THREAD

1. To start the thread, begin by holding the bobbin in your dominant hand (photos are for right-handed tiers) and the loose tag end of the thread in the other. Hold the tag end of the thread below the hook on the near side of the hook shank with the bobbin above the hook. The thread should be somewhat taut between your two hands and pressed against the hook shank. Hold onto the tag end of the thread under the hook and bring the thread coming from the bobbin down around the hook shank and up again to the top of the hook.

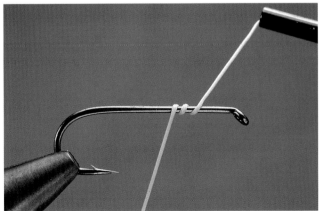

2. Make another turn of thread with the bobbin, working slightly forward and angling the wraps toward the hook eye. In the photo, I have exaggerated this angle. You can start the thread over a short length of hook shank by butting the wraps more closely together.

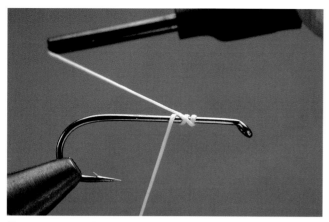

3. Once you have two turns of thread angled toward the hook eye, make a sharply angled wrap with the bobbin back over the first two turns of thread to lock them down.

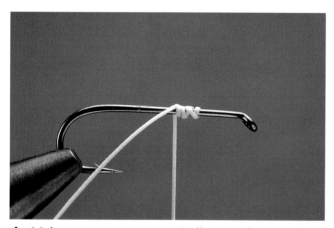

4. Make one more turn vertically over the top of the hook to further secure the tag end of the thread.

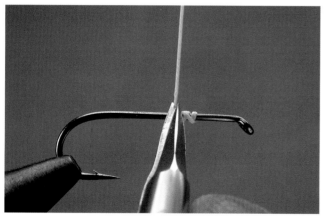

5. Lift the tag end of the thread above the hook and trim it as close as possible.

THE QUICK START

You can also start the thread using the quick start method. The quick start saves you the step of cutting off the tag end of the thread, which can add up over a dozen or more flies. It takes a little getting used to, but you may want to try it just to help speed things along later. It also uses less thread.

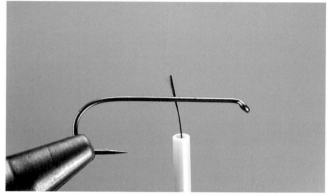

1. Start with a very short length of thread extending from the tip of the bobbin. Place the tip of the bobbin and the protruding thread on the backside of the hook shank with the thread touching the shank.

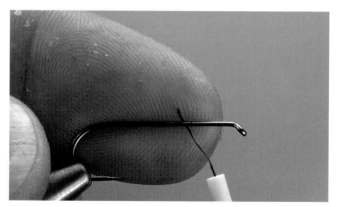

2. Press the tip of your index finger up against the thread, trapping it against the backside of the hook.

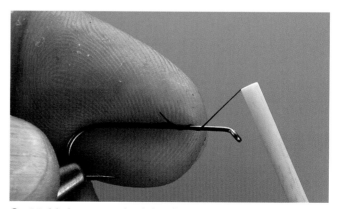

3. Hold the tag end of the thread against the shank and make two wide turns of thread forward on the hook shank.

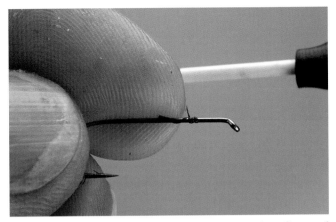

4. Once you have made the two turns going forward on the shank, make another two turns back over those turns just as you would in a normal thread start. The quick start merely eliminates the tag end of the thread, saving you the step of clipping it off as well as the few inches of thread that are normally wasted here.

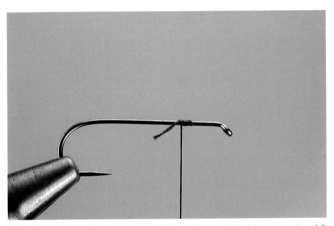

5. Once you have crossed the thread back over itself, you can release your index finger from the tag end.

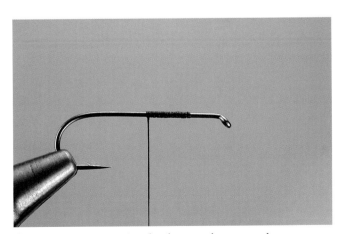

6. Continue wrapping back over the tag end.

THREAD TORQUE

One of the first things you discover when you begin to tie flies is the concept of thread torque, also known as "dang, it's hard to get stuff attached to the hook." Thread torque is the tension on the thread pushing or pulling on the material you are trying to tie down. The number-one trick in fly tying is learning to counteract this torque and make it work for, rather than against, you.

In the following text and photos, I show several ways of attaching materials to the hook without allowing the thread to wreak havoc. Outsmarting thread torque is the first step in becoming a great tier, and I use most of these techniques on the flies in the rest of the book.

If you allow thread torque to get the better of you, you may give up tying altogether. If the materials you are tying in seem skewed to one side, cant the material toward you a bit before you tie it in. Wings and tails have a nasty propensity to slide off center if you are not conscious of thread torque when tying them in.

Good tiers learn to use thread torque to their advantage by placing the material ahead of where the thread wants to pull it, and then let the thread slide the material into position. A great example of this is the legs on a Copper John. If you place a clump of hen fibers along the side of the hook and wrap the thread tightly over them, the thread would push the legs about a quarter to half turn around the shank, making them end up on either the top of the shank in the case of the near side leg clump, or the bottom in the case of the far side clump. If we outsmart this thread torque, the answer is easy. If the thread is going to push the material a quarter turn on the shank, just place the material on your side of the hook a quarter turn ahead of where the thread will push it and tie it in there, allowing the tension on the thread to move the material into, not out of, place.

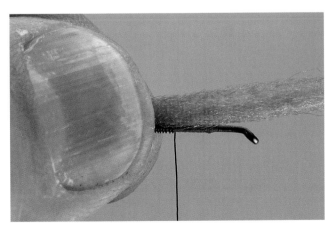

1. If I place a material atop the hook shank . . .

2. and make a tight wrap of thread over it, . . .

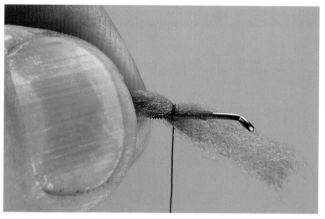

3. thread tension pushes the material, particularly the loose front end, around the hook and out of position.

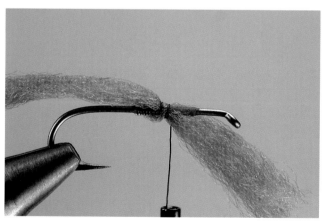

4. This makes it hard to tie a nice fly, because all the parts are skewed to the far side of the hook and the underbodies end up all lumpy and bumpy.

THE RIGHT-ANGLE TECHNIQUE

The right-angle technique is a little trick I developed over the years to attach any stiff material to the hook shank. It works great for materials like wire and hackle stems but can be used with any rigid material. It is a quick, easy method of capturing materials against the shank. In the following photos, I am using small black wire in place of thread for photo clarity.

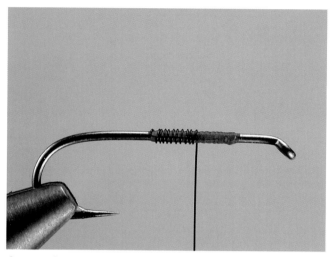

1. Let the tying thread hang precisely where you want to start anchoring the material in place. Note there is a right angle where the hook shank and the hanging tying thread meet on the underside of the hook.

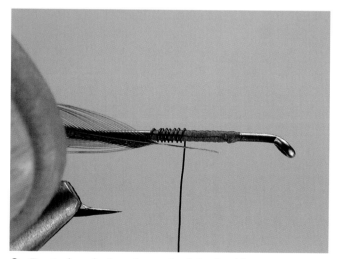

2. Begin by placing the end of the hackle stem or wire into the front side of this right angle. The material will be on the front side of the thread on the underside of the hook.

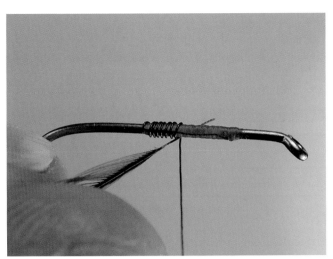

3. Turn the long end of the material toward you to cross the butt end of the feather at a sharp angle to the hook shank. Think of this as an X-Y-Z axis. The shank is at a right angle to the thread, the thread is at a right angle to the material, and the material is at a right angle to the shank *and* the thread. Everything is at a right angle to everything else.

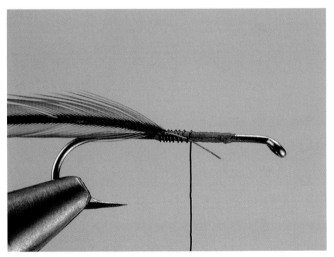

4. Hold the material in place in the corner of the right angle formed by the thread and the hook shank and bring the thread smoothly up and over the material and down again on the far side of the hook. The thread will trap the material in that corner and the hook shank will block the material and keep it from rolling over the top of the hook.

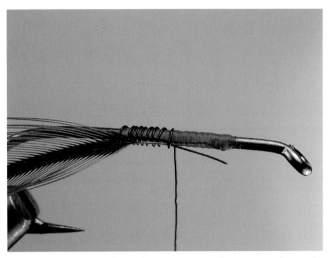

5. The right-angle technique traps the material nearly on the underside of the hook, but once trapped, the material can then be manually maneuvered to any quadrant of the shank. With wire, I typically pull the long front end down to length once I have trapped it and allow it to slide up along the side of the hook in-line with the side of the hook shank.

Once you practice and become more comfortable with this technique, you can touch the material to the underside of the shank as you wrap and trap it all in one fluid motion.

THE PINCH WRAP

If you need to trap material on the top of the shank, such as to mount the wings on an RS2, use a pinch wrap instead of the right-angle technique. Hold the material in place on the top of the shank and form a loose loop of thread over it inside your fingertips. Draw the thread loop down tight over the top of the pinched material, trapping it against the top of the hook.

3. Bring the tying thread up between your thumb and near side of the material. Push the end of the bobbin tube back toward your material hand to slide the thread well back between your fingertips. Pinch the thread where it comes above the hook in the tops of your fingertips.

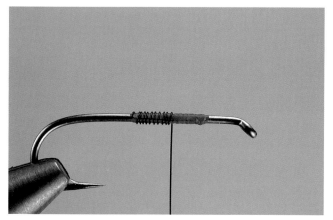

1. Begin with the thread hanging exactly where you want to tie in the material.

2. Pinch both the material and the hook shank in your fingertips with the material snugged right down to the top of the shank. Be sure to leave a small length of the material sticking out of your fingertips so you have enough to catch with the thread.

4. Drop the thread over the far side of the hook, forming a loop over the material within your fingertips.

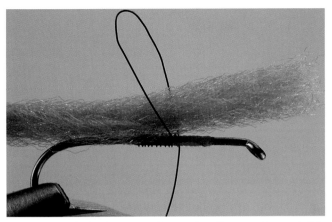

5. View of the loop without the fingers. In real life your fingers will be on either side of the loop, pinching the loop and the material between them.

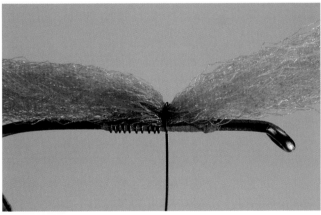

6. Pull straight down on the thread under the hook to close the loop around the top of the material, locking it on top of the hook shank. I always follow a single pinch wrap with another one to form a complete revolution of thread around the material before releasing my fingers from the material.

The **reverse pinch wrap** is a variation of this technique using the thread hand to hold the material while the material hand works the thread. The reverse pinch is useful when mounting materials that point out over the hook eye or materials so short that you can't transfer the butt ends from one hand to the other easily, like wings on an Adams.

SOFT LOOP

A soft loop or loose wrap is used to roll the material into place on the shank, allowing the thread to pull the material to its desired location. I couple this with a variation of the right-angle technique known as the angled butts technique. The loose wrap allows you to sneak the thread over the material and angling the butt ends allows the thread to pull the material to the top of the shank rather than over to the far side.

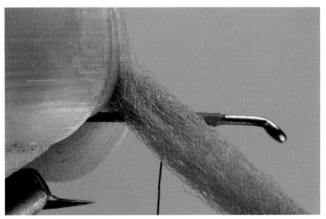

1. Start by laying the material at an angle across the top of the hook shank. I angle the butt ends of the material toward my thread hand side and slightly down.

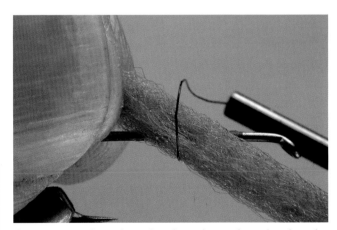

2. Using a short length of working thread, relax the tension on the thread and come over the top of the material with a soft loop. You don't want the thread to go completely slack until you approach the top of the thread wrap. The wire used in these photos illustrates the soft loop as it comes over the top of the material.

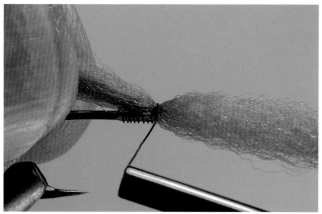

3. Draw the thread sharply toward you on the underside of the shank, allowing the loop to close around the material, and pull the butt ends of the material to the top of the hook shank. The soft loop is loose all the way around the shank until you reach the near bottom side of the hook, where you apply tension and close the loop. Angle the butt ends across the shank to use the hook to block the material from rolling over prematurely. I use this technique to attach tails on most flies, as it works when you don't have enough shank to hold for a pinch wrap.

CHEATER

The cheater was introduced to me by one of my tying-class students. He used this method to attach the fine tailing fibers on an RS2, and upon seeing this trick I couldn't find any reason not to use it in tight spots like this. The cheater lets you slide the material up under the thread to the top of the shank rather than wrapping the thread over the material. This works great for attaching Krystal Flash or any small slippery material at a precise location to the shank.

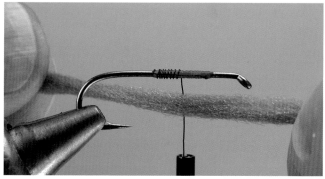

1. Place the material under the shank and behind the thread. Reach over the back of the hook and grab the far end of the material.

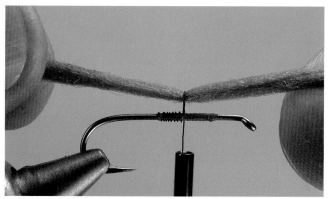

2. Bring the material to the top of the shank, lifting the thread with it as you go.

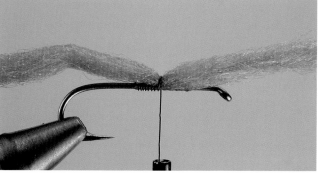

3. Let the weight of the bobbin draw the thread and material down to the top of the shank. You never have to touch the bobbin.

WRAPPING MATERIALS

All wraps of thread, material, and hackle always go over the top of the hook away from you. With that in mind, I will illustrate the hand-to-hand wrapping technique used to move materials along the shank.

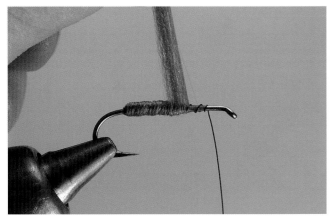

1. Once you attach a material to the hook, bring the thread forward to the point at which you want the material to end and let it hang. Hold the material in your material hand and bring it to the top of the hook shank. I generally try to keep the material wraps as upright as possible and slightly overlapping to help form a smooth body. This method is the same whether you are wrapping peacock herl, floss, or yarn (and nearly any other material).

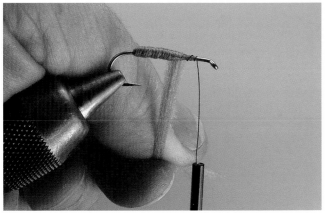

2. Drop the material over the far side of the shank while keeping it under complete tension. Do not let the turns of material go slack at any time.

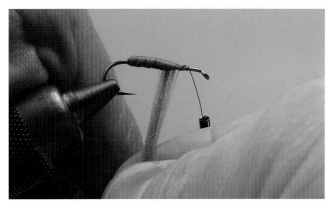

3. Reach in with your thread hand and transfer the end of the material from your material hand to your thread hand on the underside of the hook. Bring the material to the near side of the hook in your thread hand. You have to reach behind the tying thread to grab the material in your thread hand.

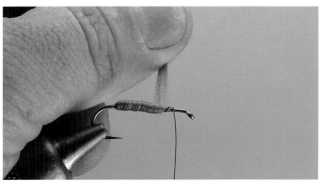

4. Bring your material hand back around the near side of the shank and transfer the material back into your material hand.

5. Repeat the above process as you wind the material forward on the shank to the awaiting thread. Materials must always be wrapped with two hands. You should have to work around the hanging bobbin to wrap the material, and if you find that you can smoothly wrap the material forward using just your thread hand you will also find that your thread is hanging at the wrong end of the hook. The thread must be waiting at the front of the hook to tie the material off, causing you to work around the hanging thread in this process.

TIE OFF

To tie a material off to the hook shank, you need the thread to cross the material and anchor it to the hook shank, which will involve switching the material into your thread hand and working the thread with your material hand. Wrapping the thread back over the front edge of the wrapped material without changing hands doesn't allow the thread to cross the material and makes for a much less durable fly.

1. Wrap the material up to the waiting thread and transfer it to your thread hand. Hold the material taut above the shank and pull it slightly forward so it angles out toward the hook eye.

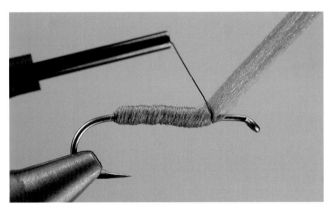

2. Pick up the bobbin in your material hand and wrap the thread over the material where it crosses the hook shank. Make a two firm wraps here to securely anchor the material.

3. Note how the thread crosses the material and binds it to the shank. Also notice the minimal bulk at the tie-off point.

TRANSFER MEASUREMENT

Measuring materials against the hook shank can be a bit confusing. To view the shank as you measure the hair, you'll need to hold the hair (or material being measured) in your thread hand to get an idea of how its length correlates to the shank's length. You'll then often need to transfer the material to your other hand to tie it in. Essentially, I just butt the ends of my fingers together to transfer the measured hair from one hand to the other. You must be careful not to let the hair shift in your fingertips as you switch hands, but with practice this technique becomes second nature. Here is how I go about measuring and transferring materials from one hand to the other without changing their measured length.

1. I am using a clump of moose hock hair in these photos, but the method is the same regardless of the material. Hold the hair against the top of the hook shank with the tips extending the length you desire. In this case, you want the hair to be a shank-length long, so push the tips back to the hook bend while holding the butt ends even with the back edge of the hook eye. Use the extreme edge of your thumb to visually mark the length of the hair as you hold it in your thread hand.

2. Bring your material hand in and butt the fingertips of both hands together at the rear edge of the hook eye. Grab the hair slightly behind the one-shank-length point so that you have a useable amount of material in front of your material-hand fingertips to attach to the shank when you tie it in.

3. Let go of the hair with your thread hand, so you now have it pinched in the fingertips of your material hand with the pre-measured tips inside your fingers. The hook eye should still be exposed beyond your fingertips, but your index finger is now marking that length on the backside of the hair clump.

4. Pick the hair up and move the pinched butt ends to the hook bend, using the edge of your forefinger to mark where the butt ends meet the shank at the bend.

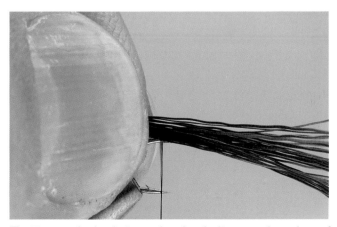

5. To attach the hair to the shank, line up the edge of your fingertip with the hanging thread to assure that the one-shank-length point on the hair lines up with the thread at the bend.

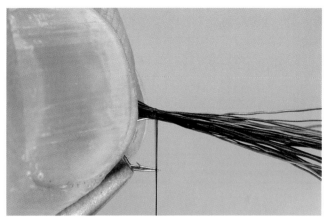

6. Wrap over the hair and anchor it at the hook bend with a few turns of thread.

7. The tips of the hair now extend beyond the hook shank one shank-length, forming a perfectly proportioned tail.

8. From this point, you can wrap the thread forward over the butt ends of the hair, forming an underbody and anchoring the hair in place as you go. If the butt ends want to roll around the shank as you wrap forward over them, use the tip of the index finger on your material hand along the backside of the shank to hold them atop the hook and keep them from rolling over.

WHIP-FINISHING

A whip-finish is the knot you use to tie off the thread once you are done tying the fly. It is exactly the same as the nail knot you use to tie your leader to the end of your fly line. Some tiers use half-hitches rather than a whip-finish, reasoning that a few half-hitches are the same as a single whip-finish. This just isn't true. The whip-finish is a much more secure knot. Take the time to learn this knot now because you'll use it on every fly you'll ever tie. I will do my best to photograph and explain the steps for using a Matarelli whip-finish tool, but if you have trouble, go to your local shop and get a short lesson from one of the salespeople. This knot is simple when you see it in person.

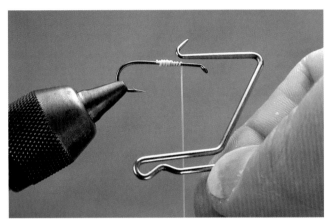

1. Begin with the whip-finisher in your thread hand. Hold the tool at the ball below the head with the hook and the notch pointing toward the hook bend. Bring the tool down on the front side of the thread.

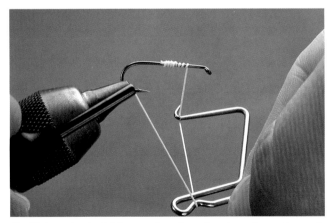

2. Bring the bobbin up, drawing the thread up through the notch at the base of the tool while simultaneously catching the thread with the hook on top of the tool.

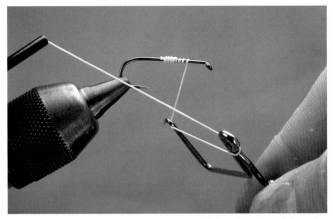

3. Let go of the ball at the base of the head and let the tool rotate down and then toward you.

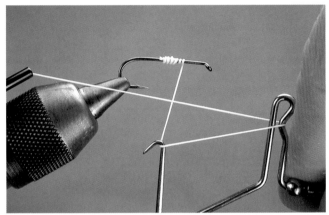

4. Invert the tool under the hook, forming an upside-down figure-four.

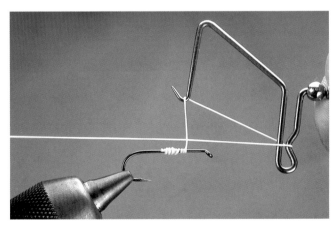

5. Turn the tool to the top of the hook, moving the figure-four to the top of the shank. The horizontal strand of thread should now be on the backside of the vertical strand.

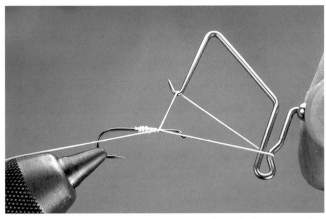

6. Draw the intersection of the thread down to the hook shank, placing it where you want your knot.

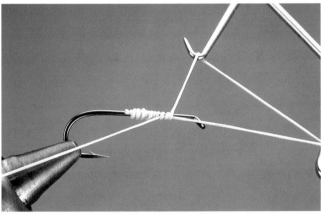

7. Turn the tool around the shank, wrapping the vertical strand of thread over the hook shank and the horizontal strand from three to five times. The horizontal strand does not travel around the shank and should stay on the near side of the hook and in-line with the shank.

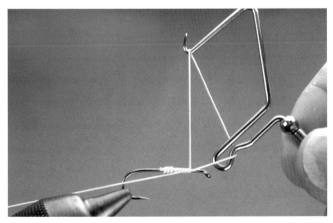

8. Draw the working thread out toward the bend while lifting the tool up until the thread pops off the notch.

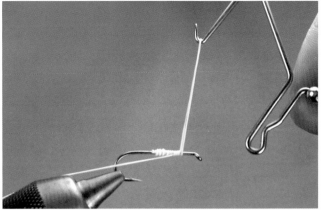

9. Once the thread pops off the notch, draw the working thread tight while holding it in the hook of the tool.

10. Draw the slack from the loop by pulling back on the working thread, lowering the hook on the tool down to the shank. Keep the thread in the hook until it is drawn all the way down to the shank to keep from trapping any errant fibers on your fly.

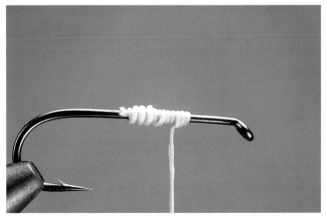

11. Slip the hook out of the loop and draw the bobbin back tightly toward the bend to cinch the knot.

CHAPTER 5

Dubbing

In fly tying, the word "dubbing" has at least two meanings. As a noun, "dubbing" refers to fur, natural or synthetic, or even a mix of the two, twisted around the tying thread and then wrapped on the hook to build bodies. As a verb, it means the actual act of twisting fur onto thread. You can choose from a plethora of different dubbing types. Animal furs like rabbit, beaver, muskrat, and opossum are all readily available in a variety of natural and dyed colors. Natural fur dubbings offer good translucency, are easy to work with, and come in a variety of textures. They also have an attractive natural mottling, even when dyed, that breaks up the color pattern on the fly. The fur from water animals like muskrats are purported to be more buoyant than furs from land animals, but to be honest I have seen no real difference between

them. Natural dubbings have short underfur and longer guard hairs, and the mix of the two produces a wonderfully animated dubbing with a buggier look than flies tied with synthetics.

Synthetic dubbings are available with short and long fibers. Dry fly dubbings have fine, long fibers that are waterproof and easy to work with. The shorter stuff works well for buggy nymphs and flies that you shag out with a dubbing brush like scuds or streamers. These dubbings pick out well and create lifelike gills and legs on flies that breathe in the water. Some synthetic dubbing are made from flashy materials or have flashy materials added to them. Adding a bit of sparkle to a fly can be a great way to make it stand out, but like salt and pepper, too much flash can ruin a fly. I try to limit my use of

Dubbing is both a material and a technique. Most tiers try to attach too much to the thread at one time.

flashy dubbings to small heads or thoraxes, rather than dubbing the entire fly with them. Synthetics also have consistent color and texture. If I run out of a particular kind of synthetic dubbing, I just run over and get another pack that is exactly the same as the last one. No mixing colors, shearing hides, or trying to pick out a particularly good package from the peg on the wall. I do prefer synthetic dubbings that are a mix of colors, however, as the mottling adds a hint of life to my patterns.

Though not always an easy task, it is important to pick the right dubbing for the job. Some dubbing is short and coarse and makes shaggy bodies, while others are fine and long, creating smooth, slick bodies. Some dubbings are buoyant; some sink. Generally, I prefer fine dubbings like Super Fine, Antron, and beaver fur for dry flies and short, coarse dubbings like hare's mask, rabbit, and Ice Dub for nymphs. Run by your favorite fly shop, pick out a few different types of dubbing, and play with them a bit. You can take some dubbing out of the package and roll it in your fingers a bit to get the overall idea, but until you have tied a few flies and dubbed a bit of thread, it is hard to get a good idea of the nuances and variances in each type. Start with the dubbings in this book and expand on them if you wish.

Super Fine is a long-fiber, waterproof, synthetic dubbing that works as well as any dubbing I have found. It comes in a large variety of hatch-matching colors, but not in any bright attractor shades. I use Super Fine for most of my dry fly patterns. Antron dubbing is another synthetic with long, fine fibers. Antron soaks up a little bit of water, and it can be used on either dry flies or nymphs. Antron is available in a rainbow of both natural and bright attractor shades. This dubbing is slicker and more slippery than Super Fine and as such requires a tight pinch and roll to twist it onto the thread. Antron dubbing is great for flies like the Stimulator because it comes in a wide variety of hot colors.

Hare's-mask dubbing, or hare's ear, is a short-fiber natural dubbing with outstanding mottling and spiky guard hairs. Hare's mask also has some short, soft underfur that helps to bind it to the thread when you dub. Unlike Super Fine, the short fibers in hare's mask need more and tighter twisting to wrap them around the thread, and it helps to apply this dubbing in smaller increments. Hare's-mask dubbing is great for nymph patterns, but it is not particularly buoyant. It can be used on some low-floating dry flies, however, as its shaggy guard hairs can mimic legs, and modern floatants will counteract its propensity to soak up water—for awhile at least. Hare's masks are available in a variety of dyed colors, all of which still feature the prominent barring and variegation of the natural mask. While you can purchase pre-packaged dubbing, I only use the stuff straight from the mask—the store-bought version is but a shadow of the real thing (see the Gold Ribbed Hare's Ear chapter for more information).

Dubbing fur onto thread is really a simple skill, but in my eyes it is a good indicator of a fly tier's prowess. The difference between a decent tier and a good tier can often be boiled down to the quality of their dubbing skills. The most common mistake I see is that new tiers use too much dubbing. I have joked in my fly tying classes that I am going to start charging $50 for a package of dubbing so the students will start conserving it. Most standard trout flies require such a small amount of dubbing that an average pack of Super Fine should last a recreational tier most of his life. I once kept track of how many flies I could get out of one pack of Super Fine and found that I could tie over 500 dozen #20 RS2s from it. I often make a game out of how little dubbing I can get away with. Peel eight or ten individual fibers from the dubbing clump and twist them onto the thread. You'll see that is plenty for a small fly and produces a thin, smooth body with a very slight taper. Using too much dubbing bulks up the flies and throws off the proportions. Remember, it is much easier to add a bit of dubbing than it is to remove it. When in doubt, use less.

By too much dubbing, I mean both a dubbing strand that is too long and a dubbing strand that is too thick. A proper strand of dubbing (particularly for a small fly) should be just slightly thicker than the thread. Of course, there are exceptions to this and every other rule, but as a general guideline, try to spread a little bit of dubbing over a longer length of thread to keep a thin strand. The dubbed thread should just look furry, and the dubbing should just add texture and color to the thread with little additional diameter. Fine-tuning this technique involves spreading even less dubbing over a much shorter length of thread to build ultra-small bodies.

Bigger flies require more dubbing, so do what needs to be done to form proportionate bodies. You can wrap a heavy yarn or Furry Foam underbody to build bulk on bigger flies, and then dub over the yarn to create the color and texture you want. You can also build larger fly bodies by adding more dubbing to the thread. If you do this, make sure the fur is adequately twisted around the thread so that it wraps tightly. Loose dubbing doesn't stay on the fly when you fish it. There are applications that call for loose, soft turns of dubbing, but frankly these are most commonly used on flies that don't appeal to me. Dubbing should be applied tightly to the thread and wrapped tightly on the fly. If I want a shaggy fly, I pick out the fibers with a dubbing brush once the fly is done rather than trying to dub loosely in the beginning.

Loosely wrapped dubbing loses its shape and falls apart too easily.

I apply nearly every type of dubbing in the same way, making adjustments as needed. Essentially, dubbing properly involves twisting the fur around the thread strand in a smooth, even application. Think of dubbing as paint, rather than spackle. You want to color and perhaps texture the thread without bulking it up too much. In the photos below I am using Super Fine, which has long, fine fibers. Always align the fibers parallel to the thread. If you align them perpendicular to the thread, you'll end up with a dubbing rope that looks like a segmented cord when wrapped on the hook (which is fine and dandy if that's what you're after). Shorter-fiber dubbings can be dubbed in a perpendicular fashion without altering their overall effect too much, but if your dubbing fibers are long, align them parallel with the thread.

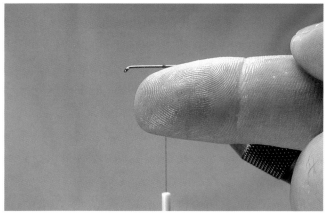

2. If you can see wax on your fingertip, you have too much. If you have dry hands, as I do, dubbing wax is a great help, but if you are one of those sweaty-hand prewaxed kind of people, you may not need any.

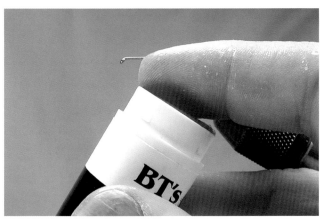

1. Before you sit down to tie any fly, wash your hands. Clean hands prevent any crud from rubbing off your fingers and onto the dubbing or thread when you tie. Once your hands are clean and dry, run the tip of your right (dominant) index finger across the top of the dubbing wax to give it a light coating of wax, then rub the tip of your index finger against your thumb so that both fingers have a very light coat of wax. This wax is only to help you gain traction on the dubbing, not to stick it all together or adhere it to the thread.

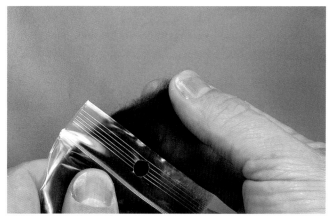

3. I use the little zip bags as dubbing dispensers and rarely take an entire clump of dubbing out of the original package. I like that I can draw a length of dubbing from the top of the bag without getting the fibers twisted or curled up. The little fly boxes with holes drilled in them that are sold as dubbing dispensers are one of the worst things in the world for long-fiber, fine dubbings like Super Fine. Balling a pack of Super Fine up in a knot and stuffing it in a little box should be punishable with forty lashes in my book. Cramming the dubbing in these little spaces assures that it gets crumpled and will never lie straight again. The dubbing is put into the plastic baggie packages so that it aligns with the long side of the bag, ready to draw out in smooth, straight portions. These little baggies take up minimal space and file away nicely in a drawer. Leave them as they are.

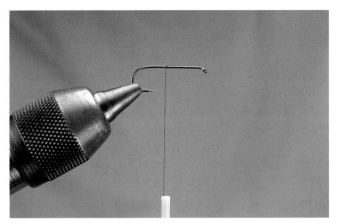

4. To prepare for a dubbed abdomen, pull enough thread from the bobbin tube to form the body and apply it to the hook easily. Make aure that the thread is not so long that you have to make giant circling turns with your arm as you wrap it.

I typically don't care where exactly the thread is hanging on the hook shank when I twist the dubbing onto the thread, as long as it's not right where I want the dubbing to start on the shank. I usually move the thread to the midpoint on the hook if it's not already there before I dub an abdomen. There is, invariably, a short length of bare thread, a half inch or so, between the top of the dubbing strand and the hook shank. I use this bare thread to work back to the bend, placing the first turn of dubbing right at the hook bend. If I leave the thread hanging at the bend and still have this bare thread, I have to pile up several turns of bare thread at the hook bend to work the dubbing up to the hook, creating a lump of thread at the back of the body. This is not conducive to forming a tapered body that starts off small.

If you are dubbing a head, you just have to try to start the dubbing as close to the hook as you can to keep from having a bunch of bare thread to work onto the fly before you start wrapping dubbing. Try to avoid the hook point as you twist the dubbing onto the thread up close to the hook—it will reach right out and grab you when you least expect it.

Some tiers will just slide and pull the dubbing strand up the thread to the shank before they start to wrap, but I find that sliding the dubbing loosens it and makes for a ragged body. If you dub the fur onto the thread tightly, you probably won't be able to move it anyway, particularly if it's a long-fiber dubbing like Super Fine.

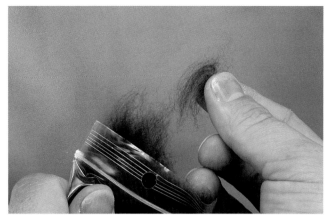

5. Open the dubbing package and pull a few fibers off one corner of the dubbing bunch. Toss these few fibers in the trash. Hanging from the bag should be the straight ends of the dubbing fibers, all aligned parallel to each other and ready to go.

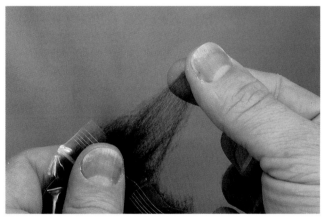

6. Pinch a small amount of this dubbing in your thumb and forefinger and pull it straight out of the pack.

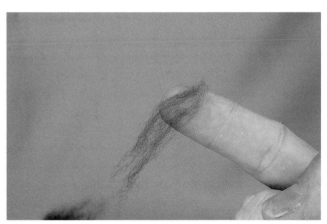

7. Note its overall inverted triangle shape. The end you grabbed is the wide end, and when you tore it away from the main clump, it tapers into a point on the other end.

8. Turn this clump of dubbing over, so the fine-tapered end is facing up toward the hook. This does two things. It gives you the smallest amount of dubbing possible to start twisting on the thread, which in turn makes your first wrap of dubbing as small as it can be. The first turn of dubbing on the shank is the base line of any tapered body, so the thinner this first wrap, the thinner you can make the rest of the body without throwing off the overall shape. Doing this also tapers the actual dubbing clump so the bottom of the dubbing strand will be slightly thicker, helping to taper the front end of the finished fly.

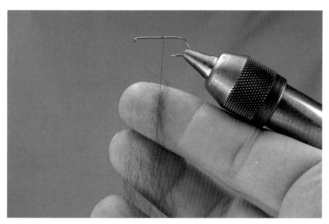

9. Lay the tapered end of the dubbing on the tip of your dominant index finger, letting it lightly adhere to the wax you rubbed on there earlier. You want the sparsest amount of dubbing possible at the top of your finger. Bring this finger in behind the thread, with the dubbing between your finger and the thread.

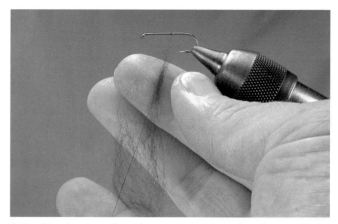

10. Pinch your thumb against your index finger at the first knuckle. You are not touching the dubbing with your thumb yet.

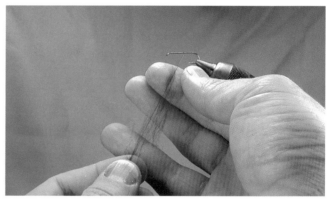

11. Grasp the base of the dubbing clump with your left hand and draw it down along the thread just enough that it spreads out into a long strand. You don't want to pull the dubbing clump apart, just feed it out over the length of the thread so it is evenly distributed from the top to the bottom of the thread. Hold the base of the dubbing loosely in your left hand as you go on to twist the top end onto the thread. You can pull down slightly on the bottom end of the dubbing to spread the clump out as you twist the top end to help distribute the dubbing evenly over the thread.

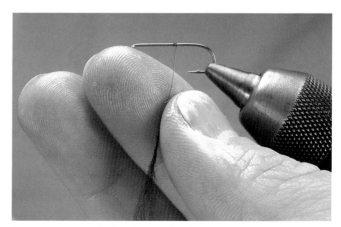

12. Pull your index finger back . . .

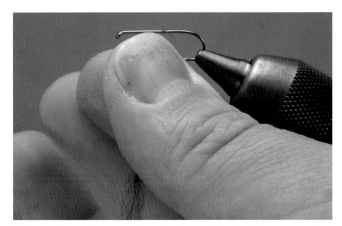

13. and push your thumb forward, pinching your fin-gers together *as tightly as you can,* and let them roll over the top of the dubbing, from right to left for a right-handed tier. Open your fingers and repeat the above process over the top of the dubbing. Make sure you only twist and roll the dubbing in one direction—in this case, clockwise—around the thread. If you twist going for-ward and back without releasing your fingers from the thread in between, you'll roll the dubbing onto the thread, then roll it off, then roll it on, then off again. We want the dubbing on the thread, so just roll one direc-tion. The direction you roll makes no difference, but you have to pick one way and stick with it.

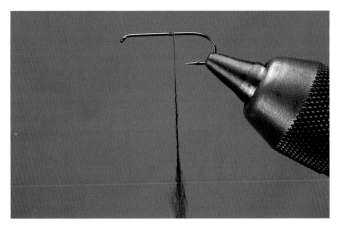

14. Once the top end of the dubbing clump is firmly twisted around the thread, pull down on the bottom of the dubbing clump with your other hand to spread the dubbing in an even layer.

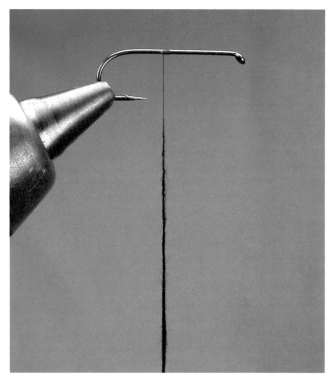

15. Continue twisting the dubbing onto the thread, working from the top on down the strand until you run out of dubbing. If you feel that you have enough dub-bing on the thread to shape the body of the fly, yet still have dubbing left in the clump at the bottom, go ahead and tear away any extra dubbing before you twist it all down tight to the thread. Just because you pulled the dubbing from the package doesn't mean you have to use it all. Make a mental note of how much you used this time and reduce that amount for the next fly.

Make certain that the top and bottom ends of the dubbing are tight on the thread and tapered to a point. If the ends of the dubbing are loose, they will wrap that way on the hook and make an unkempt body.

To start the dubbing, use the bare thread between the top of the dubbed thread and the hook shank to wind back to the hook bend. Space the wraps of bare thread so you use it up along the way back and run out of thread. Make the first turn of dubbing at the hook bend and continue wrapping the dubbed thread forward to form the body. I cover building tapers and shapes in depth on the patterns as we tie them, but the above is basically how I apply any type of dubbing. Shorter-fiber dubbings like hare's ear and rabbit are still applied in the same way, but in smaller batches and increments as you work down the thread. I use my left hand to distribute and feed the dubbing into my right hand, which does all the twisting. Practice this technique and keep at it, alter-ing the amount of dubbing and the length of thread you are twisting it on until you figure out what works for you.

CHAPTER 6

Brassie

MAIN FOCUS

Forming a smooth thread base and underbody • Learning the right-angle technique
Pulling a material to length • Wrapping wire • Dubbing basics

One of the easiest flies to tie, the Brassie is a realistic midge larva imitation in small sizes and a good caddis larva pattern when tied in slightly larger sizes and appropriate colors. I like to tie these in the traditional copper color and in black, chartreuse, red, blue, green, wine, and many other colors.

One of the reasons the Brassie is so effective is because the wire gives it enough weight to stay down along the bottom where the fish tend to feed. Many anglers have trouble casting weight on their leaders and thus use the smallest amount possible. While this can be a fatal mistake in many fishing circumstances, the Brassie allows many folks to get away with it. The inherent weight of the Brassie also makes it a great fly to use as a dropper under a dry fly. I have even started tying them with small tungsten beads in front of the dubbed head to add a bit more weight to really get them down. I call this version of the fly a Poison Tung.

Many pattern guides call for peacock or ostrich herl to be wrapped for the head of the Brassie. I substitute

The Brassie is a distinctive Colorado pattern developed by Gene Lynch and friends for the South Platte River. The original pattern was tied with the familiar copper wire body but had a somewhat chunky piece of heat-shrink tubing for a head in place of the now-common dubbing or peacock herl.

By changing the wire color, you can tie Brassies to imitate a wide range of midge and caddis larvae.

dubbing for two reasons: dubbing makes it easier to control the size and shape of the head and is far more durable than peacock herl. Peacock and ostrich herl, while beautiful and effective materials, are not durable and are often too bushy on a small fly. Dubbing the head solves both of these troubles. I often use oversized wire on my Brassies for the extra segmentation and weight.

I like to use the Tiemco 100 or Tiemco 100SP-BL, both technically dry fly hooks, for Brassies and many other small nymphs. Most standard nymph hooks aren't

available smaller than size 20. Using the dry fly hook gives me the flexibility to tie smaller flies than the nymph hooks' range allows and keeps them in proportion to the larger flies. For instance, if I were to tie Brassies in sizes 16–20 on a Tiemco 3761 (a 1X-long, heavy-wire nymph hook available down to a size 20), then switch to a Tiemco 100 (a standard shank length, wide-gap dry-fly hook available to size 26) for flies smaller than that, there would be a large gap in the actual physical size difference between the size 20 Tiemco 3761 and the size 22 Tiemco

PROPORTIONS AT A GLANCE

HEAD:
10 to 15 percent of
the hook shank

BODY:
85 to 90 percent
of the hook shank

BRASSIE

Brassie materials

Hook: #14–24 Tiemco 100, 101, 9300, 2457, 2487, 2488, 2488H, 200, or 100SP-BL
Thread: Black 8/0 Uni-Thread
Body: Copper Ultra Wire (#22–26, small; #18–20, Brassie; #14–16, medium)
Head: Black Super Fine, Ice Dub, rabbit, muskrat, or other

Note: Change wire color for a range of different patterns.

100. This size difference is a result of the Tiemco 3761 (a 1X-long hook) having a longer shank than the standard-length Tiemco 100.

To alleviate this, I have settled on tying small nymphs on dry fly hooks and haven't ever had a problem bending the hooks, as long as they are high quality and the tippet size stays relative to the hook size (dividing the hook size by three or four gives you the X size of tippet you should be using, but you can even fudge this one size up or down). Tiemco 100SP-BL hooks provide the perfect chassis for many of my small nymph patterns. While we still have the size issue to contend with (the 100SP-BL isn't available smaller than a size 20 at the moment), this slightly heavier-wire hook fits perfectly into the size pattern of the standard 100.

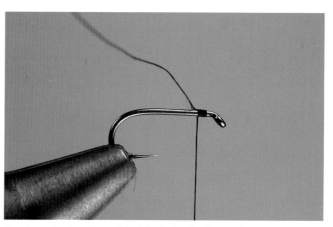

1. Attach the thread behind the index point.

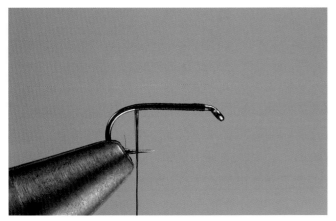

2. Trim the tag end, and wrap a smooth, even layer of thread back to the bend.

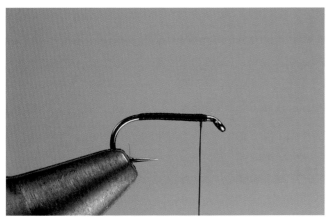

3. Return the tying thread to the back of the index point with more tightly spaced concentric wraps.

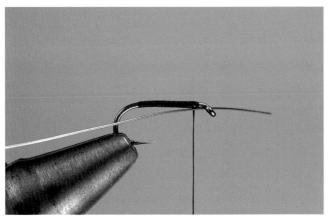

4. Clip from 6 to 8 inches of wire from the spool. Hold the wire in your material hand about an inch or so from the end. Place this end of the wire under the hook in the corner of the right angle (formed by the hanging thread and the hook shank), in front of the thread, so that it passes from the near side of the hook, behind the far side eye, and is pointing directly away from you.

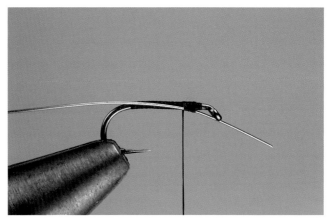

5. Wrap the thread up and over the end of the wire in one motion, trapping the wire against the bottom of the hook as you wrap. Continue wrapping the thread two or three more turns, one right next to the other, toward the hook bend.

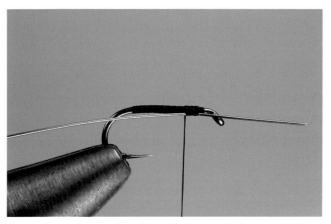

6. Pull the front end of the wire toward the near side of the hook so it is on your side of the hook eye.

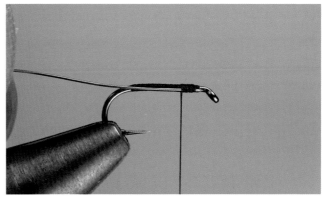

7. With your material hand braced against the vise, pull the long end of the wire back, shortening the front end that is sticking out over the hook eye until the front end is flush against the thread turns holding it down. If you accidentally pull the wire out from under the thread wraps, unwrap the thread and start over. Twist the wire to the near side of the hook so it is in-line with the shank.

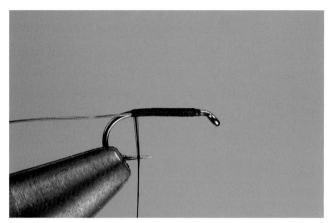

8. Continue wrapping the thread in tight, concentric (touching) wraps over the wire back to the hook bend. Keep the wire along the near side of the hook shank the entire way back to the bend to keep a smooth underbody. To do this, pull the wire slightly downward as you wrap over it with the thread so the thread torque pulls the wire to the near side of the hook.

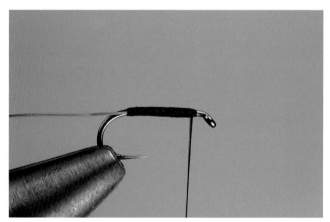

9. Return the thread to the back of the index point with tight concentric turns. Make certain the wraps nearest the hook bend are particularly tight to keep the wire from crawling around the hook when you begin to wrap it. At this point the thread should be hanging at the index point and the wire should be hanging off the hook bend.

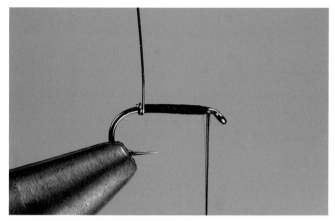

10. Wrap the wire over the top of the hook with your material hand. Make the first turn of wire perpendicular to the hook shank by pulling up hard as you begin the first turn. Pull the wire straight down on the far side of the shank. Reach under the hook and behind the thread with your other hand and transfer the wire to your thread hand. Hold the wire on the bottom side of the hook with your thread hand as you bring your material hand back around the near side of the shank to grasp the end for the next turn.

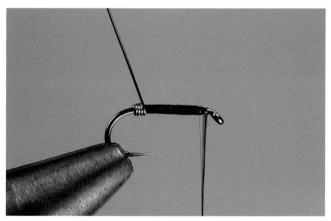

11. Continue wrapping the wire in touching turns with this hand-to-hand technique all the way to the rear edge of the index point. As you wrap, tilt the wire toward the hook bend as it makes its way around the shank so the previous wrap of wire guides the next. Roll the wire off the front edge of the previous wrap and it will fall into place next to it.

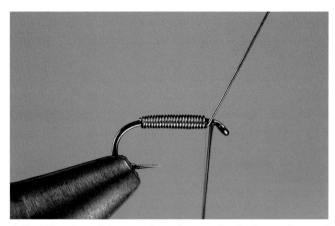

12. The thread is now hanging at the index point and the wire should be right behind it. Pull the wire above the hook and switch hands so it is now in your thread hand.

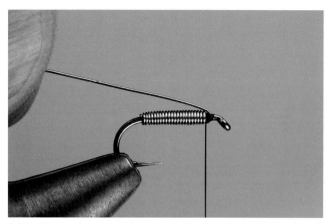

15. Twist it around in a circle parallel to the hook shank (as if it were a helicopter propeller) until it breaks off.

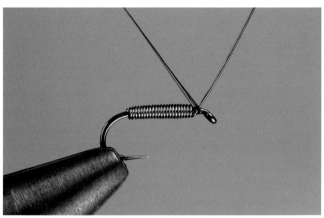

13. Pick up the bobbin with your material hand and make a turn of thread directly behind the long end of the wire (the one in your thread hand) tying the wire down to the hook shank. Make three or four more tight wraps at this point to secure the wire.

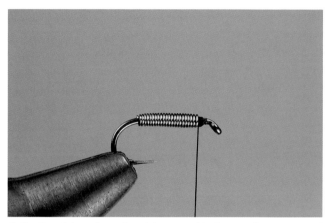

16. Breaking the wire this way eliminates the wear and tear on your scissors and leaves no stub end to contend with later. If you were to trim the end of the wire with your scissors, you would both dull your scissors and leave a stub of wire sticking out from the shank.

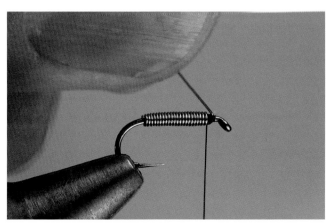

14. Hold the bobbin tightly in your thread hand and grasp the loose end of the wire with your material hand.

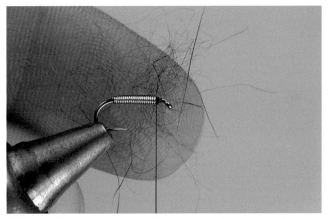

17. Pull down on the bobbin to feed out about 4 inches of thread. Tease a tiny amount of black rabbit dubbing from the package and place half of that amount on the table in front of you. Touch your right index finger to the top of your dubbing wax to pick up just the slightest amount of wax.

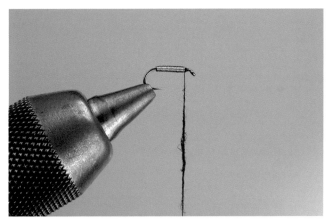

18. Pick up the dubbing you reserved earlier and apply a small amount at a time to the thread working from the top (closest to the hook) down, twisting it on in one direction only. Try to make a long (about one and a half inches), thin, even layer of dubbing on the thread with no lumps or bumps and no bald spots. This dubbing only adds a little texture and not much bulk.

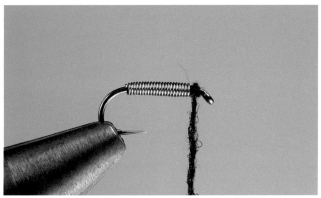

19. Begin wrapping the dubbed thread around the hook at the midpoint of the index point.

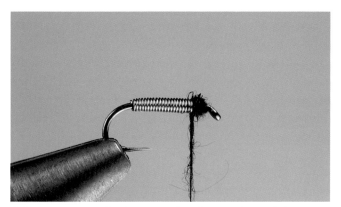

20. Continue back onto the front edge of the wire body. The diameter of this dubbing ball should be about 1 ½ times the diameter of the wire body.

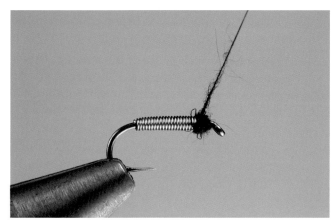

21. As you near the end of your dubbing strand, prepare to end with the bare thread on the bare hook shank immediately behind the hook eye. Do this by angling the last complete revolution of dubbing forward toward the hook eye, taking care not to let any bare thread cross over the dubbed head, which could catch in a fish's teeth and break, causing your fly to fall apart.

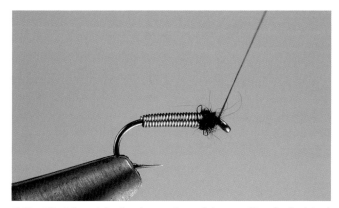

22. Finish with the bare thread immediately behind the hook eye in the index point. If you have too much dubbing on the thread, there is no law that says you have to use it all. Pull any extra dubbing off the thread, re-twist the end of the dubbing to tighten it, and continue on.

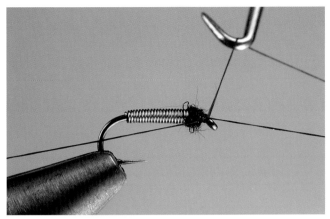

23. Whip-finish the thread at the index point (between the hook eye and the front edge of the dubbing).

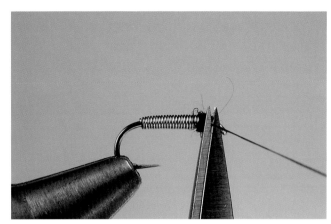

24. Clip the thread flush against the hook eye. You are the proud owner of your first Brassie.

PATTERN VARIATIONS

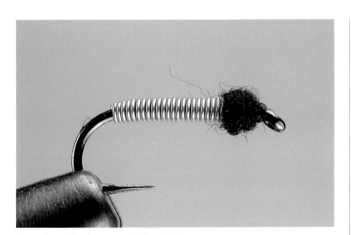

Brassie with chartreuse Ultra Wire.

Brassie with red Ultra Wire.

Brassie with green Ultra Wire.

Brassie with black Ultra Wire.

CHAPTER 7

Black Beauty

MAIN FOCUS

Ribbing and building a smooth thread body • Tying wire in without a thread base

Pat Dorsey, Colorado's illustrious South Platte River guide, popularized the Black Beauty in recent years. The Black Beauty is the ultimate guide fly—quick and easy to tie, durable, and it catches fish. The Black Beauty imitates midge larvae or pupae and is the basis for a number of other effective midge larva patterns.

Tie it with white thread and a black or gray dubbed head and you've got a Miracle Nymph; substitute silver wire for the rib and you have a Zebra Midge; red thread and no head makes a Blood Midge. You get the idea: a simple thread body ribbed with wire for segmentation and flash and a small dubbed head combine to match a variety of midge larvae. You can tie up a complete size

and color range to match midges anywhere using this fly as a pattern. Pat really likes the small glass Mercury Beads for this pattern and many others. I don't know why these work so well, but I'm now smart enough not to care.

I use the Black Beauty on a dropper behind a Pheasant Tail or RS2 much of the time and in tandem with a Brassie, Poison Tung, or other midge variation during the winter. Fishing a fly like the Black Beauty—something small and subtle that imitates prevalent foods—can sometimes be just the ticket when fishing to fish that are pounded or off the bite. Midge larvae are present in most rivers all year, and there aren't any other insects that the trout are so accustomed to seeing. This staple food is always a good bet, regardless of season or conditions.

The Black Beauty is the ultimate guide fly—quick and easy to tie, durable, and it catches fish.

PROPORTIONS AT A GLANCE

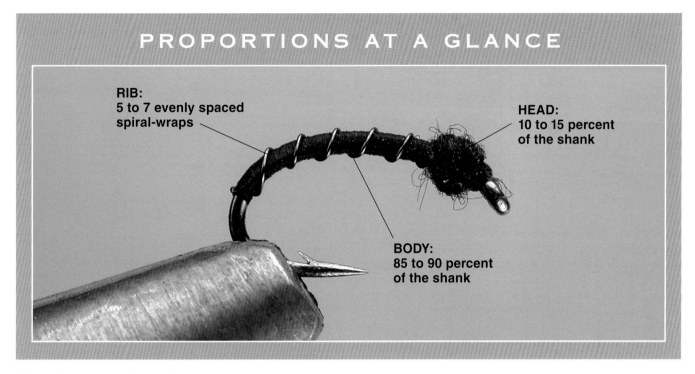

RIB:
5 to 7 evenly spaced
spiral-wraps

HEAD:
10 to 15 percent
of the shank

BODY:
85 to 90 percent
of the shank

1. Attach the thread behind the index point and clip the butt end. Leave the thread hanging at the rear edge of the index point.

2. Clip 6 inches of wire and tie it in (using the right-angle technique) at the rear edge of the index point. There should only be a small layer of thread on the hook at the index area. A thread base down the shank creates unnecessary bulk. The thread you use to tie down the wire and return to the index will create plenty of body on a small slender fly like this.

BLACK BEAUTY

Black Beauty materials.

Hook:	#16–24 Tiemco 2487 or 2488
Thread:	Black 70-denier Ultra Thread
Rib:	Lagartun copper wire (fine or extra fine)
Body:	Thread
Head:	Black Super Fine or any fine black dubbing

Note: The 70-denier thread makes a really shiny, smooth body and builds quickly. For flies smaller than #22, I typically switch to the narrower 8/0 Uni-Thread. Olive, brown, white, chartreuse, red, and gray are all good midge colors.

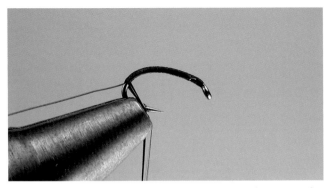

3. Wrap the tying thread over the wire (keeping the wire along the near side or the top of the hook) all the way to the hook bend, forming a smooth, even body. In the case of the Tiemco 2487, wrap the thread body back to about a third of the way down the bend.

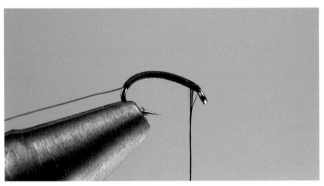

4. Return the thread to the rear of the index point, forming a smooth thread body with tight, concentric wraps.

5. Reposition the hook in the vise so the area immediately behind the eye is parallel to the tying surface. This will help keep the thread from trying to jump off the front of the hook in the next few steps. You may also have noticed that the tying thread is spread out and flattened at this point on the fly. This is because I wrapped the thread to form the body from the eye to the bend and back again, and with my left-handed wraps, have counter-spun the thread as I did this. I am using the ribbonlike 70-denier Ultra Thread for this fly, and it is not uncommon to have the thread spread out in this manner. The flattened thread creates a smooth, slick body and creates little bulk on the hook.

6. Wrap the wire ribbing forward with five to seven spiraling turns to the index point. Once there, grasp the end of the wire in your thread hand and hold it above and slightly in front of the hook.

7. Take the bobbin in your material hand and make three or four tight wraps of thread over the long end of the wire where it meets the hook (which should be at the rear of the index point).

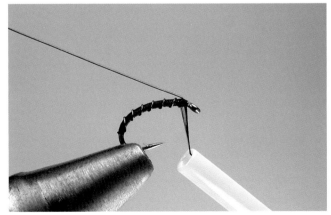

8. Pull down on the bobbin below the hook and tug the tag end of the wire sharply to the rear.

9. This motion should snap the wire off cleanly at the tie-down point. If not, you are probably using wire that is too big.

10. Pull a small amount of dubbing from the package and apply a bit of dubbing wax to your fingertips. Twist a 1-inch length of dubbing tightly onto the thread.

11. Wrap this dubbing onto the hook from the rear edge of the index point up onto the body slightly and forward again to just behind the hook eye. Form a small ball, and end with bare thread hanging at the index point.

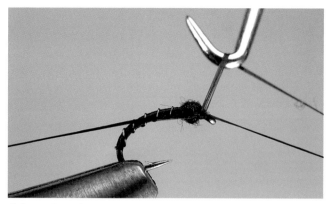

12. Whip-finish and clip the thread.

13. The finished fly.

PATTERN VARIATIONS

ZEBRA MIDGE

Hook: #16–24 Tiemco 2487 or 2488
Thread: Black 70-denier Ultra Thread
Rib: Lagartun silver wire (fine)
Head: Black Super Fine

BLOOD MIDGE

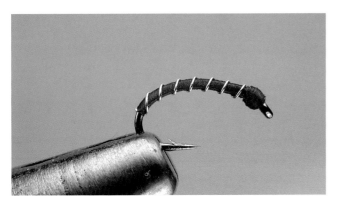

Hook: #16–24 Tiemco 2487 or 2488
Thread: Red 70-denier Ultra Thread
Rib: Lagartun silver wire (fine)
Head: Tying thread

GREEN MACHINE

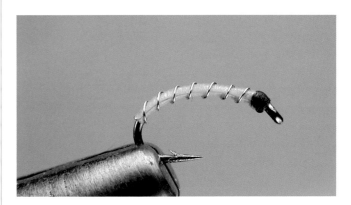

Hook: #16–24 Tiemco 2487 or 2488
Thread: Fluorescent-green 70-denier Ultra Thread
Rib: Lagartun silver wire (fine)
Head: Tying thread colored with black Sharpie
              marker

ZEBRA MIDGE EMERGER

Hook: #16–24 Tiemco 2487 or 2488
Thread: Black 70-denier Ultra Thread
Rib: Lagartun silver wire (fine)
Wing: Bright white Antron yarn
Head: Black Super Fine

OLIVE THREAD MIDGE

Hook:	#16–24 Tiemco 2487 or 2488
Thread:	Olive 6/0 Danville
Rib:	Black Ultra Wire (extra small)
Head:	Tying thread

BROWN BEADHEAD MIDGE

Hook:	#16–24 Tiemco 2487 or 2488
Bead:	¹⁄₁₆" copper-colored tungsten
Thread:	Camel 8/0 Uni-Thread
Rib:	Lagartun copper wire (fine)
Head:	Brown Super Fine

OLIVE MIDGE EMERGER

Hook:	#16–24 Tiemco 2487 or 2488
Thread:	Olive 6/0 Danville
Rib:	Black Ultra Wire (extra small)
Wing:	Bright white Antron yarn
Head:	Olive-brown beaver dubbing

MIRACLE NYMPH

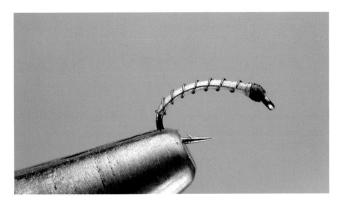

Hook:	#16–24 Tiemco 2487 or 2488
Thread:	White 70-denier Ultra Thread
Rib:	Lagartun copper wire (fine)
Head:	Tying thread colored with black Sharpie marker

DEEP BLUE POISON TUNG

Hook:	#16–24 Tiemco 2488
Bead:	2mm silver-colored tungsten
Thread:	Gray 8/0 Uni-Thread
Rib:	Blue Lagartun wire (fine)
Head:	UV gray Ice Dub

CHAPTER 8

RS2

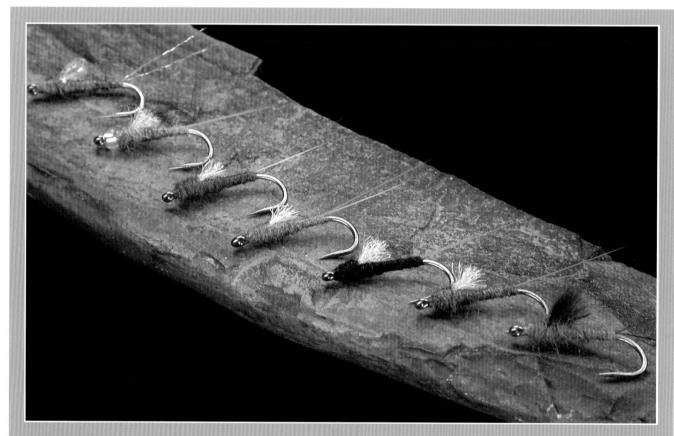

MAIN FOCUS

Splitting tails with the thread tag • Dubbing a separate abdomen and thorax
Tying in an emerger-style wing

The RS2 is one of my favorite flies. If you have ever had the pleasure of watching Rim Chung and his unconventional nymphing technique work through a run, this fly might become one of your favorites as well. This guy catches fish like nobody's business. Rim uses an old Sage LL rod in the 389 configuration (8-foot, 9-inch, 3-weight), a thin-diameter level line, and a long leader. He weights the leader with split shot or putty and uses no indicator. I could say that

Chung's deadly technique is reminiscent of the now-popular Czech nymphing style, but I believe I would have to say it the other way around, since Chung has been at this game long before I ever heard of Czech nymphing. Chung is a gracious and gentlemanly angler and is a pleasure to share the water with.

When I guided on the South Platte River it seemed that at least one of my clients always had an RS2 on, and I would bet that half the fish my clients caught were vic-

The RS2 (Rim's Semblance, version 2) is a simple, yet effective fly developed by Rim Chung for Colorado's South Platte River.

tims of this fly. Confidence in a pattern can make all the difference, and I have a lot of confidence in the RS2. The pattern that we will tie here is not Rim's original, but a variation that I developed over the years using alternative synthetic materials. Synthetics are, in my opinion, more durable, cheaper and easier to get, and more consistent than their natural counterparts.

I've incorporated a few special techniques into my RS2 variation after years of tying these flies. The first is to split the tail with the tag end of the thread. I first saw this method used by Scott Sanchez in *Tying Flies with Jack Dennis and Friends*. It is so simple and obvious (once you see it) that it will leave you slapping your forehead and wondering why you didn't think of it first.

The second trick, which is especially useful on flies smaller than #18, is to cut the Super Fine dubbing clump in half across the center of the bunch. Super Fine's long fibers make it hard to control the taper and density of the body. Cutting the dubbing lets you add it in smaller increments, allowing more control over its application.

The third trick is burning or melting the Antron wing clump. If you tie your RS2s with Antron wings, you quickly find out that you can only tie a few flies from a length of Antron before it starts to fall apart and become unusable. This trick prevents this and makes for more efficient use of both your time and materials. Clip a length of Antron from the package, so it is as wide as the card it came on, which is about 3 inches. Hold one end of the Antron up to a flame and melt the ends a bit. Take the flame away and quickly pinch the hot end (be careful) to fuse the end together. Now you have a "wing blank" that will tie a dozen flies without falling apart. You tie the loose ends of the Antron to the hook, so the melted end will always be toward the rear of the hook and stay intact for the next fly.

Rim Chung's original RS2.

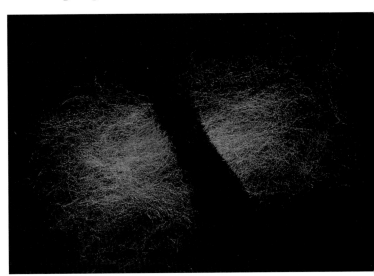

Cutting the dubbing clump in half, or even in thirds, makes it much easier to draw out and apply a very thin strand of dubbing for small flies.

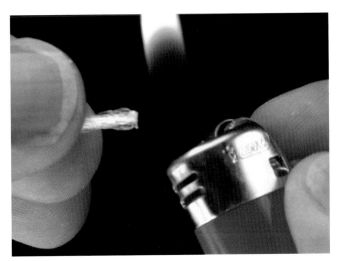

1. Melt ends.

2. Quickly pinch the ends.

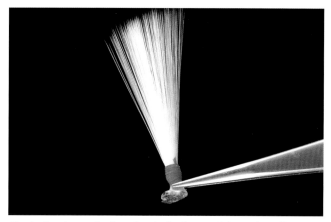

Stack the tips and whip-finish the butts of the tailing fibers.

When you buy a pack of these fibers, they are typically taped to a paper card and slightly stuck together at their base. The fibers separate and become hard to handle and the tips are never even.

To alleviate the trouble with unruly synthetic tailing fibers, take a brand new pack of tailing fibers and remove the tape and the paper card, then cut the gooey bases off. Put the entire clump in your hair stacker and tap them a few times to even them. Remove the fibers from the stacker and bind the ends with heavy thread (use brightly colored thread so you can find the clump more easily), just like you would on a fly. Tie a whip-finish around the bases and clip the thread. Melt the butt ends of the clump with a flame and press the hot end against your workbench to form a small nub. Now you have clean, nicely stacked tailing fibers that won't separate for years to come.

The RS2 is the first fly in this book that uses the front-to-back dubbing technique. After tying in the wing, the wing butts will create bulk on the hook that forms a slope toward the hook eye. If you were to try to dub from the base of the wing forward to the hook eye, the dubbing would slide down the hill and pile up at the hook eye. To counteract this, dub from the rear edge of the index point up to the base of the wing and then back to the index. This allows you to climb the dubbing up that slope using each wrap to support the next, instead of collapsing on top of one another. This also assures the abdomen and thorax tapers flow together.

The RS2 is a great mayfly emerger pattern that can be fished from the stream bottom to the surface. I most often dead-drift it on the bottom as a nymph, but it can be effective on the swing also. I typically rig a #20 RS2 in a two-fly rig with a Pheasant Tail or Barr Emerger on the front end with the RS2 on a 12- to 15-inch dropper off the bend of the first fly. I have also fished the RS2 as an emerger pattern in the surface film. I have taken to fishing it behind a Parachute Adams or other visible dry so I can spend less time searching for the fly and more time catching fish. While the standard RS2 color is gray, this fly is also a killer in black, brown, and olive.

RS2

RS2 materials.

Hook:	#16–24 Tiemco 101
Thread:	Gray 8/0 Uni-Thread
Tail:	White Mayfly Tails, Microfibbets, or other synthetic tailing fibers
Abdomen:	Gray Super Fine
Wing:	Bright white Antron
Thorax:	Gray Super Fine

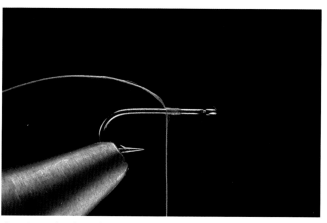

1. Attach the thread at the 75 percent point on the hook, leaving a long tag end.

PROPORTIONS AT A GLANCE

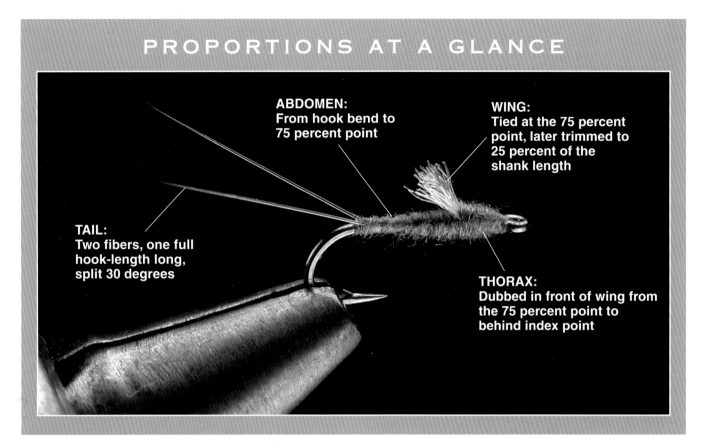

ABDOMEN:
From hook bend to 75 percent point

WING:
Tied at the 75 percent point, later trimmed to 25 percent of the shank length

TAIL:
Two fibers, one full hook-length long, split 30 degrees

THORAX:
Dubbed in front of wing from the 75 percent point to behind index point

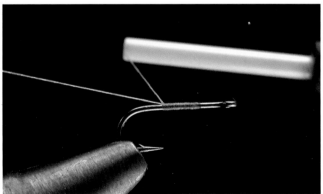

2. Wrap back over the tag end toward the hook bend, taking care to keep the tag end along the top of the hook by lifting it slightly toward you.

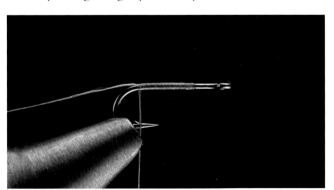

3. Thread torque should pull the tag to the top of the shank.

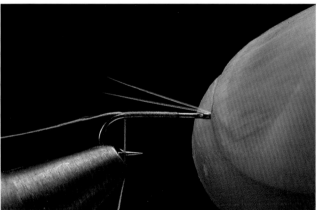

4. Select two fibers from the bundle of tailing material and even the tips. Measure these against the hook shank so that they are a full hook-length long and grasp them at this point with your material hand. The tapered ends should be in your fingertips with the butt ends sticking out toward the hook eye.

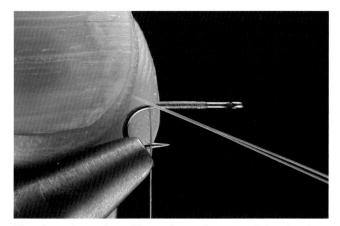

5. Place the tailing fibers along the top of the shank at the bend at an angle that points the butt ends at your thread-hand-side shoulder.

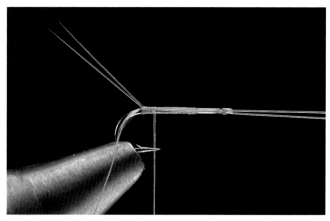

8. The tails should be separated and on top of the hook. Make sure the tails are not crossed up or tied down on one side of the hook shank. If the tails are off to one side, splitting them will become much more difficult.

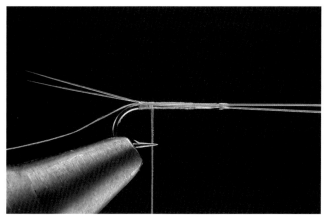

6. Wrap the thread up and over the tail fibers, allowing the thread torque to twist the tail fibers to the top of the hook shank. Make another two turns of thread over the butt ends of the tail up to the hook point.

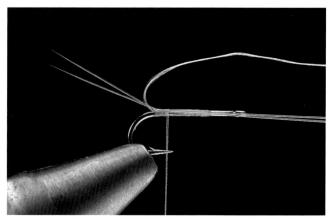

9. Lift the tag end of the thread that was hanging off the hook bend up between the tails.

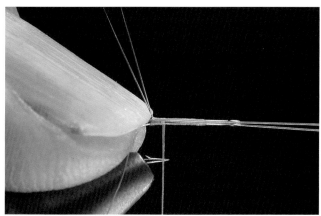

7. Press your thumbnail up under the tails to lift and splay them out.

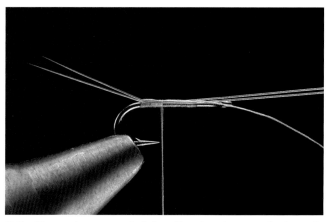

10. Draw the tag end tight, allowing it to push the tails apart. You may need to maneuver the tag to the left or right side of the hook to manipulate the tail fibers so they are split evenly. Tie the tag end down at the hook point with a turn or two of thread. All the thread turns are traveling forward one in front of the other to eliminate bulk at the rear of the fly.

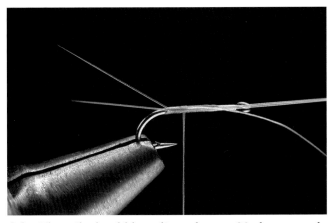

11. The tails should be split at about a 30-degree angle to each other and be slightly elevated.

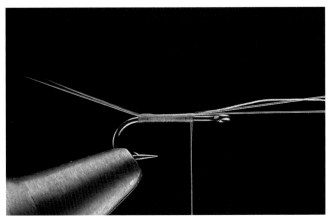

12. Continue wrapping the working thread forward to the 75 percent point, one turn in front of the other.

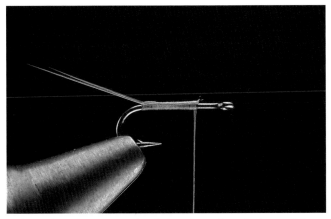

13. Clip the tag end of the thread and the tail butt ends.

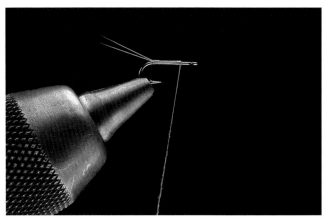

14. Dub the thread with a thin, slightly tapered strand of gray dubbing. There should be ½ to 1 inch of bare thread between the top of the dubbing strand and the hook shank.

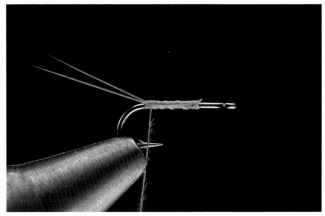

15. Use this bare thread to work back over the shank to the hook bend. Notice the widely spaced spiraling wraps of thread from the front to the back of the hook.

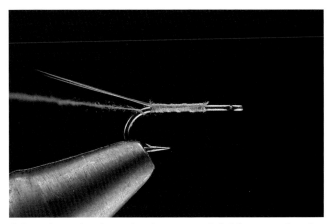

16. Place the first, slender turn of dubbing under the tails by wrapping around the shank just as you normally would . . .

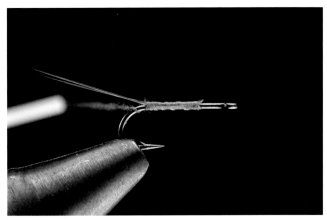

17. but wrap the dubbing under and behind the tails.

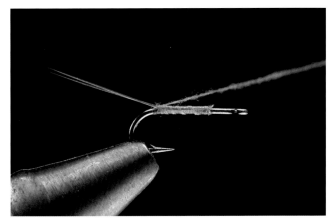

18. Draw the dubbed thread forward as you come around the backside of the hook shank, pulling the first turn of dubbing up against the base of the tails. This turn should prop the tails up and cover the tag end of the thread that you used to split the tails. Once the dubbing is tight against the tails, drop the bobbin to bring the thread under the hook shank in front of the base of the tails.

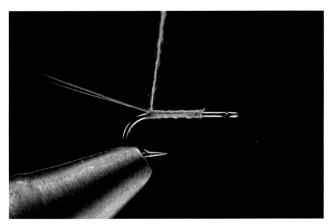

19. Make the next turn straight up over the top of the shank at the front edge of the tails. A thin strand of dubbing is required for the slightly tapered body.

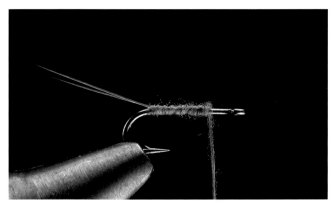

20. Wrap the dubbing forward in a single layer to the 75 percent point on the shank. The trick to making a slightly tapered body such as this with a single, thin layer of dubbing lies in the angle of the first few turns. I wrap the first three turns of dubbing at a dramatic angle toward the front of the shank, almost spiraling the thread forward. About halfway up the body, I start to make the wraps more perpendicular to the shank, allowing the dubbing to bulk up.

21. Wrap the remaining dubbing back over the front half of the abdomen, creating a second thin layer of dubbing.

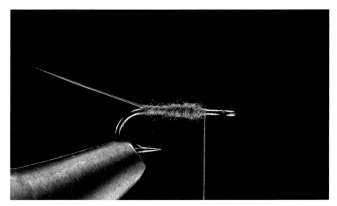

22. Move the last of the dubbing forward from the midpoint of the abdomen to the 75 percent point by making two spiraling turns forward. Strive for an even taper with no lumps, bumps, or gaps. End with the bare thread at the front edge of the abdomen on bare shank.

23. Wrap a smooth, flat thread base up to the hook eye.

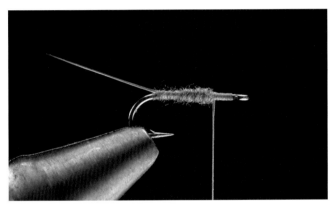

24. Wrap back to the front edge of the abdomen to cover the shank with a thread base for the wing to adhere to.

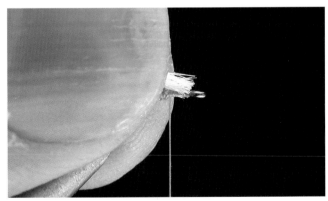

25. Pick up the Antron wing blank you prepared at the beginning and clip the loose ends square. Hold the loose ends of the Antron between your thumb and forefinger of your material hand as close to the tips as you can. Place the yarn flush against the top of the hook shank with the stub ends facing forward. You do not want any space between the Antron and the hook shank. They should be touching, and the thread should be hanging directly at the front edge of the dubbed abdomen. I always use an entire strand of Antron yarn for the wing, rather than thinning it down for smaller flies. Fewer fibers don't form the same wing profile, and besides, the Antron compresses well on the hook and creates little bulk.

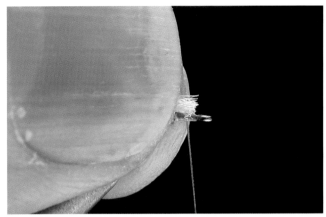

26. Bring the working thread up above the hook and push the bobbin tube toward the hook bend, sliding a length of thread in between your fingertips on the near side of the Antron. Drop the bobbin over the far side of the hook, but keep tension on the thread loop in your fingertips so it doesn't draw tight just yet. You should have a loop of thread up and over the material inside your fingertips. This is the beginning of a pinch wrap and allows you to tie the Antron down onto the top of the shank without the thread twisting it to the far side.

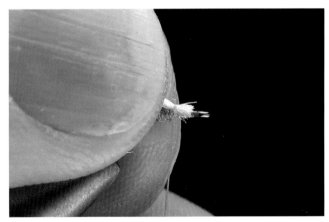

27. Draw the bobbin straight down, closing the loop within your fingertips so it catches the Antron against the top of the hook shank. Do this whole maneuver one more time before letting go of the yarn. It takes two turns like this to make a complete thread revolution around the hook to lock things down.

28. The loose ends of the Antron should be well behind the hook eye. If they are not, pull the butt ends to shorten the ends so they are.

29. Wrap forward over the ends of the Antron up to the hook eye. Let the thread hang in the index point.

30. Twist a bit more dubbing onto the thread.

31. Begin wrapping the dubbing from the back edge of the index point up to the base of the wing. Wrapping the dubbing up the slope from the front to the back of the hook prevents the dubbing from sliding down the hill you created with the butt ends of the wing.

32. Wrap the remaining dubbing forward to the back edge of the index point, ending with bare thread behind the hook eye, so that you have a descending taper with the thickest point at the base of the wing. Overall, the whole fly should look like an elongated teardrop when viewed from the bottom, with no seam or gap at the wing.

33. Whip-finish and clip the thread.

34. The wing is now ready for trimming.

36. Clip it straight across at the back edge of the hook eye.

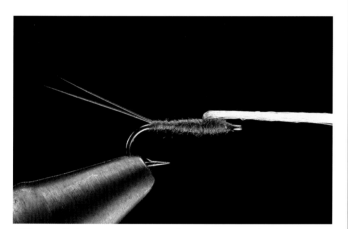

35. Pull the wing straight forward over the hook eye.

37. Another view of the finished fly.

PATTERN VARIATIONS

BLACK RS2

Hook:	#16–24 Tiemco 101
Thread:	Black 8/0 Uni-Thread
Tail:	White Mayfly Tails or Microfibetts
Abdomen:	Black Super Fine
Wing:	Bright white Antron
Thorax:	Black Super Fine

BROWN RS2

Hook:	#16–24 Tiemco 101
Thread:	Brown 8/0 Uni-Thread
Tail:	White Mayfly Tails or Microfibetts
Abdomen:	Brown Super Fine
Wing:	Bright white Antron
Thorax:	Brown Super Fine

SPARKLE WING RS2

Hook:	#16–24 Tiemco 101
Thread:	Gray 8/0 Uni-Thread
Tail:	Two strands of white Fluoro Fibre
Abdomen:	Gray Super Fine
Wing:	Pearl Lagartun Mini Flat Braid
Thorax:	Gray Super Fine

MERCURY RS2

Hook:	#16–24 Tiemco 101
Bead:	Mercury Bead (extra small)
Thread:	Gray 8/0 Uni-Thread
Tail:	White Mayfly Tails or Microfibetts
Abdomen:	Gray Super Fine
Wing:	Bright white Antron
Thorax:	Gray Super Fine

OLIVE RS2

Hook:	#16–24 Tiemco 101
Thread:	Olive 8/0 Uni-Thread
Tail:	White Mayfly Tails or Microfibetts
Abdomen:	Olive Super Fine
Wing:	Bright white Antron
Thorax:	Olive Super Fine

CHAPTER 9

Gold-Ribbed Hare's Ear Nymph

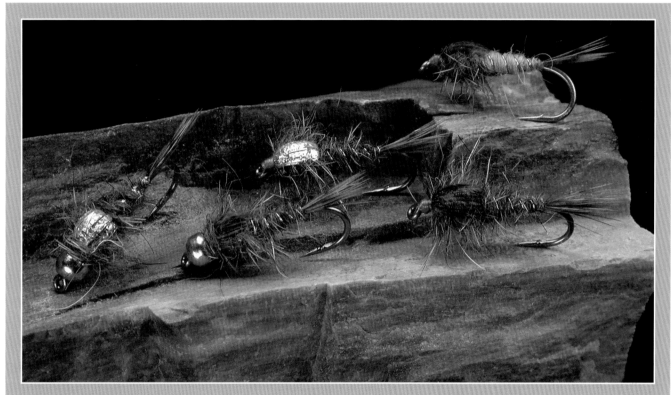

MAIN FOCUS

Correct abdomen and thorax proportions • Working with a coarse, natural dubbing
Tying in a wing case and tail

Some flies, such as the Gold-Ribbed Hare's Ear, have an inherent "fishiness" about them. A nondescript, buggy compilation of fur and feathers, the Hare's Ear won't win any beauty contests, but it is one of those flies that you don't want to be without. While I know I won't win any originality awards by including the Hare's Ear in this book, its purpose here is twofold. The Hare's Ear encompasses virtually all the parts of a standard nymph and teaches traditional proportions. You will learn to measure and tie in tails, cut and blend dubbing fur,

wrap a rib, dub a tapered abdomen, tie in and fold a wing case, dub a thorax, and form a thread head all on this one simple fly. Once you learn these procedures, you'll have all the skills to tie a huge variety of nymphs by varying the materials. Even if you're not fond of the Hare's Ear, for your own good, tie a few to become familiar with the techniques and proportions.

While the Hare's Ear is not a perfect match for anything, it looks a little like a lot of things. I like to use Hare's Ears in large sizes (#6–12) as a simple stonefly

The Gold-Ribbed Hare's Ear Nymph can be tied in many configurations including everything from chunky stonefly nymphs to soft-hackles.

nymph pattern, tied in both light (natural, bleached, or dyed gold) and dark (black, brown, and olive) color schemes and in smaller sizes to match anything from *Callibaetis* in lakes to Green Drake nymphs in rivers. I simply alter the color, hook style, and size to match the insect I have in mind. This flexibility is one of the reasons the Hare's Ear enjoys such popularity.

I use hen saddle feathers for the tail of this fly (rather than the traditional guard hairs from the ears of a hare's mask) because they are much easier to work with and simply make a better looking tail. They are also inexpensive and last much longer than what little bit of fur you can get off the hare's ears.

The ribbing on the Hare's Ear can be made from many different materials, but I am fond of gold wire because it is much more subtle than the traditionally used oval tinsel. While the wire doesn't seem terribly apparent when the fly is dry, it comes alive once the fly is wet and creates just the right amount of sparkle and segmentation. Don't be afraid to rib this fly with some

of the newly available colored wires. Adding a shot of color can sometimes be just what the doctor ordered.

I also dub the fly with real hare's mask fur cut from the mask of a real English hare. Jackrabbit and cottontail won't cut it here; they're a whole different critter. The mix of nicely marked guard hairs and soft underfur from the hare creates a buggy dubbing that is still easy to apply. The commonly available pre-packaged hare's-mask dubbings just aren't the same stuff, no matter what the label says. The fur from a real hare's mask has a perfect blend of well-colored, spiky guard hairs and soft, workable underfur that mix together and create a soft yet spiky dubbing unmatched by any others. The soft underfur dubs easily onto the thread and carries the otherwise tough-to-dub guard hairs along with it. Most of the stuff you find in a pre-mixed bag labeled "Hare's Mask" is just plain old rabbit fur, which is much longer and doesn't create the same effect at all. Incidentally, the lighter fur on the cheeks of the hare's mask can be cut and mixed into a separate batch of dubbing for use on other patterns, but don't mix it up with the darker fur from the center of the mask. This fur from the edges of the mask is much longer than the fur in the center and will dub much more tightly onto the thread, killing the spiky look that we are after.

GOLD-RIBBED HARE'S EAR NYMPH

Hare's Ear materials.

Hook:	#4–22 Tiemco 5262, 5263, 3761, 200, 760 TC
Thread:	Tan or brown; 6/0 for #4-16, 8/0 for #18 and smaller
Tail:	Mottled-brown India hen saddle feather fibers
Rib:	Gold Ultra Wire (small)
Abdomen:	Dubbing from an English hare's mask
Wing case:	Turkey tail feather slip
Thorax:	Hare's-mask dubbing

PREPARING THE DUBBING

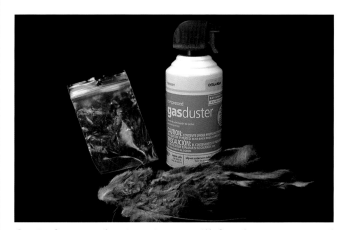

1. Before you begin tying, you'll first have to cut and mix the hare's mask into useable dubbing. I came up with the method I'll describe here during a long phone call. A can of air was sitting on my desk and idle hands found a handy fly tying use for these commonly available items.

PROPORTIONS AT A GLANCE

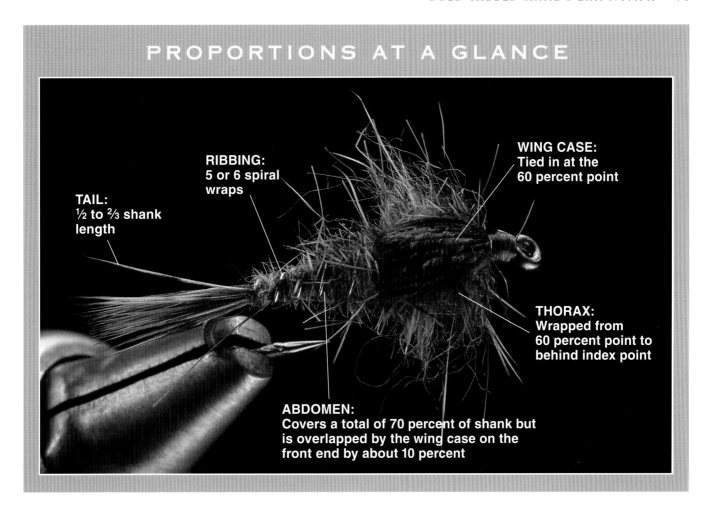

RIBBING:
5 or 6 spiral wraps

TAIL:
½ to ⅔ shank length

WING CASE:
Tied in at the 60 percent point

THORAX:
Wrapped from 60 percent point to behind index point

ABDOMEN:
Covers a total of 70 percent of shank but is overlapped by the wing case on the front end by about 10 percent

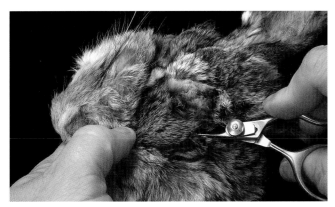

2. Start with a new hare's mask and begin trimming all the fur from between the eyes, along the forehead, and down to the tip of the nose. All of the short, darker-colored hair should be cut off the mask. Make the cuts as close to the hide as possible and run your scissors in against the grain of the hair to help things along. The longer fur along the cheeks can be cut and used in a different batch of dubbing, but you don't want to mix it in with the shorter fur from the middle of the mask. You can use some of that longer, softer cheek fur from the hare's mask to make a lighter-colored abdomen in the Two-Tone Hare's Ear.

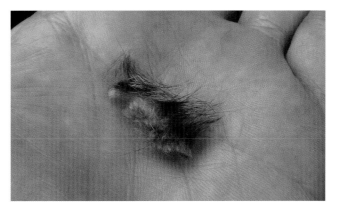

3. The shorter fur has guard hairs mixed with short soft underfur. The inherent bugginess of hare's-mask dubbing comes from this mixture of stiff guard hairs and soft underfur. Mixing the longer fur into the short stuff "cuts" the guard hairs a bit much for my taste and eliminates the scraggly fibers that I equate with true hare's-mask dubbing.

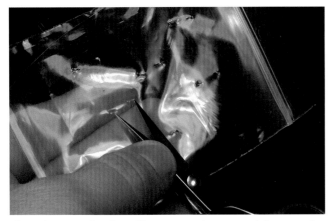

4. Take a Ziploc bag, like most tying materials come in, and poke a few holes in it with the tips of your scissors. You don't want these holes to be too big—just enough to let some air circulate in and out of the bag. The bag the hare's mask came in is perfect for this, though I am using a smaller bag here.

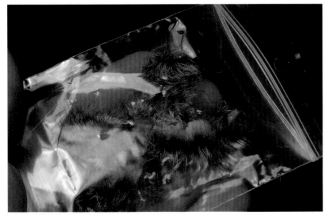

5. Put the cut fur from the mask into the baggie.

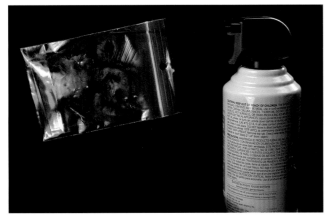

6. Put the air nozzle into one corner of the baggie and close it all the way down around the tip of the tube.

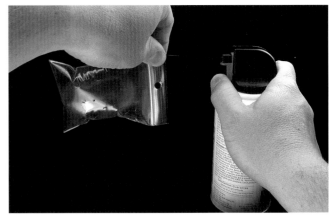

7. Pinch the opening around where the nozzle goes into the dubbing bag and blast a long shot of air through the dubbing.

8. The air stirs the dubbing together, intermixing the guard hairs and underfur into a nicely mixed dubbing ball. This method works for nearly all types of dubbing and is quicker and easier than the old coffee grinder technique.

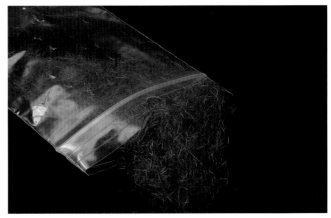

9. Now you have a bag of pre-mixed hare's-mask dubbing. Mark the contents so you remember what you did later.

GOLD-RIBBED HARE'S EAR STEPS

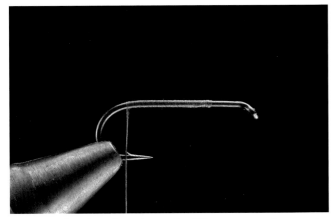

1. Start the thread at about the 75 percent point on the hook shank, and wrap a thread base back to the bend.

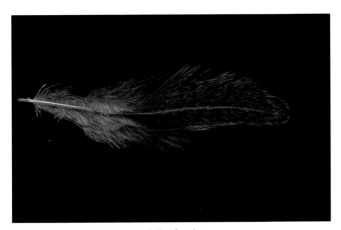

2. Select a large hen saddle feather.

3. Cut the fluff from the base. Preen a few fibers out to the side of the stem to even the tips.

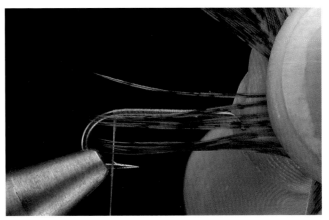

4. As a rule of thumb, you want a clump of fibers more or less equal to the hook's gap width. Grasp these fibers near their base and peel them from the feather stem, taking care to keep the tips even. Fold the fibers into a small bundle.

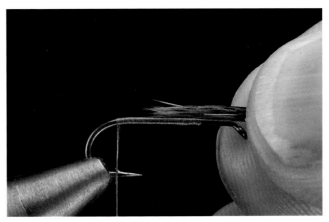

5. Measure the tips of the bundle against the hook so they are equal to half the shank length. Transfer the fibers into your material hand, grasping them at the base of measured length.

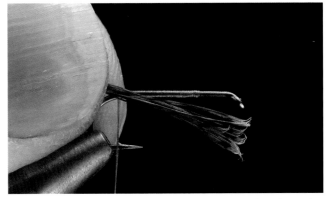

6. Place the base of the tail against the shank at the hook bend with the butt ends pointing slightly down. This angle is important because you will use the hook shank to block the fibers from rolling over the shank.

7. Bring the tying thread up and over the tail material, trapping it against the top of the hook shank. You'll need to lighten up on the thread tension as you come over the top of the hook to trap the material in place. Use the tip of your index finger on your material hand to hold the material on top of the shank as you wrap the thread forward three or four turns. Check the length of the tail at this point to be sure it is still only as long as half the hook shank.

8. Press the tip of your material hand index finger along the far side of the shank as you wrap the thread forward over the butts. Your fingertip should keep the material from rolling to the far side of the hook as you wrap the thread. Wrap over the butt ends of the hen fibers to the 75 percent point. Clip the excess hen fiber butts.

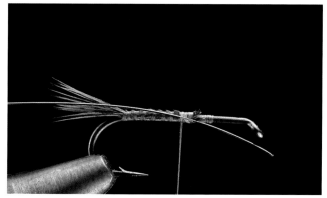

9. Break a length of gold wire from the spool and tie it in at the 75 percent point on the shank.

10. Pull the front end of the wire down to the 75 percent point and wrap over the back end of the wire to the base of the tail. Try to keep the wire along the near side of the hook shank as you wrap back over it. Anchor the wire at the bend with several tight turns of thread.

11. Return the thread to the midpoint on the shank and apply a thin layer of dubbing to the thread. Hare's-mask dubbing is considerably coarser than Super Fine, so it requires more twisting than synthetic dubbing. Pinch small portions onto the thread at a time, and try not to get too much on in one place at a time.

12. Make the first turn of dubbing at the base of the tail.

13. Continue wrapping the dubbing forward to the 75 percent point on the shank, forming a slight taper as you go. With hare's mask, I find it easiest to sort of pile and overlap the dubbing wraps a bit closer together as I get toward the front of the hook to build a taper.

14. If you have a bit of extra dubbing left on the thread, work the dubbing back over the front edge of the abdomen to fill out the taper, if needed.

15. Spiral-wrap the wire forward over the dubbing with five or six turns and tie the wire off at the front of the abdomen.

16. Helicopter the wire to break off the long end.

17. Wrap the tying thread back over the front of the abdomen, overlapping it to the 60 percent point on the shank. This gives you a larger base to tie a wide, flat wing case to, rather than a skinny bare hook shank that will split the wing case.

18. Cut a slip (section) from a turkey tail feather that has a tip end about as wide as the hook gap. This piece will become your wing case.

19. Cut the ragged tips of the turkey slips square. You'll be tying the feather tips to the hook, as the butt end is much thicker in cross section and more prone to splitting than the thin tip portion.

20. Place the tip end of the slip on top of the hook with the inside of the feather facing up. Ultimately, you will fold this feather over the thorax, exposing the outside of the feather to the fish's scrutiny, so you want the pretty, outside of the feather facing down. No self-respecting fish will eat the fly if the wing case is upside down, so make sure you get this part right.

21. Press your material-hand thumb down on top of the turkey slip to hold it flat along the top of the fly. This wide section is nearly impossible to pinch into place, but the thumb-on-top technique works nicely here. Note that the tip of the feather is clearly behind the hook eye, with enough room for a thread head.

22. Make a turn or two over the tip end of the turkey feather while still holding it in place with your thumb at the 60 percent point. Make sure the feather stays flat and centered across the top of the hook as you wrap over it.

23. You may need to work back and forth with the thread to smooth things out. Continue wrapping forward over the remaining stub end to the back edge of the index point.

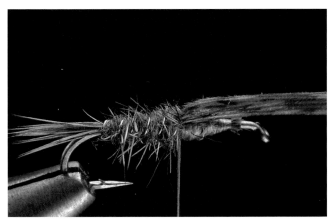

24. Pull the turkey wing case section forward, making sure there is no thread showing along its back edge. If there is, lay the feather slip back and wrap over it a bit more. The turkey feather slip should butt up to the abdomen dubbing at the 60 percent point.

25. Dub another pinch of dubbing onto the thread and start wrapping it around the hook at the back edge of the index point to form the thorax. You have a taper on the front end of the hook where you overlapped the abdomen, so you want to dub up this hill from the front to the back rather than back to front. Wrapping the dubbing from the base of the wing case forward, going down the hill, would allow the dubbing wraps to slip down the tapered thread base and pile up behind the hook eye. Dubbing up the hill allows the first turn of dubbing to support the second and so on, providing a good foundation to build a nicely shaped thorax.

26. Continue wrapping the dubbing to the base of the wing case, building an elongated ball shape.

27. Once you reach the front edge of the wing case (60 percent point), return the dubbing to the back edge of the index point and end with bare thread behind the hook eye.

28. Pull the turkey slip taut over the top of the thorax. Pick up the bobbin with your material hand and make a turn of thread over the wing case at the back edge of the index point. Don't let this wrap pull the wing case down tight. Let it hang on top of the turkey slip up away from the hook for the time being. This loose wrap will allow the wide wing case to close down around the shank as you tighten the thread, instead of pushing the wing case up on the near side of the hook as a taut wrap of thread would do.

29. Pull the bobbin toward you to close the loop of thread around the wing case. You may need to pull the long end of the wing case slightly toward you as you tighten this wrap to counteract thread torque. The wing case should be directly on top of the thorax. Make a couple more tight wraps of thread to anchor the wing case at the index point.

30. Check that the wing case is lying flat over the top of the thorax and there is a nice wide strip of turkey showing on top of the dubbing.

31. Clip the butt ends of the wing case as close as you can.

32. Build a smooth thread head to cover the butt ends of the wing case at the index point. Build the head with the minimum number of thread turns required to cover any stubs. You don't want to create a lot of bulk. Whip-finish and clip the thread. Add a small drop of Gloss Coat.

33. The fly before creating legs.

34. Use a dubbing brush to pick out some of the dubbing along the sides of the thorax to mimic legs.

35. Finished fly.

PATTERN VARIATIONS

BEADHEAD HARE'S EAR

Hook:	#4–18 Tiemco 5262
Bead:	Gold, copper, or black, sized to hook (see page 103)
Thread:	Tan or brown; 6/0 Danville for #4–16, 8/0 Uni-Thread for #18 and smaller
Tail:	Mottled-brown India hen saddle feather fibers
Rib:	Gold Ultra Wire (small)
Abdomen:	Hare's-mask dubbing
Wing case:	Turkey tail feather slip
Thorax:	Hare's-mask dubbing

FLASHBACK HARE'S EAR

Hook:	#4–18 Tiemco 5262
Thread:	Tan or brown; 6/0 Danville for #4–18, 8/0 Uni-Thread for #18 and smaller
Tail:	Mottled-brown India hen saddle feather fibers
Rib:	Gold Ultra Wire (small)
Abdomen:	Hare's-mask dubbing
Wing case:	Six or eight strands of pearl Fire Fly
Thorax:	Hare's-mask dubbing

FLASHBACK BEADHEAD HARE'S EAR

Hook:	#4–18 Tiemco 5262
Bead:	Gold, copper, or black, sized to hook (see page 103)
Thread:	Tan or brown; 6/0 Danville for #4–18, 8/0 Uni-Thread for #18 and smaller
Tail:	Mottled-brown India hen saddle feather fibers
Rib:	A single strand of pearl Fire Fly
Abdomen:	Hare's-mask dubbing
Wing case:	Six or eight strands of pearl Fire Fly
Thorax:	Hare's-mask dubbing

TWO-TONE HARE'S EAR

Hook:	#4–18 Tiemco 5262
Thread:	Tan or brown; 6/0 Danville for #4-16, 8/0 Uni-Thread for #18 and smaller
Tail:	Mottled-brown India hen saddle feather fibers
Rib:	Gold Ultra Wire (small)
Abdomen:	Light-colored hare's-mask dubbing from the cheeks of the mask
Wing case:	Turkey tail feather slip
Thorax:	Hare's-mask dubbing from the center of the mask

CURVED HARE'S EAR

Hook:	#10–18 Tiemco 2457 #10–18
Thread:	Tan or brown; 6/0 Danville for #4–16, 8/0 Uni-Thread for #18
Tail:	Mottled-brown India hen saddle feather fibers
Rib:	Gold Ultra Wire (small)
Abdomen:	Dubbing from an English hare's mask
Wing case:	Turkey tail feather slip
Thorax:	Hare's-mask dubbing

SKINNY HARE'S EAR

Hook:	#12–18 Tiemco 5263
Thread:	Tan or brown; 6/0 Danville for #4–16, 8/0 Uni-Thread for #18
Tail:	Mottled-brown India hen saddle feather fibers
Rib:	Copper Ultra Wire (extra small)
Abdomen:	Dubbing from an English hare's mask
Wing case:	Turkey tail feather slip
Thorax:	Hare's-mask dubbing

HARE'S EAR STONE

Hook:	#6–16 Tiemco 200R
Thread:	Tan or brown 6/0 Danville
Tail:	Brown goose biots
Rib:	Gold Ultra Wire (small)
Abdomen:	Light-colored hare's-mask dubbing from the cheeks of the mask
Wing case:	Turkey tail feather slip
Thorax:	Hare's-mask dubbing from the center of the mask

HARE'S EAR GOLDEN STONE

Hook:	#4–18 Tiemco 200R
Thread:	Tan or brown; 6/0 Danville for #4–16, 8/0 Uni-Thread for #18
Tail:	Brown goose biots
Rib:	Gold Ultra Wire (small)
Abdomen:	Light-colored hare's-mask dubbing from the cheeks of the mask
Wing case:	Turkey tail feather slip
Thorax:	Hare's-mask dubbing from the center of the mask
Legs:	Mottled-brown India hen saddle, wrapped as hackle

OLD SCHOOL HARE'S EAR

Hook:	#12–20 Tiemco 3761
Thread:	Tan 6/0 Danville; 8/0 Uni-Thread for #18 and smaller
Tail:	Mottled-brown India hen saddle feather fibers
Rib:	Lagartun copper wire (fine)
Body:	Hare's-mask dubbing, picked out

HARE'S EAR SOFT-HACKLE

Hook:	#14–16 Tiemco 760 TC
Thread:	Tan 6/0 Danville
Tail:	Sparse mottled-brown India hen saddle feather fibers
Rib:	Lagartun copper wire (fine)
Body:	Hare's-mask dubbing
Hackle:	Mottled-brown India hen saddle

CHAPTER 10

Pheasant Tail Nymph

MAIN FOCUS

Working with pheasant-tail fibers and peacock herl • Creating a tapered thread underbody
Forming legs

Originated by Frank Sawyer on the other side of the pond, the original Pheasant Tail used no thread and was tied completely with copper wire. It had no legs and a copper wire thorax. Al Troth developed what we now know as the American Pheasant Tail Nymph. The Troth adaptation streamlined the fly into the present-day version, which I find infinitely more compelling than the original, and is the pattern I present here. Al Troth, incidentally, also gave us the venerable Elk Hair Caddis, which I cover later in this book.

The dark brown color and slender profile of the Pheasant Tail create a highly realistic mayfly imitation. Although it can be tied in larger sizes, I prefer this fly in sizes 16 through 24 because smaller-size Pheasant Tails match Blue-Winged Olive and Pale Morning Dun nymphs. The Hare's Ear lends itself better to imitations in larger sizes. I have streamlined the process for tying Pheasant Tails over the years. I like to keep this fly pretty slender. Most books show the Pheasant Tail using three or four separate bunches of fibers to form the tail, body,

The Pheasant Tail is the quintessential mayfly nymph pattern. The dark brown color and slender profile create a highly realistic mayfly imitation.

wing case, and legs. This creates too much bulk on the hook and makes a simple fly more complicated than it needs to be. I use the same four fibers of pheasant tail for all of these parts.

Proper selection of both the pheasant-tail fibers and the peacock herl used in this pattern is critical. Not all pheasant-tail feathers are created equal. Some have bushy fibers, like oversized hackle, that create too much bulk on the hook. Some have thin, short fibers that work beautifully for small flies. I am not talking about the actual fibers themselves, but the flues that radiate from the stem of these fibers. The feathers that these fibers come from tend to look ratty and ugly, not full and bushy like the pretty feathers you'd like to put in a hat. The ratty ones are the feathers you want to select for your Pheasant Tails. I didn't say broken, chewed, or bent, just thin—as though they came from a bird that didn't do too well last winter.

As for the peacock, I use only the herls that extend directly out from the tip of the eyed quill. These herls are smaller and finer than the stuff that is below the eye and have a nice velvety texture on a small fly while keeping the thorax in proportion to the rest of the fly. In keeping with the "thin to win" philosophy, I pull only one fiber of pheasant tail back along each side of the thorax to imitate legs. Most tiers pull back two per side, but I think that creates too much bulk on a slender fly.

Regular (left) and eyed herl.

The Pheasant Tail can be fished in a variety of ways. I usually fish it as a nymph on the stream bottom with split shot on the leader, often in tandem with an RS2 or Black Beauty. This fly can be deadly when fished in the surface film, greased with floatant and hanging on a 10-inch dropper behind a more visible dry fly. During many hatches, fish eat the emerging nymphs just as they reach the surface of the water, and a Pheasant Tail fished high in the water column is often the answer to tough fish.

PROPORTIONS AT A GLANCE

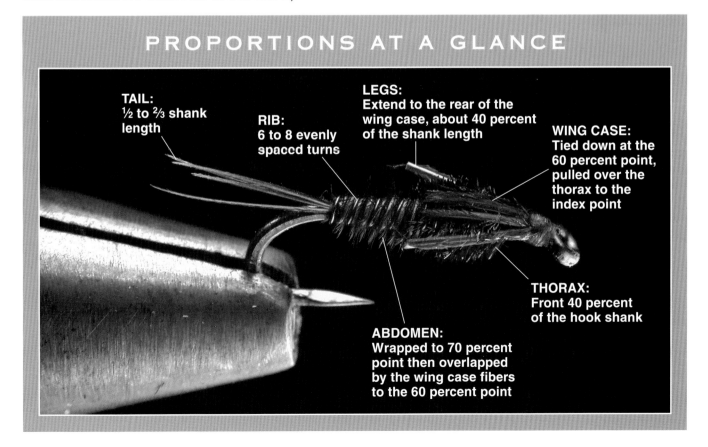

TAIL:
½ to ⅔ shank length

RIB:
6 to 8 evenly spaced turns

LEGS:
Extend to the rear of the wing case, about 40 percent of the shank length

WING CASE:
Tied down at the 60 percent point, pulled over the thorax to the index point

THORAX:
Front 40 percent of the hook shank

ABDOMEN:
Wrapped to 70 percent point then overlapped by the wing case fibers to the 60 percent point

PHEASANT TAIL NYMPH

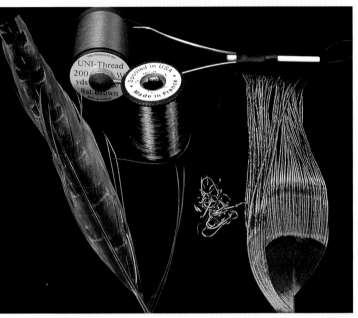

Pheasant Tail materials.

Hook:	#14–24 Tiemco 100, 9300, 100SP-BL, or 3761
Thread:	Rusty brown 8/0 Uni-Thread
Tail:	Ringneck pheasant tail fibers
Body:	Ringneck pheasant tail fibers
Rib:	Lagartun copper wire (fine)
Thorax:	Peacock herl
Wing case/Legs:	Ringneck pheasant tail fibers

Note: Olive, black, red, and bleached pheasant tails are all effective colors.

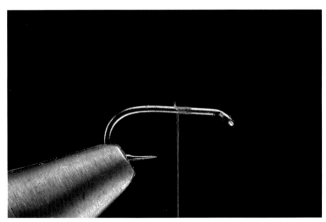

1. Attach the thread at the 75 percent point and clip the tag end. Do not move the thread back to the bend.

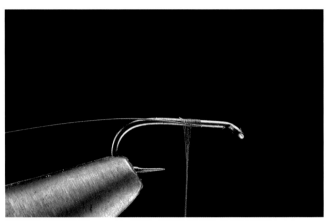

2. Tie in a 6-inch length of fine copper wire at the 75 percent point. Pull the front end of the wire down flush against the front edge of the thread wraps.

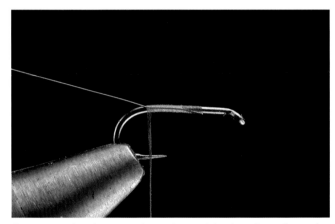

3. Wrap back over the wire with the thread to the bend, keeping the wire along the near side of the hook.

4. Select a pheasant tail feather with fine fibers, appropriate for the hook size. Pull four fibers out from the center quill so that their tips are even and strip them from the feather. Stripping the fibers, rather than cutting them, will leave little hooks on the butt end of the feather that help hold the fibers together during the tying process to follow.

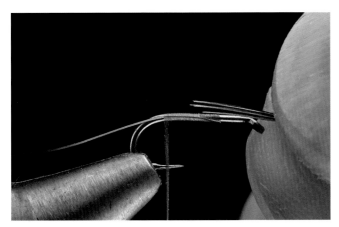

5. Measure the tips of the four pheasant tail fibers against the hook shank so they are half a hook shank long (slightly longer is fine). If the tail is too long, the entire fly looks bigger, which is not what we are after here.

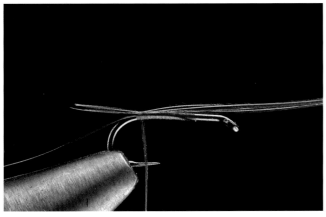

6. Transfer the pheasant tail fibers to the material hand and tie them in with one turn of thread at the hook bend. The tips should extend back about half a shank length beyond the bend.

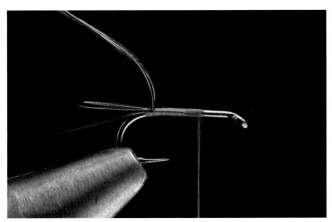

7. Lift the butt ends of the pheasant tail fibers up and back (out of the way of the thread) while you wrap the thread forward to the 75 percent point.

8. Work the thread back and forth over the hook shank, creating a slight taper. This is an underbody taper and should be considerably smaller than what you hope the finished body to be.

9. Wrap all four pheasant tail fibers forward at the same time, one turn in front of the other, up to the 75 percent point. Tie them off with two tight turns of thread. Because you are wrapping all four fibers together, it should only take about four turns on a size eighteen hook to reach the 75 percent point. Try to make the fibers lie flat like a ribbon as you wrap so they cover the maximum amount of shank with the least amount of bulk.

10. Grab the wire and make the first turn under the tail to lift it.

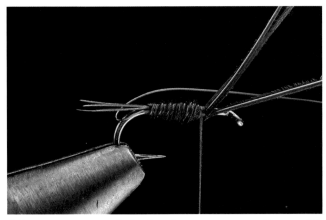

11. Come around the hook as you normally would, but under the tail and down on the far side of the shank.

12. Bring the wire up from the bottom of the shank and over the top of the body at the base of the tail.

13. Continue spiral-wrapping the wire forward with six to eight turns over the pheasant tail abdomen up to the 75 percent point. Once at the front of the abdomen, hold the ribbing wire in your thread hand and wrap the thread over the wire with the other hand to anchor the wire at the front of the body.

14. Snap the wire off flush with the shank rather than cutting it with your scissors. To do this, first pull down on the thread and then pull back on the wire at a steep angle.

15. Give the wire a sharp tug upward and slightly back, and it will snap off cleanly at the tie-down point.

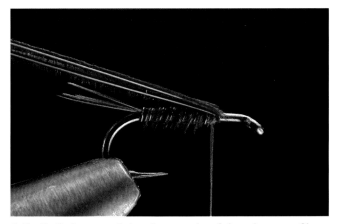

16. Pull the remaining butt ends of the pheasant fibers back over the top of the abdomen.

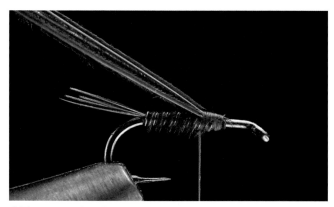

17. Wrap the thread back over them, overlapping both the fibers and the front edge of the abdomen back to the 60 percent point. These leftover butt ends become the wing case in the next few steps.

18. Select six or eight small peacock herls from the eye of the quill. Clip the tip ends square and tie them in at the base of the wing case with a few tight turns of thread. (Always tie peacock herl in by its tip ends.) Make sure the tips are behind the back edge of the index point to retain that bare shank up at the front. You're going to need it later.

19. Wrap forward over the short ends of the peacock herl, binding them down to the back edge of the index point. You may even smooth out the thorax taper with another smooth, light layer of thread. Leave the thread hanging at the back edge of the index point.

20. Wrap all the peacock herls forward at the same time, forming the thorax. Just as with the pheasant-tail fibers in the abdomen, you want these herls to lie side by side as you wrap, so just cover the thread with a light coating of peacock herl. You don't need any bulk from this herl, just its texture and color. It should take no more than three turns of herl to move from the front edge of the abdomen to the back edge of the index point. Once you reach the back edge of the index point, tie off the herl with two solid wraps of thread. If you break a herl or two in the process, it's no big deal—that's why you tied in a bunch rather than a few.

21. Clip the remaining herl flush against the hook.

22. Pull the wing case fibers forward over the top of the peacock thorax, making sure they aren't twisted and are flat across the top. Tie the wing case down at the back edge of the index point with two turns of thread.

23. To form the legs, separate one strand of the wing-case fibers from the clump. Pull the one on the far side of the bunch back along the far side of the hook and bind it in place with a single taut turn of thread at the back edge of the index point. This leg should be in-line with the hook shank and not tilt up or down from center. You can tweak the legs into position, but be careful of breaking them off. Again, if one does break, you've got two extras waiting for you up front.

24. Separate a fiber from the clump on the near side of the hook and pull it back along the near side of the hook. Bind this fiber in place with another single turn of thread. You don't need a lot of thread turns here, as from here on out the wraps become cumulative. You have two turns over the first leg on the far side and one turn over the leg on the near side. All of these wraps are within the index point area, so be careful of bulking things up.

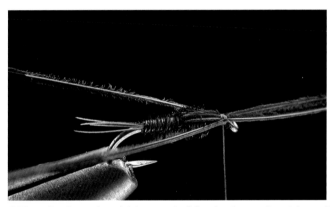

25. The legs should be angled back along the sides of the fly. If they are sticking out to the side, the thorax is too fat or you need to move the thread back over the base of the legs.

26. Don't cut the two leftover wing-case fibers. Just pull down firmly on the bobbin and pull them up and back as you did with the wire, and they will break off cleanly behind the hook eye.

27. The leg fibers on each side should look like this.

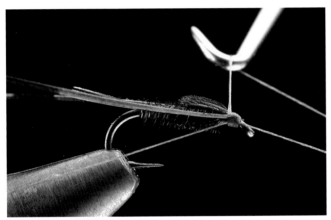

28. To maintain a small head on this fly, use the whip-finish wraps to actually build the head, rather than thread wraps followed by a whip-finish. This reduces bulk and provides a nice neat head. Make a three-turn whip-finish to cover the butt ends of the wing case and clip the thread.

29. Trim the legs slightly longer than the wing case. I turn the fly in the vise and trim both the legs at the same time. Make sure your scissors are absolutely perpendicular to the shank when you trim the legs so they come out the same length.

30. Add a tiny drop of head cement all the way around the thread head.

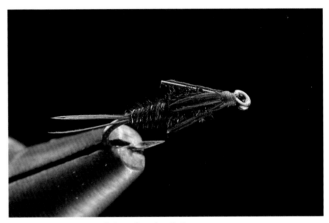

31. Top view of the finished fly.

PATTERN VARIATIONS

FLASHBACK PHEASANT TAIL

Hook:	#14–20 Tiemco 100SP-BL
Thread:	Rusty brown 8/0 Uni-Thread
Tail:	Ringneck pheasant tail fibers
Body:	Ringneck pheasant tail fibers
Rib:	Lagartun copper wire (fine)
Thorax:	Peacock herl
Wing case/Legs:	Pheasant tail fibers topped with three or four strands of pearl Flashabou

BEADHEAD PHEASANT TAIL

Hook:	#14–20 Tiemco 100SP-BL
Bead:	Copper- or gold-colored brass or tungsten bead, sized to hook
Thread:	Rusty brown 8/0 Uni-Thread
Tail:	Ringneck pheasant tail fibers
Body:	Ringneck pheasant tail fibers
Rib:	Lagartun copper wire (fine)
Thorax:	Peacock herl
Wing case/Legs:	Ringneck pheasant tail fibers

BEADHEAD PHEASANT TAIL (VARIATION)

Hook:	#14-20 Tiemco 100SP-BL
Bead:	Copper-colored tungsten, sized to hook
Thread:	Rusty brown 8/0 Uni-Thread
Tail:	Ringneck pheasant tail fibers
Body:	Ringneck pheasant tail fibers
Rib:	Lagartun copper wire (fine)
Thorax:	Peacock herl
Wing case/Legs:	Ringneck pheasant tail fibers

BEADHEAD FLASHBACK PHEASANT TAIL

Hook:	#14–20 Tiemco 2488
Bead:	Copper- or gold-colored brass or tungsten bead, sized to hook
Thread:	Rusty brown 8/0 Uni-Thread
Tail:	Ringneck pheasant tail fibers
Body:	Ringneck pheasant tail fibers
Rib:	Lagartun copper wire (fine)
Thorax:	Peacock herl
Wing case:	Opal Mirage tinsel (medium)
Legs:	Ringneck pheasant tail fibers

CDC PHEASANT TAIL

Hook:	#10–16 Tiemco 5262
Bead:	Copper-colored tungsten
Weight:	.015-inch-diameter lead wire
Thread:	Rusty brown 70-denier Ultra Thread
Tail:	Dyed orange or other color pheasant tail barbs
Rib:	Copper-brown Ultra Wire (small)
Flashback:	Pearl Flashabou
Wing case:	Lagartun Mini Flat Braid (pearl)
Thorax:	Peacock herl twisted with fine copper wire
Collar:	Natural dun CDC wrapped as a collar

CHAPTER 11

Hackle

H ackle feathers are generally referred to as the neck (cape) or back (saddle) feathers of a chicken, although there are also body and rump feathers used for hackling and feathers from many other types of birds. Here we will only deal with the feathers from the neck and back of chickens. Typically, hackle is used for collars on dry flies, although it is certainly not limited to them. A hackle collar is formed by wrapping a hackle feather around the hook, causing the barbs of the feather to splay out around the hook or around the wing post in the case of a parachute fly. Hackle serves a variety of purposes ranging from flotation (on dry flies) to movement (on nymphs) to imitating the legs of the insect (both dry flies and nymphs). Hackle feathers can come from the neck, body, or back of the bird as well as from roosters and hens. All of these have different characteristics that make them suitable for different uses.

Grizzly dry fly neck (left) and saddle.

Genetic rooster necks (above) come in a wide range of colors.

TYPES OF HACKLE
Genetic Rooster Necks

A genetic rooster neck or cape comes from a male chicken bred and raised specifically to grow long, slender feathers with stiff barbs and thin quills that make them perfectly suited to tying dry flies. These are not your ordinary, barnyard roosters. Some of these birds have longer bloodlines than you or I. Rooster necks provide the fullest size range of feathers with long, thin, and stiff barbs with little web (the soft, downy portion at the base of the feather) and rectangular, supple stems—all you could ask for in a dry fly feather.

Dry fly necks are graded Gold, Silver, or Bronze, or 1, 2, or 3 depending on the breeder. The grades are based on criteria involving overall feather length, absence of web, size range of the feathers, feather quantity, and the overall condition of the cape (i.e. broken feather tips). Gold or #1 grade capes have the best, longest feathers and the widest size range with no flawed feathers. But, they can be hard to find and aren't getting any cheaper. The Silver (#2) and Bronze (#3) capes are of outstanding quality and are more than adequate for most people's tying needs. The only downside to buying hackle these days is that next year's batch is going to be even better.

The rate at which genetic dry fly hackle has improved has been incredible over the past few years and shows no signs of slowing. The best way to get around this is to tie lots of flies and use those necks up before the next new wave leaves you wanting.

Whiting Farms located in Colorado produces some of the best dry fly capes available today. The Metz Hatchery in Pennsylvania also produces capes of outstanding quality. I would stay away from off-brand feathers. No matter what your cheap friends say, they just aren't as good as quality name-brand hackles.

Genetic Rooster Saddles

Saddles come from the back of the rooster and are the longest feathers available for tying dry flies. These feathers are often long enough to tie six or eight flies, but what you gain in length with a saddle you give up in size range. Saddles generally provide a huge quantity of feathers in a narrow range of sizes. This can be just what the doctor ordered if you tie all your flies in the same narrow size range, but it is not all that hot if you tie a large variety of sizes. Saddles are graded on the same scale and system as rooster necks, with many of the same considerations going into the overall grade.

Dry fly saddles have a huge amount of feathers with very long lengths but lack the size variations that necks produce.

Dry fly rooster necks in grizzly and natural brown.

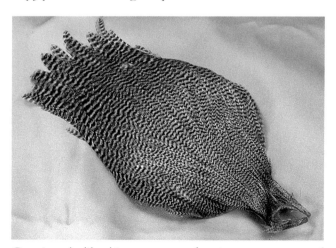

Generic necks like this one are great for wings on streamers and tails on bass bugs but aren't stiff enough to hackle a dry fly adequately.

Where to Find Useable Feathers on a Neck

The narrow end of the neck (the top) has the smallest feathers, and the sizes get bigger as you go toward the bottom of the cape. The most useable size range of feathers, from size 28 up to about size 10, are located from the top down to about the midpoint on the cape. The feathers on the edges of the cape at its widest point, called spade hackles, have long stiff barbs that are excellent for tailing on dry flies. Contrary to popular belief, spade hackles are still present and even abundant on modern genetic necks. The largest feathers found along the base of the neck are not all that useful but can be used for some streamers like Woolly Buggers.

Generic Domestic, Chinese, or India Necks

These necks are from birds that have had either no genetic engineering to breed desirable dry-fly characteristics or are bred specifically to produce wider, softer feathers. They are suited for nymphs, streamers, and wet flies but are really perfect for tailing and winging on bass and saltwater flies. These feathers lack the stiffness and length to be useful on dries and typically have much thicker stems, which makes it hard to wrap a nice collar-style hackle. These feathers do make excellent beards and tails and are great for featherwing streamers like the Lefty's Deceiver and the Platte River Special.

Generic Rooster Saddle

These feathers are much wider and have more web than their genetic counterparts and are typically used for palmering Woolly Buggers and other streamers or for

CHOOSING A DRY FLY NECK OR SADDLE

Long useable feather length. A long uniform width portion of the feather. This is what you have left to work with after trimming the fluff and web from the base, so the longer it is the easier it will be to work with and the more of it you can wrap on the fly.

Lack of webbing. Web is the soft downy portion at the base of the feather that extends up into the useable portion along the quill. The web will soak up water and prevents the fibers from splaying properly when wrapped on the hook. A minimum amount of web is okay.

Barb length. The actual length of the barbs on the feather. Ideally, you want short barbs on a long

feather. Make sure they fall into the size range of the flies you intend to tie. Necks have a wide variety of sizes while saddles tend to have a much narrower range.

Barb stiffness. Stiff barbs float a fly higher, don't soak up water, and resist crushing.

Quill shape and suppleness. Thin, roundish to rectangular quills wrap the best. Oval or flat stems roll out on their side as you wrap them and cause the feather fibers to splay out of position. Thick stems can split and crack, breaking at the least opportune time. A thin, round quill will make wrapping hackles go much smoother.

Detail of hen neck feather (right) and a genetic rooster neck feather showing differences in length and web.

Note the shadowy web near the base of this feather. Webbing will soak up water and prevent your fly from floating well.

tails and wings on large saltwater and bass flies. Generic saddle feathers tend to taper from the butt to the tip of the feather, which creates a nicely flowing and tapered silhouette on flies like the Woolly Bugger.

Hen Necks

Hen neck feathers are shorter, softer, and webbier than rooster neck feathers and are used for wings on dry flies like the Adams or for hackle on nymphs like the Prince. For dry-fly wings you want feathers with broad, rounded tips for a good wing silhouette. For hackling a nymph, any tip shape, even if they are broken, is okay because you discard the tip. Whiting Farms sells Winger Necks, specifically grown for their heavy web and round tips. These feathers make great hen-hackle-tip wings and are a must on many flies. The standard Whiting line of hen necks

Soft, wide feathered saddles like this are perfect for flies like Woolly Buggers.

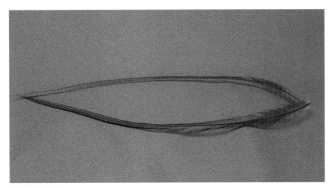

2. The inside and outside of the feather are terms I use to eliminate some of the confusion stemming from the traditional terms of "shiny" and "dull" side. The inside of a feather is the side that faces the inside of the bird, or the concave side. The outside of the feather faces toward the outside of the bird and is the convex side of the feather. The shiny and dull descriptions have always caused confusion with my tying students because the inside of the feather is actually a bit shinier than the outside, although the color itself is duller, particularly when used to reference turkey tail feathers and the like. The outside of the feather is the pretty side, used by the bird to camouflage itself or show off. The inside of the feather is the other side.

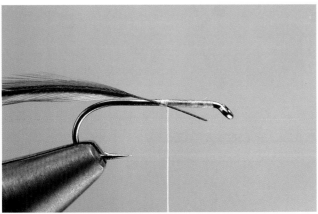

3. The outside of the feather is facing up, and the inside is facing down toward the hook shank (be it from the top, the near side, or the far side). You want to tie a hackle feather in this way so it wraps with the outside facing the hook eye and the inside (concave side) facing the bend to ensure a cleanly wrapped, tightly wound hackle collar.

4. When we tie the feather in this way, the fibers tilt slightly toward the rear of the fly and allow a clear space for the next turn of hackle.

5. If you tie the feather in inside forward, the fibers lean forward into the space where you need to make the next wrap of hackle and get bound down with the feather, resulting in a ratty looking collar. I must admit, I have done a pretty fine job of wrapping a hackle the wrong way in the above photo, although I used a thin stemmed saddle feather to make sure it looked clean and illustrated my point. With a regular neck feather or thicker-stemmed saddle feather, the stem tends to roll on the hook shank, throwing hackle fibers awry.

Don't try to "stretch" a feather by leaving some of the web or a thick portion of the quill attached to the useable portion. This defeats the purpose of using good hackle. If, after preparation, the feather is too short to make enough turns of hackle, buy a better neck or use two feathers.

WINDING HACKLE

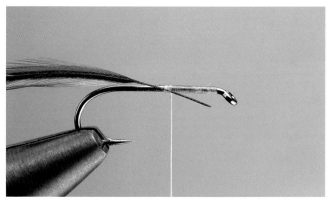

1. Select, size, and prepare a hackle feather as shown above. Lay the stripped butt end of the feather along the side of the hook and capture it with the thread using the right-angle technique that you used to secure the wire on the Brassie.

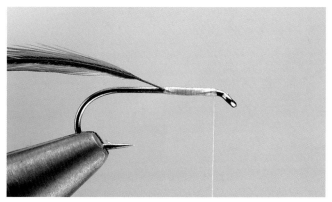

2. Wrap forward over the stub end of the feather to the hook eye. Note there is exposed bare stem behind the tie-in point. I have slightly exaggerated the amount of bare stem here to make sure it is clearly shown. Also be sure that the outside of the feather is facing out from the hook shank. In this particular case, the outside of the feather is facing up.

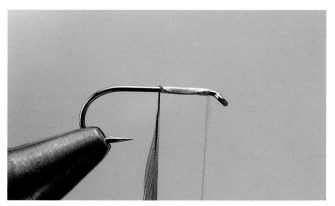

3. Wrap the feather tightly over the top and down again on the far side of the hook using your material hand. Try to make this turn as vertically as possible.

4. Bring the feather up again on the near side of the hook, laying this wrap right up against the front edge of the first turn of bare stem. Note that there are still not any hackle fibers radiating from the stem. The bare stem prevents you from having any hackle fibers pointing back along the hook shank and makes for a much more squarely wrapped hackle.

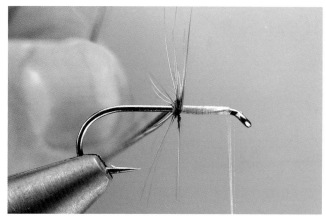

5. Make another tight turn of hackle against the front edge of the last turn. This turn should start the hackle fibers splaying out around the shank. Be sure this wrap is absolutely vertical. You may even pull the feather tip slightly back as you wrap it, like you did with the wire on the Brassie, to help butt the turns together.

6. Continue wrapping the feather forward in tight, abutting, concentric turns.

7. Wrap the feather to the hook eye and end by pulling the feather above and slightly out over the hook eye.

8. Hold the feather taut above the hook and bring the thread up and over the stem of the feather with your material hand. Make two or three turns to securely anchor the feather.

9. Once you tie off the feather, reach in with your thread hand and pinch the tip of the feather and any loose strands of hackle in your fingertips.

10. With your fine-point scissors, clip the tip of the feather along with any of the stray hackle fibers that may be pointing out over the hook eye. Pull up on the hackle tip and push the scissor blades down against the hook shank to assure a flush cut.

11. You should have just the shortest of stub ends left on the shank.

12. Make several smooth wraps of thread to cover them.

13. Whip-finish and clip the thread.

14. This photo is of a properly wound hackle feather that has been trimmed to the stem. Look closely at the stem where it is wrapped around the shank and note how the turns are butted closely together, just as they are in the wire wraps on the Brassie.

CHAPTER 12

Beadhead Prince Nymph

MAIN FOCUS

Adding beads and lead wire • Working with goose biots • Mounting a split-biot tail
Wrapping a peacock herl body • Selecting and wrapping a folded hackle collar

The Prince Nymph was developed by Doug Prince back in the 1930s, and over the last twenty years or so it has become a go-to pattern for many anglers across the country. The recent addition of a brass or tungsten bead has made this fly even more popular and effective. I tie the Prince (and any other fly with a bead) with lead wire shoved into the bead to add weight and to hold and center the bead on the hook. I use nothing but tungsten beads on my nymphs these days, as the added weight keeps the fly down where the fish feed, which is critical to catching fish. Heavy flies aren't pushed up and around by the current as easily as their non-weighted counterparts and stay in the zone much better. Some flies don't lend themselves well to being weighted. The wire adds bulk and diameter that can be overpowering. In this case, I will fish these skinny

The Prince is a general-purpose nymph that can imitate anything from stoneflies to caddis to mayflies.

BEADHEAD PRINCE NYMPH ■ 103

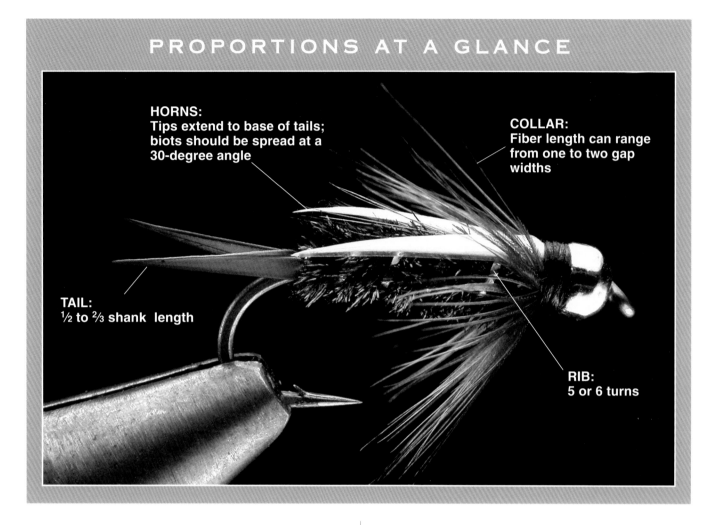

PROPORTIONS AT A GLANCE

HORNS:
Tips extend to base of tails;
biots should be spread at a
30-degree angle

COLLAR:
Fiber length can range
from one to two gap
widths

TAIL:
½ to ⅔ shank length

RIB:
5 or 6 turns

flies behind a larger, more heavily weighted pattern like the Prince to keep them down in the strike zone.

Material selection is important. Starting with the biot tails, I use only goose biots selected near the tip of the feather, where they tend to be thinner and are easier to tie in than the biots at the base of the quill, which are wider and hard to anchor along the sides of the hook. I also look for biots with a good degree of natural curve. Straight biots can be tied in correctly and still the tails won't look right. Goose biots are much stiffer and more durable than turkey biots in this application.

Unlike the Pheasant Tail, you want bushy, full peacock herl for this fly. Strung peacock or herls from the eyed quill are fine as long as they are full-fibered. Dyed peacock in bright green or purple adds a nice, subtle touch of color on the finished fly. Peacock herl comes from the tail feathers of the male peacock, and these long feathers drag the ground for the entire life of the bird. Dirt (and worse) gets rubbed into the feathers, matting the fibers. Most of the herl you'd buy in a fly shop has been washed, but I always go to the trouble to wash it again. To assure your peacock herl flies all come out looking their best, wash your herl or peacock eyes in

BEAD TO HOOK SIZE

Diameter	Hook Size
¼" bead	#2–4
⁷⁄₃₂" bead	#2–8
³⁄₁₆" bead	#4–8
⁵⁄₃₂" bead	#8–12
⅛" bead	#10–14
⁷⁄₆₄" bead	#14–16
³⁄₃₂" bead	#14–18
⁵⁄₆₄" bead	#18–22
¹⁄₁₆" bead	#22–26

BEADHEAD PRINCE NYMPH

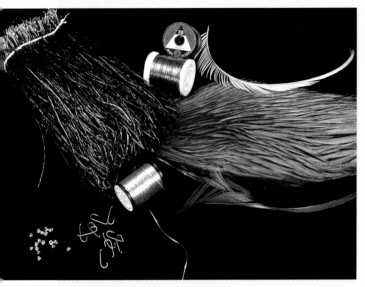

Prince Nymph materials.

Hook: #4–18 Tiemco 5262, 5263, or 3761
Thread: Black 6/0 Danville for #4–14; 8/0 Uni-Thread for #16 and smaller
Bead: Brass or tungsten
Weight: Lead wire, sized to hook per chart
Tails: Brown goose biots
Rib: Lagartun gold oval tinsel (small)
Body: Peacock herl
Hackle: Brown hen neck or saddle (in larger sizes)
Horns: White goose biots

LEAD WIRE TO HOOK SIZE

Diameter	Hook Size
.035"	#4 and larger
.030"	#4–6
.025"	#6–10
.020"	#12–14
.015"	#14–16
.010"	#16 and smaller

Note: **Some areas prohibit the use of lead in flies (Yellowstone National Park for instance). You can use lead-free wire, but it is not as heavy as real lead.**

the sink with some warm water and dish washing liquid, then blow dry them outside, as there will undoubtedly be some "fallout," and the mess is hard to hide. Aside from getting all that nastiness off the feathers, the blow dryer will puff up the barbules on the herls and make for a much thicker, juicier looking body. Now you know my secret.

For big Princes (#12 and larger) I often use hen saddle feathers for the collar, but on smaller flies, a genetic hen neck is necessary to get the proper size. Folding sweeps the hackle fibers back along the fly in a soft arc, creating a beautiful collar, and we are going to tie the collar on the Prince that way here. Finally, for the white biot horns at the head of the fly, I use the wider biots at the base of the feather. Their width helps to hold them in place as you tie them down and adds durability.

I would be hard pressed to say exactly what the Prince imitates, but if I had to hazard a guess I would have to say a stonefly nymph. The biot tails are what lead me this way, but I've seen this fly work under so many different hatch conditions, from mayflies to caddis, and in both rivers and lakes, that I think I would be safer to lump it into the attractor nymph category. A big Beadhead Prince is a guaranteed fish catcher during the winter months on many freestone streams here in Colorado, and during the summer, a Prince fished under a Stimulator is a common rig. This is a great little bug that still catches fish after all these years. Sometimes, the good stuff just never wears out.

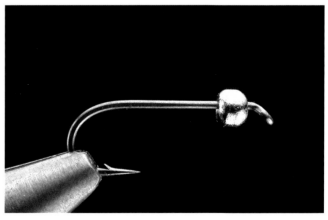

1. Before placing the hook in the vise, take a bead and place the hook point in the small hole, which is on the opposite side of the larger hole. The reason for this is so the bead will have enough clearance to make it around the sharp corner of the hook bend. Thread the bead onto the hook through the small hole. This will put the small hole against the hook eye. Slide the bead around the bend all the way to the hook eye. Now, mount the hook in the vise.

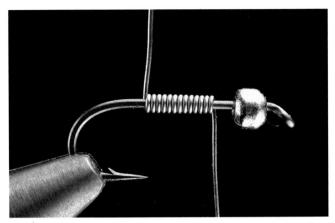

2. Pull 6 inches of lead wire from the spool, break it off, and wrap it around the hook in tight concentric turns from just in front of the hook point to just behind the bead. Make about a dozen turns. The lead doesn't need to be tied in because it is malleable and holds its shape around the hook as you wrap it.

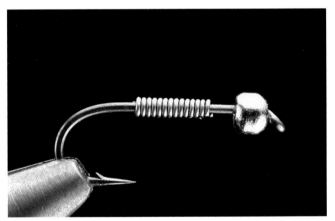

3. Break off the stubs on both ends with your fingernail or just by pulling on it. Lead wire is soft and will break easily. If there is any tag end left, fold it down against the shank with your finger or the tips of your scissors.

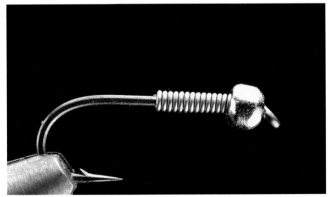

4. Shove the lead wraps into the bead. This helps keep the bead centered on the hook and holds it in place.

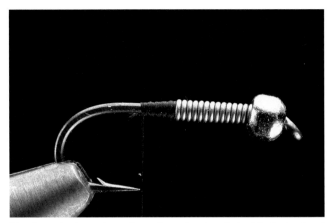

5. Attach the tying thread to the hook behind the lead wraps and clip the tag end of the thread. Form a thread dam from the bare hook up to the diameter of the lead wraps to provide a smooth transition from the bare hook to the wire and keep the lead wraps pressed tightly together.

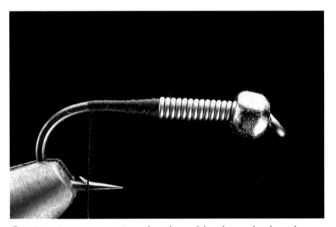

6. Continue wrapping the thread back to the bend.

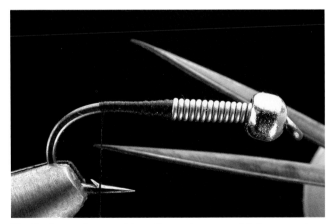

7. Peel two brown biots from the stem. Make sure they are separated at their bases. Lay the two biots back to back so they curve away from each other.

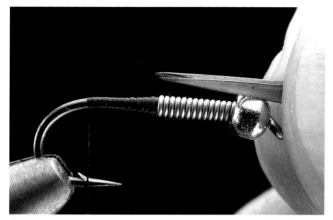

8. Even their tips and measure the two opposed biots against the hook shank so they are equal to half the length of the hook shank.

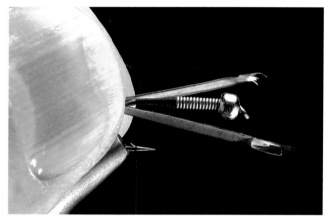

9. Transfer the tips of the biots to your material hand and place them on either side of the hook shank. Rather than setting the biots in place at top dead center, which is where you want them to ultimately end up, place the biots on a slight angle toward the near side of the shank, about a quarter turn toward you. Thread torque will twist the biots to the top of the hook.

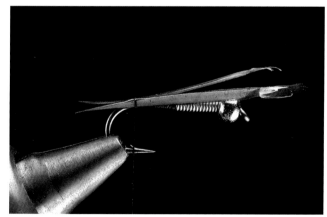

10. Put a single turn of thread over the biots, without letting go of the tips. Bring this wrap of thread over the top of the shank and back underneath so the bobbin is on the near side of the hook.

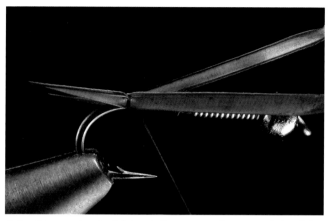

11. Draw the bobbin tight as you let go of the biot tips, allowing the thread to twist the biots to the top of the shank.

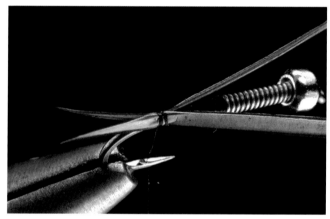

12. Once the biots are centered on top of the hook, make another loose wrap of thread over the base at the hook bend. Pull this wrap tight once it comes all the way around the shank to lock everything in place.

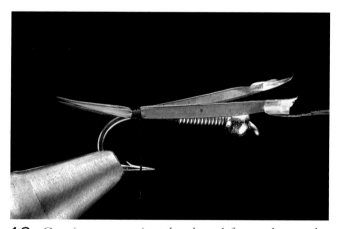

13. Continue wrapping the thread forward over the butt end of the biots, forming a short, tight band of thread.

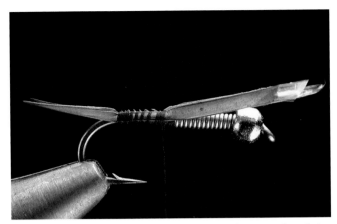

14. Spiral-wrap the thread over the butt ends of the biots up to the back of the lead wraps.

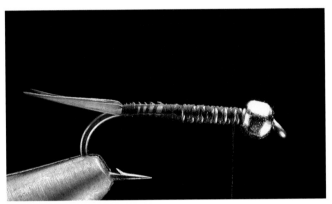

15. Clip the butt ends of the biots where they meet the lead wraps. Continue wrapping the thread forward over the lead up to the bead and back again to the rear edge of the lead. Make these wraps at an angle so the thread doesn't slide down between the wraps of wire.

16. Cut 8 inches of oval tinsel from the spool. You can use your good scissors, because tinsel is not wire and won't damage them. It has a strong silk core under the Mylar tinsel. Tie the tinsel in like wire, but make the first few thread wraps somewhat lightly so you can still pull the front end down to length. If you wrap too tight, the thread turns pull the tinsel off the core. Tie the end of the tinsel in about an eye length back from the bead.

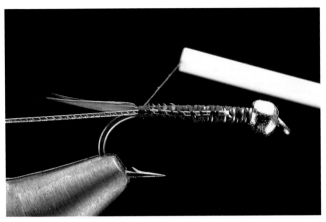

17. Wrap back over the tinsel to the hook bend, keeping the tinsel on the near side of the hook.

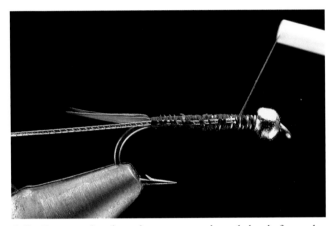

18. Return the thread to one eye-length back from the bead.

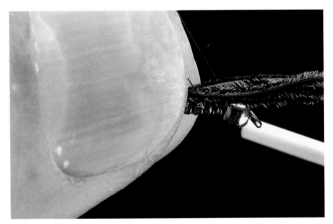

19. Select six to eight peacock herls and clip their tips square. Tie these in behind the bead with a pinch wrap.

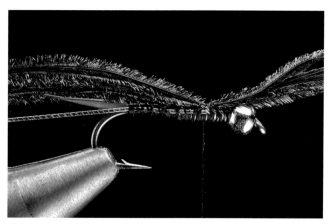

20. Properly tied in peacock.

21. Pull the long ends of the peacock toward the bend to draw the tips back behind the bead.

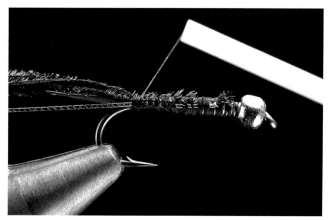

22. Wrap back over the peacock to the hook bend.

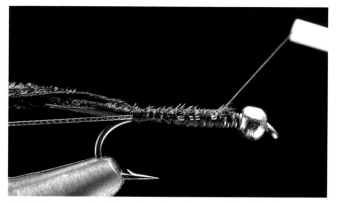

23. Return the thread to the front of the shank.

24. Place a drop of Gloss Coat or Zap-A-Gap on the shank and smooth it from the bead back to the bend with your bodkin or other applicator. This undercoating helps lock everything in place on the underbody and helps strengthen the peacock overbody.

25. Wrap the peacock herl forward from the hook bend to just behind the bead. Do not twist the peacock into a cord, just let it lie flat along the hook shank as you wrap. Twisting the herl into a rope toughens it a bit but also makes for a much blockier body. The lead wire under-body helps to taper the underbody, if you angle the first few turns of peacock forward sharply as you wrap. As you get up to the lead wraps, start to make the peacock turns more upright and perpendicular to the shank. Leave space behind the bead for the hackle and wing yet to come.

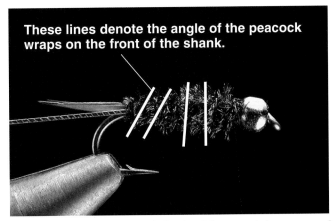

These lines denote the angle of the peacock wraps on the front of the shank.

26. Tie off the peacock herl with two tight turns of thread.

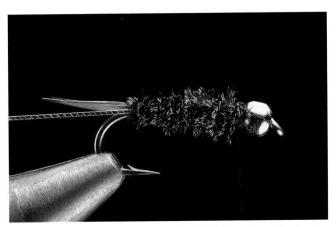

27. Clip the excess peacock herl flush against the back of the bead.

28. Spiral-wrap the tinsel forward over the peacock body with five or six turns. Don't get carried away with the ribbing here. The tinsel is pretty bright, so less is more. Tie the tinsel off behind the bead with several tight turns of thread and clip the excess.

29. Select, size, and prepare a brown hen neck feather with hackle fibers equal to about 1 ½ hook gaps. Trim the fibers along the base of the feather into short bristles to help secure the base of the feather to the hook. This step is usually not necessary to tie in hackles, but you are about to put some pressure on the feather when you fold it, and you want it as secure as possible.

30. Tie in the base of the hen feather behind the bead with several tight turns of thread. You want the concave (inside) side of the feather to face the rear of the shank and the shiny, outside of the feather to face toward the front.

31. Grasp the tip of the feather in your hackle pliers, being sure to grip the center stem in the jaws. Pull the feather straight up above the hook shank and hold the feather taut.

32. To fold the hackle feather, wet the tip of your thumb and forefinger of your material hand. Close your fingers together in front of the feather and draw the feather through your closed fingertips, forcing all the fibers back to one side of the feather stem. Pinch hard on the fibers as they pass through your fingers and perhaps even work them up and down to crease them back to the rear side of the quill.

33. Fold about an inch or so of the feather. You only need a few turns of hackle, so you don't have to fold the entire feather. You don't have to fold the feather, but I think it makes for a much cleaner hackle that is beautifully swept back over the body.

34. Make the first turn of hackle at the front edge of the peacock herl as upright as possible.

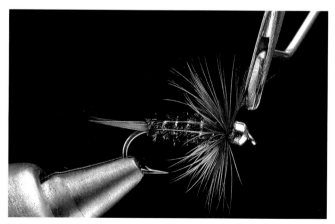

35. Make a second complete turn of hackle immediately in front of the first. It may help to stroke the wrapped portion of the hackle back as you wind the second turn to prevent trapping any stray fibers.

36. Pick up the bobbin and make a few tight wraps of thread behind the tip of the hackle feather to tie it off.

37. Clip the remaining tip as close as possible.

38. Close the thumb and forefinger of your thread hand around the hackle, trying to keep it 360 degrees around the shank, and pinch it down hard against the shank. Hold the hackle flat like this for a moment until the next step.

39. Reach in with your material hand and grasp the tips of the hackle fibers against the body of the fly. Hold these fibers in place and make several thread wraps over the front edge of the hackle.

40. These wraps should help hold the hackle in a swept-back position. Note that you still have about an eye length of thread space right behind the bead. You are about to need that space, so make sure it's there.

41. Pick two white biots from the stem. Do not oppose the two feathers, just cross them like scissor blades. The curve of the feathers should be facing down toward the body.

42. Measure the biots so the tips reach the base of the tail and the point at which the biots cross is right behind the bead. Place the biots on top of the hook shank with your thread hand. Press your thread hand thumb down on top of the biots.

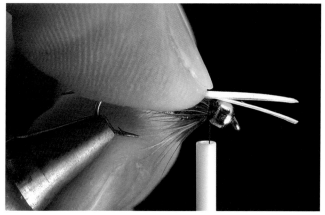

43. Bring your material hand thumb up on top of the biot tips and press them down flat on top of the body. These two feathers are hard to hold in place with any sort of a pinch wrap.

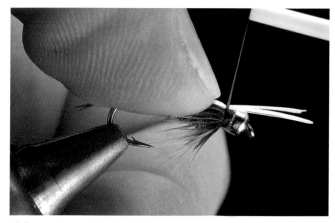

44. Make a few tight turns of thread over the base of the biots as close to the hackle as possible. There is not much room in here, but you want these initial wraps to be as far back from the bead as possible to leave a bit of room to trim the butt ends of the biots closer than you could otherwise.

45. Clip the butt ends of the biots as close to the bead as you can. Use those fine-tip scissors you bought to do this. You did buy the fine-tip scissors, didn't you? Wide-tip scissors just can't cut close enough to the bead to eliminate a big fat stub end. Go ahead, try it and see.

46. Wrap several tight turns of thread over the butt ends of the biots to anchor them in place and cover the stubs.

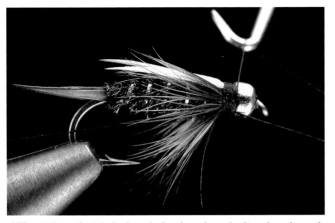

47. Whip-finish behind the bead and clip the thread.

48. Run a bead of Gloss Coat around the thread head.

PATTERN VARIATIONS

FLASHBACK PRINCE NYMPH

Hook:	#10–18 Tiemco 5262
Bead:	Gold-, black-, or copper-colored tungsten or brass, sized to hook
Weight:	Lead wire, sized to hook
Thread:	Black Danville 6/0 or 8/0 Uni-Thread
Tail:	Brown goose biots
Rib:	Lagartun gold oval tinsel (small)
Body:	Peacock herl
Hackle:	Brown hen neck hackle
Horns:	Opal Mirage Flash (small)

PURPLE PRINCE NYMPH

Hook:	#10–18 Tiemco 5262
Bead:	Gold-, black-, or copper-colored tungsten or brass, sized to hook
Weight:	Lead wire, sized to hook
Thread:	Black Danville 6/0 or 8/0 Uni-Thread
Tail:	Brown goose biots
Rib:	Lagartun gold oval tinsel (small)
Body:	Purple Holographic Ice Dub
Hackle:	Brown hen neck hackle
Horns:	White goose biots

LIME PRINCE NYMPH

Hook: #10–18 Tiemco 5262
Bead: Gold-, black-, or copper-colored tungsten or brass, sized to hook
Weight: Lead wire, sized to hook
Thread: Black Danville 6/0 or 8/0 Uni-Thread
Tail: Brown goose biots
Rib: Lagartun gold oval tinsel (small)
Body: Chartreuse Ice Dub
Hackle: Brown hen neck hackle
Horns: White goose biots

HOT WIRE PRINCE NYMPH

Hook: #10–18 Tiemco 5262
Bead: Gold-, black-, or copper-colored tungsten or brass, sized to hook
Weight: Lead wire, sized to hook
Thread: Black Danville 6/0 or 8/0 Uni-Thread
Tail: Brown goose biots
Rib: Lagartun gold oval tinsel (small)
Body: Green and gold (or other combinations) Ultra Wire
Hackle: Brown hen neck hackle
Horns: White goose biots
Thorax: Peacock herl

Note: Use one color wire in Brassie size and the other in small to create the variegated abdomen.

CHAPTER 13

Copper John

MAIN FOCUS

Compiling previous techniques into one fly
Installing a strip of flash to form a flashback wing case • Working with epoxy

The Copper John is the most popular fly in the country right now. Developed by my dear friend, John Barr, the Copper John is perhaps one of the most perfect combinations of materials ever adhered to a hook. John is a talented, no-nonsense kind of guy when it comes to fly design, so if you find a material on one of his patterns, you can be sure that it has a good reason for being there. John has related to me that he,

and perhaps he alone, has never fished with such common flies as the Prince Nymph or Pheasant Tail but instead came right out of the gate with many of his own creations. I find this idea compelling because many of us are so influenced by what others tie that it clouds our own creativity. Keep this in mind as you continue tying and branch out into developing your own ideas and patterns.

The Copper John: Perhaps the most perfect combination of materials ever tied to a hook.

115

Barr chose the biot tails over softer hen or partridge fibers because they are much more durable. The wire body adds shine, weight, durability, and many color options. A strip of flash over the top of a synthetic Thin Skin wing case creates a fish-attracting sparkle, highlighted with a topcoat of epoxy to bring out the color in the flash and toughen the fly. Peacock herl is mandatory on a fly like this, so the thorax material was an easy choice. Hen hackle fibers have replaced the original Hungarian partridge fiber legs, because hen feathers are cheaper and more durable than the Hun. Combine these components with a heavy lead-wire underbody and tungsten bead and you have what may be the World's Most Perfect Fly.

The Copper John is our first compilation fly in this book. I chose this pattern to demonstrate that even a challenging pattern can be broken down into simple steps that you are already familiar with. I think you'll be surprised at how many of the techniques used in the Copper John are already second nature to you by now. The bead, lead, and biot tails are mounted just as they were on the Beadhead Prince Nymph. The copper wire is tied in and wrapped just as we did on the Brassie, and the thorax is wrapped with peacock herl in much the same way that we formed the thorax on the Pheasant Tail. The Thin Skin wing case is mounted in the same manner as the turkey tail slip in the Hare's Ear tutorial. The only new tricks on this fly are the additional back strap of flash over the top of the wing case, the side mounted legs (which not surprisingly are similarly connected to the tailing fibers on the Hare's Ear), and the epoxy overcoat.

After guiding on the South Platte for so many years, I have developed an aversion to watching yarn strike indicators float down a river. Make no mistake; I have no argument against the efficacy of Bozo Heads—they are an incredibly sensitive indicator and I admit that I always have a hank of yarn in my pack just in case. But, these days I much prefer the Hopper/Copper/Dropper (HCD) rig to any sort of conventional indicator. The HCD rig consists of a large buoyant dry fly like a Charlie Boy Hopper or BC Hopper fished on the end of a 6-foot 3X leader. To the bend of the Hopper is tied a 2- to 4-foot section of 4X fluorocarbon tippet. At the business end of this tippet section, I attach a Copper John, sized to get down along the bottom of the river and stay there. Think of the Copper as a weight in this instance and vary its size

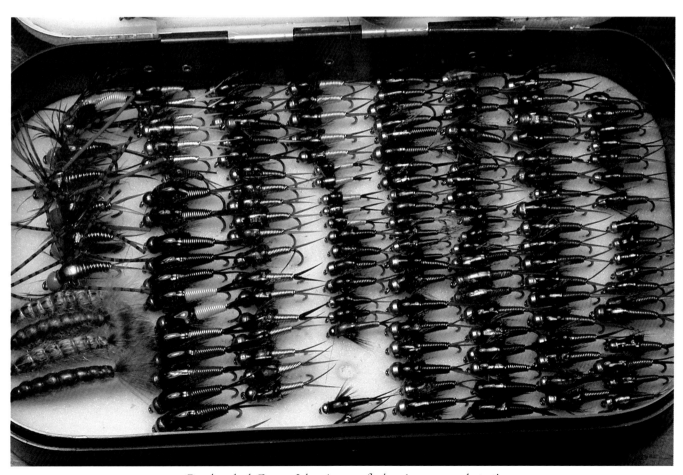

One hundred Copper Johns in your fly box is . . . a good start!

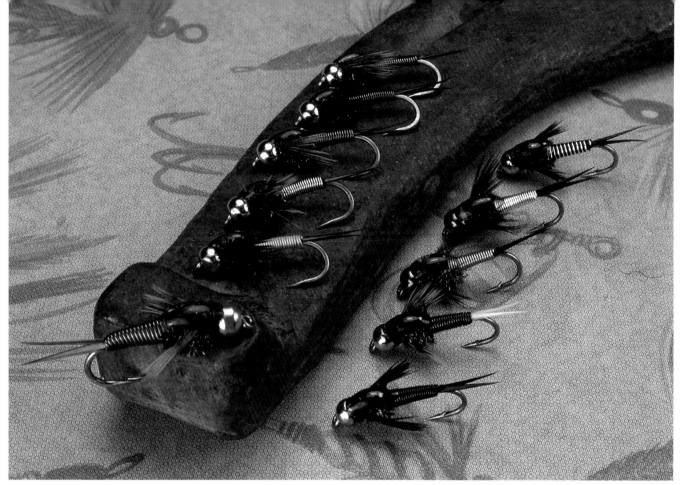

Copper John colors are limited only by your imagination and wire supply.

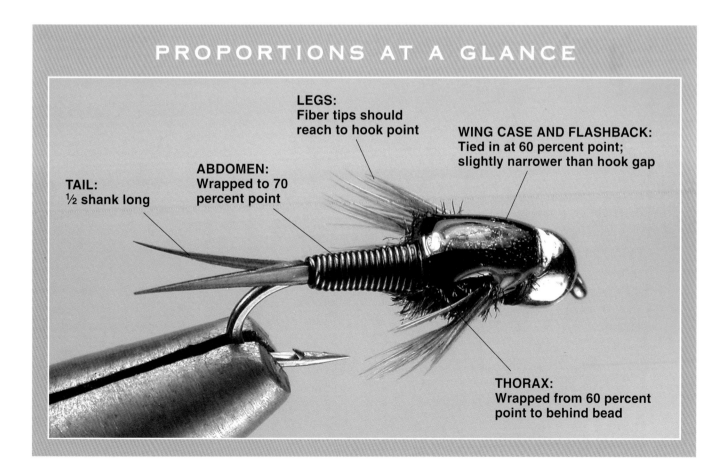

PROPORTIONS AT A GLANCE

LEGS:
Fiber tips should
reach to hook point

WING CASE AND FLASHBACK:
Tied in at 60 percent point;
slightly narrower than hook gap

ABDOMEN:
Wrapped to 70
percent point

TAIL:
½ shank long

THORAX:
Wrapped from 60 percent
point to behind bead

according to the water depth and speed, much as you would with your split shot in a conventional nymphing rig. I then tie a second, 12- to 15-inch-long section of 5X tippet to the bend of the Copper John and hang a smaller fly off the back. The third fly in this rig can be nearly anything, from another Copper John to an RS2 or Black Beauty. I try to match the dropper to the prevailing hatch. If there are *Baetis* around, I might use a Pheasant Tail or RS2; if there are lots of caddis emerging, I might use a caddis pupae pattern. If there are really lots of bugs

COPPER JOHN

Copper John materials.

Hook:	#10–18 Tiemco 5262
Bead:	Copper-colored tungsten, sized to hook (see Prince chapter)
Weight:	Lead wire, sized to hook (see Prince chapter)
Thread:	Black 70-denier Ultra Thread or 8/0 Uni-Thread
Tail:	Brown goose biots
Abdomen:	Copper brown Ultra Wire (#12, medium; #14–16, Brassie; #18–20, small)
Flash:	Pearl Flashabou or Opal Mirage Tinsel (medium)
Wing case:	Black Thin Skin
Thorax:	Peacock herl
Legs:	Mottled-brown hen saddle
Coating:	5- or 30-minute epoxy

hatching, and the fish are rising, I'll cut all this off and fish a dry without hesitation, but the Hopper/Copper/Dropper is a great way to prospect a river and cover three levels of the water column at the same time.

The more I fish this rig, the more I am convinced that the sum of the flies is greater than any of its parts. I believe each fly draws more attention to the others, and you can catch more fish covering them with the three-fly rig than you could with just one or two. I can't count how many times I have had a fish eat the Hopper, and I set the hook and fight the fish in only to discover that he has both the Hopper *and* the Copper in his mouth. I think the fish see the Copper on the way to the dry and pick it up as an appetizer to the big meal on top. I also find that this more subtle rig tends to alarm fish less than more traditional indicators. Whether the fish decides to eat the Hopper or not, they don't seem nearly as alarmed by the Hopper floating over them as they do to a conventional indicator. Of course, a Copper John can be just as deadly under old Bozo and can often be fished without any additional weight on the leader. I don't need to go any further with the merits of this fly—if you haven't gotten the idea by now, you should probably just go make a tee time.

The Copper John is tied in a huge variety of colors. I have chosen the copper brown coloration for the fly tied here as it has become one of my favorites. Red, black, green, chartreuse, and orange are on that list as well. I carry well over one hundred Copper Johns with me on any given fishing day and fish them in a variety of ways. Check out *Barr Flies* (Stackpole Books) for all the common color variations and more details on their inception.

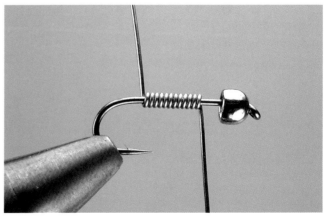

1. Place the bead on the hook and slide it up to the hook eye. Wrap thirteen turns of the appropriate-size lead wire onto the hook shank from the back of the hook to the front.

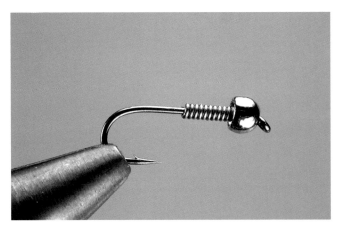

2. Break the ends off the lead on either end of the wraps by pushing on the lead with your thumbnail. Shove the lead wraps up into the back of the bead, countersinking the wraps into the recess.

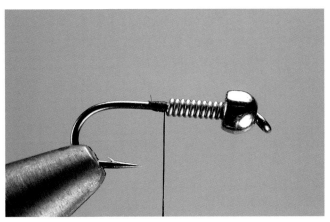

3. Start the tying thread at the back edge of the lead wraps. Build a smooth taper from the bare hook shank up to the lead wire, creating a dam to prevent the lead wraps from separating as you wrap over them later.

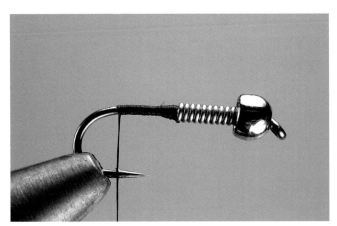

4. Continue wrapping a smooth thread base back to the hook bend.

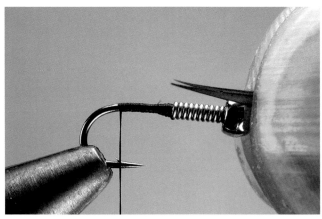

5. Select two matched biots from the quill. Pull two that are right next to each other to assure they are the same width and length. Place the biots back to back so they curve away from each other and even their tips. Measure the biots against the hook shank so they are equal to half the length of the hook shank.

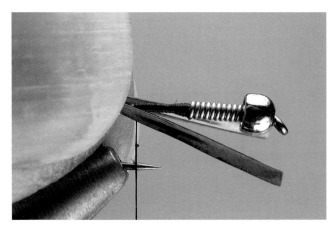

6. Place the opposed biots at the hook bend with one on each side of the hook shank.

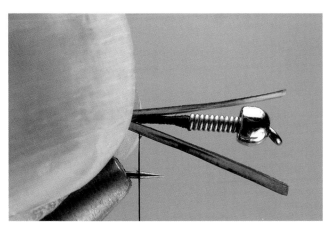

7. Turn the biots so they are slightly off-center toward the near side of the hook.

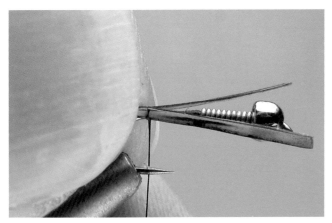

8. Wrap a single turn of thread over the biots to hold them in place on the near side of the hook. You are going to attach these biots exactly as you did on the Prince Nymph, but because this can be a tricky maneuver, I will reiterate the finer points again.

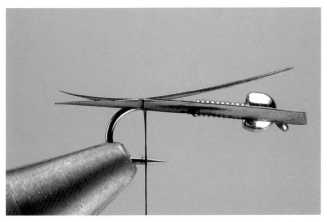

9. The biots should be on either side of the hook shank, not centered on the shank, but twisted slightly toward the near side of the hook.

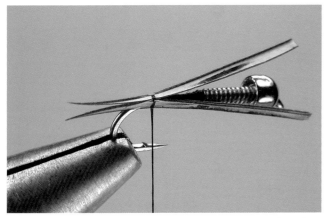

10. The biots should be parallel to each other, but canted toward the near side of the hook shank.

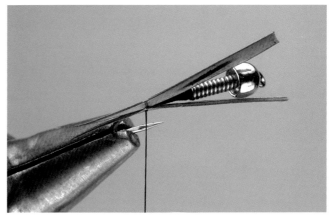

11. Another view of the properly positioned biots.

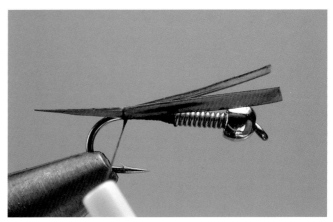

12. Pull the tying thread toward you to tighten the loop of thread going over the biots and pull the biots to top dead center on the hook shank.

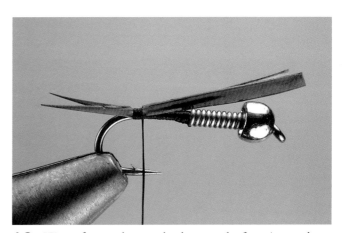

13. Wrap forward over the butt ends, forming a short band of thread to hold the tails in place.

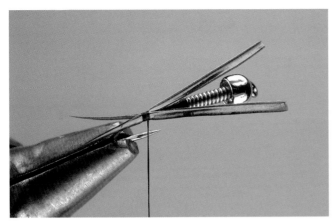

14. You should now have two biots split evenly and centered atop the hook shank.

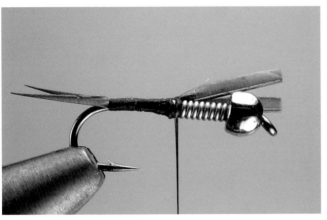

15. Continue wrapping forward over the butt ends of the biots up to and slightly onto the back edge of the lead wraps.

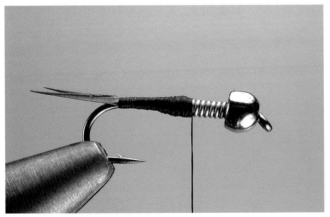

16. Clip the excess butt ends from the shank and smooth the underbody taper out.

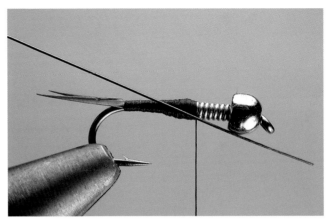

17. Cut 6 to 8 inches of copper wire.

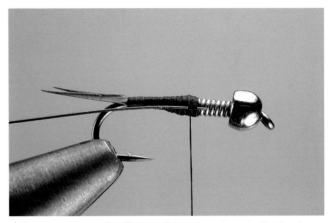

18. Tie it in at the front of the thread underbody along the near side of the hook shank using the right-angle technique.

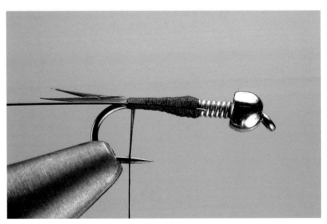

19. Wrap back over the wire to the hook bend. Make sure this underbody is as smooth as possible. The final body will mirror any lumps or bumps in it.

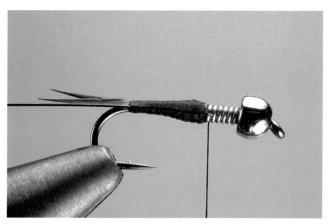

20. Return the thread to the front of the underbody. As you begin to wrap forward from the bend, make the thread wraps concentric and as tight as possible near the tail. Just like on the Brassie, make sure the wire is securely anchored at the hook bend.

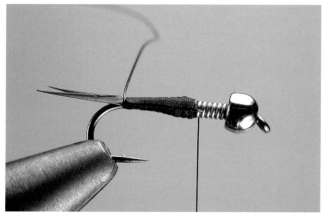

21. Bring the wire up over the top of the hook for the start of the first wrap of wire. This turn should butt against the front edge of the tails.

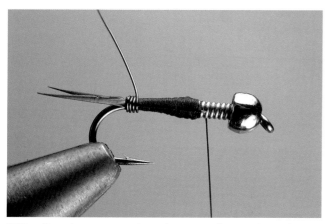

22. Continue wrapping the wire forward, with one turn directly in front of the last. Tilt the wire back as you bring it over the top of the hook to use the previous wrap of wire as a guide for the next wrap.

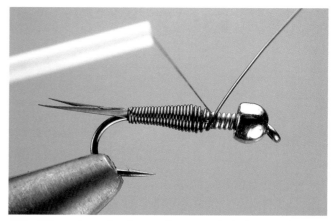

23. Wrap the wire forward to just slightly past the end of the thread underbody. Bring the end of the wire up above the hook and tie it off with a few firm wraps of thread. The descending taper will cause the wire to spread a bit, but this will eventually be covered by the thorax and wing case, so don't get worked up.

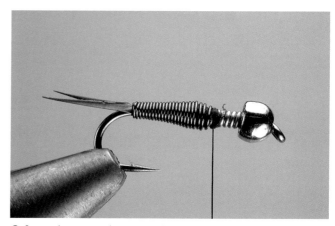

24. Helicopter the end of the wire to break it off flush.

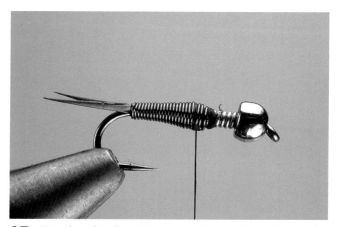

25. Overlap the thread onto the front edge of the wire abdomen back to the 60 percent point on the shank, which also, not coincidentally, is the widest part of the abdomen.

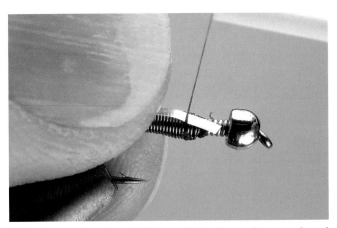

26. Cut a length of Mirage Flash from the spool and tie it in on top of the shank at the 60 percent point. Similar to the biots on the Prince Nymph, hold the flash in place with your material hand thumb slightly to the near side of the shank as you bring a wrap of thread up and over it.

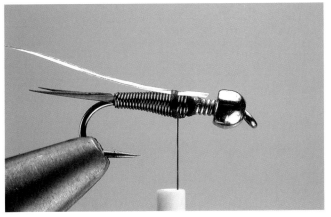

27. The thread torque will twist the flash to the top of the shank and center it.

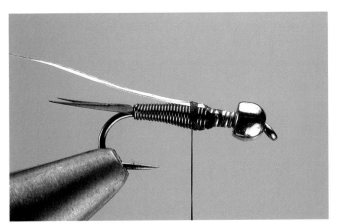

28. Wrap forward over the butt end of the flash to anchor it down. By tying this piece in with a short front end, you eliminate the need to trim it later and make for a cleaner thorax area and less bulk.

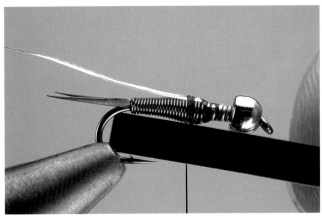

29. Cut a strip of black Thin Skin from the sheet that is just slightly narrower than the hook gap. Leave the paper backing attached while you cut the strip. If you get all fancy and try to remove the backing from the whole sheet, the Thin Skin will curl up into an unusable mess. I've warned you.

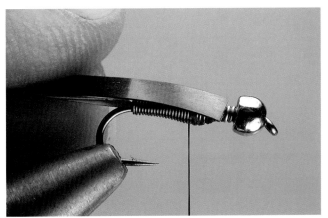

30. Remove the paper backing from the strip and lay the Thin Skin on top of the hook shank with the front end extending to just behind the bead. When you remove the backing, the Thin Skin strip will display an obvious curve. I tie the Thin Skin in so the inside of the curve is facing the hook shank. If you tie it in with the curve facing up, the other end comes around and is in the way during the rest of the tying process. It only took about a dozen flies for me to figure that out.

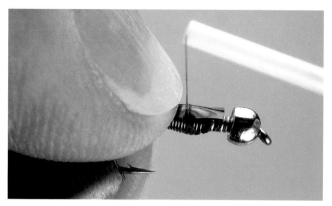

31. Press your thumb down on top of the Thin Skin and tie it in place at the 60 percent point on the shank just as you did with the flash.

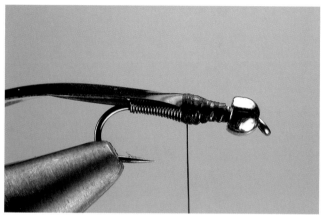

32. Wrap forward over the front end of the Thin Skin wing case to the back edge of the bead, binding it down to the shank.

33. Make sure the Thin Skin is centered on top of the hook shank.

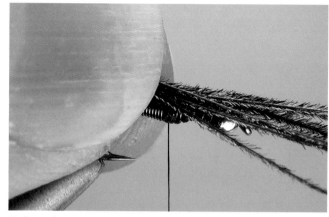

34. Select six peacock herls and clip their tips square. Tie the herls in by their tips at the base of the wing case with two taut wraps of thread.

35. Pull the butt ends of the peacock to draw the tips down behind the bead.

36. Wrap forward tightly over the tips of the peacock herl up to the back edge of the bead.

37. Wrap the peacock herl forward up to the bead. Make sure the last wrap of herl is snugged right up against the bead and tie the herl off with a few firm wraps of thread.

38. Clip the excess herl flush against the shank.

39. Select a large hen saddle feather like you used for the tail of the Hare's Ear Nymph. Prepare the feather as you did there, and preen a gap-width bundle of fibers out from the center stem so their tips are even.

40. Peel these fibers from the stem, taking care to keep the tips even, and measure them against the shank so they extend from the back edge of the bead to the hook point.

41. Reach in and pinch the hen fibers against the near side of the shank with your material hand.

42. Make two turns of thread over the base of the hen fibers at the back edge of the bead. These thread wraps should cinch down between the bead and the front edge of the peacock herl.

43. Check the length of the hen fibers to assure that they reach to the hook point and are sitting squarely on the near side of the shank.

46. Make two turns over the second clump of hen fibers on the far side of the hook before you let go of the tips.

44. Repeat the above process on the far side of the hook. Even a clump of hen fibers, peel them from the stem, and measure them so they are equal in length to the clump on the near side.

47. Check that both leg bunches are the same length. If one side is longer than the other, you can gently pull on the butt ends to shorten them slightly.

45. Pinch this second clump of fibers in place along the far side of the hook just like you did with the first bunch.

48. To trim the loose butt ends, roll the fibers in your fingertips so they twist together into a cord. This will make it much easier to cut all the fibers at once. Reach in with the tips of your fine scissors and clip the butts as close to the bead as you can.

49. Repeat this step on the far side.

50. Pull the Thin Skin wing case forward over the top of the thorax. Be sure to keep it centered on the top of the shank and put a bit of pressure on it to slightly stretch the material.

51. Hold the end of the wing case in your thread hand and make a few tight turns of thread over it right behind the bead with your material hand.

52. Pull the flash over the top of the wing case so that it is centered and tie it down behind the bead.

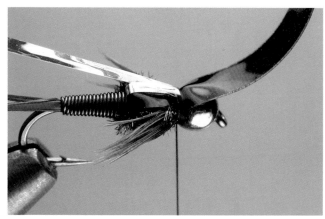

53. Fold the flash back toward the bend after you have anchored it behind the bead. Make a few more tight wraps over the fold to fix it in place.

54. Securing the flash this way assures it won't pull out later and works on flashbacks of all varieties.

55. Nick the near edge of the flash with the tips of your scissors. A small nick is all it takes.

56. Pull the flash to the far side of the hook to tear it off the hook. Tearing the flash like this makes for a much cleaner stub end.

57. The Thin Skin wing case won't tear as easily as the flash, so the best way to trim it is to use two cuts. Make the first cut up from the near side of the hook along the radius of the bead to the center of the wing case. Tilt the scissor blades across the top of the fly and down toward the far side to trim the second half of the wing case.

58. Make several turns of thread over the short stub end of the wing case to smooth out the head.

59. Whip-finish and clip the thread behind the bead.

60. Mix a small batch of epoxy. Make sure to use equal amounts of both the hardener and the resin to assure the epoxy hardens. Sometimes, I even use just a touch more hardener to assure the epoxy won't be tacky. Use your bodkin to apply a drop of epoxy across the top of the wing case, from front to back and side to side. Run the epoxy down onto the back edge of the bead and onto the last turn of wire behind the wing case. This will give the epoxy something to anchor to besides the smooth Thin Skin wing case, which doesn't adhere to the epoxy all that well.

61. Let the fly dry upright. There is no need to rotate the fly as the epoxy is only on the top of the wing case. Generally, I will tie several dozen and coat them all at once. I can get a dozen or so flies from a batch of 5-minute epoxy, and several dozen from a batch of 30-minute epoxy. Mix very small batches of epoxy, even for a larger quantity of flies. Each fly takes but a single drop of epoxy, and a common mistake I see on this fly is mixing enough epoxy to reinforce the hull of a cruise ship and wasting it.

PATTERN VARIATIONS

BLUE COPPER JOHN

Hook:	#12–18 Tiemco 5262
Bead:	Gold-colored brass or tungsten, sized to hook
Weight:	Lead wire
Thread:	Black 70-denier Ultra Thread
Tail:	Black goose biots
Abdomen:	Blue Ultra Wire
Flashback:	Pearl Flashabou or Opal Mirage Tinsel (medium)
Wing case:	Black Thin Skin
Thorax:	Peacock herl
Legs:	Black hen saddle fibers
Coating:	5- or 30-minute epoxy

HOT PINK COPPER JOHN

Hook:	#12–18 Tiemco 5262
Bead:	Gold-colored brass or tungsten, sized to hook
Weight:	Lead wire
Thread:	Black 70-denier Ultra Thread
Tail:	Black goose biots
Abdomen:	Hot pink Ultra Wire
Flashback:	Pearl Flashabou or Opal Mirage Tinsel (medium)
Wing case:	Black Thin Skin
Thorax:	Peacock herl
Legs:	Black hen saddle fibers
Coating:	5- or 30-minute epoxy

BLACK COPPER JOHN

Hook:	#12–18 Tiemco 5262
Bead:	Gold- or black-colored brass or tungsten, sized to hook
Weight:	Lead wire
Thread:	Black 70-denier Ultra Thread
Tail:	Black goose biots
Abdomen:	Black Ultra Wire
Flashback:	Pearl Flashabou or Opal Mirage Tinsel (medium)
Wing case:	Black Thin Skin
Thorax:	Peacock herl
Legs:	Black hen saddle fibers
Coating:	5- or 30-minute epoxy

ZEBRA COPPER JOHN

Hook:	#12–18 Tiemco 5262
Bead:	Silver-colored brass or tungsten, sized to hook
Weight:	Lead wire
Thread:	Black 70-denier Ultra Thread
Tail:	Black goose biots
Abdomen:	Black and silver Ultra Wire
Flashback:	Pearl Flashabou or Opal Mirage Tinsel (medium)
Wing case:	Black Thin Skin
Thorax:	Peacock herl
Legs:	Black hen saddle fibers
Coating:	5- or 30-minute epoxy

WINE COPPER JOHN

Hook:	#12–18 Tiemco 5262
Bead:	Gold-colored brass or tungsten, sized to hook
Weight:	Lead wire
Thread:	Black 70-denier Ultra Thread
Tail:	White goose biots
Abdomen:	Wine Ultra Wire
Flashback:	Pearl Flashabou or Opal Mirage Tinsel (medium)
Wing case:	Black Thin Skin
Thorax:	Peacock herl
Legs:	Brown hen saddle fibers
Coating:	5- or 30-minute epoxy

RED COPPER JOHN

Hook:	#12–18 Tiemco 5262
Bead:	Gold-colored brass or tungsten, sized to hook
Weight:	Lead wire
Thread:	Black 70-denier Ultra Thread
Tail:	Brown goose biots
Abdomen:	Red Ultra Wire
Flashback:	Pearl Flashabou or Opal Mirage Tinsel (medium)
Wing case:	Black Thin Skin
Thorax:	Peacock herl
Legs:	Brown hen saddle fibers
Coating:	5- or 30-minute epoxy

GREEN COPPER JOHN

Hook:	#12–18 Tiemco 5262
Bead:	Gold-colored brass or tungsten, sized to hook
Weight:	Lead wire
Thread:	Black 70-denier Ultra Thread
Tail:	Black goose biots
Abdomen:	Green Ultra Wire
Flashback:	Pearl Flashabou or Opal Mirage Tinsel (medium)
Wing case:	Black Thin Skin
Thorax:	Peacock herl
Legs:	Brown hen saddle fibers
Coating:	5- or 30-minute epoxy

COPPER JOHN

Hook:	#12–18 Tiemco 5262
Bead:	Gold-colored brass or tungsten, sized to hook
Weight:	Lead wire
Thread:	Black 70-denier Ultra Thread
Tail:	Brown goose biots
Abdomen:	Copper Ultra Wire
Flashback:	Pearl Flashabou or Opal Mirage Tinsel (medium)
Wing case:	Black Thin Skin
Thorax:	Peacock herl
Legs:	Brown hen saddle fibers
Coating:	5- or 30-minute epoxy

CHARTREUSE COPPER JOHN

Hook:	#12–18 Tiemco 5262
Bead:	Gold-colored brass or tungsten, sized to hook
Weight:	Lead wire
Thread:	Black 70-denier Ultra Thread
Tail:	Black goose biots
Abdomen:	Chartreuse Ultra Wire
Flashback:	Pearl Flashabou or Opal Mirage Tinsel (medium)
Wing case:	Black Thin Skin
Thorax:	Peacock herl
Legs:	Black hen saddle fibers
Coating:	5- or 30-minute epoxy

SILVER COPPER JOHN

Hook:	#12–18 Tiemco 5262
Bead:	Black-colored brass or tungsten, sized to hook
Weight:	Lead wire
Thread:	Black 70-denier Ultra Thread
Tail:	Black goose biots
Abdomen:	Silver Ultra Wire
Flashback:	Pearl Flashabou or Opal Mirage Tinsel (medium)
Wing case:	Black Thin Skin
Thorax:	Peacock herl
Legs:	Black hen saddle fibers
Coating:	5- or 30-minute epoxy

CHAPTER 14

Woolly Bugger

MAIN FOCUS

Working with marabou and chenille • Preparing and wrapping a palmered hackle
Ribbing through hackle

The Woolly Bugger was invented by Russell Blessing long enough ago that most folks don't know who he is. Mr. Blessing, perhaps inadvertently, developed what is now the single most popular streamer in the world. The Bugger is a slight variation of the ubiquitous Wooly Worm, which sports a body and hackle much like the Bugger's but either no tail at all or a short stub of brightly colored yarn. The addition of a soft, breathing marabou tail has made all the difference

in this pattern, creating a lifelike imitation of anything from a leech to a small fish.

Truly, I love the Woolly Bugger, and all its variations. If I were limited to one streamer, it would be the Bugger, with the caveat that I could exercise my right to vary it a bit here and there. I nearly always tie my Buggers with a tungsten cone or lead eyes. The heavy weight adds to the fly's jigging action and keeps it down where the fish can get to it. Some of my favorite variations on this fly are

The Woolly Bugger is one of the most popular streamers in the world and has hundreds of variations.

132

WOOLLY BUGGER ■ 133

dubbed bodies, soft schlappen hackles, and perhaps a bit of flash thrown in the tail. A gingery-cream colored variation with a pale-yellow Ice Dub body called the Vanilla Ice (developed by my good friend Dennis Collier) is a particularly good deviation. I believe this lighter color imitates the belly of a baby brown trout, and from the fish's underside view, the fly may look like a small fish making a quick escape. No self-respecting brown trout can let that happen, and the ensuing strike reminds you to hold onto the rod a little tighter.

We will tie what has become the standard edition of the infamous Bugger. This is an extraordinarily easy-to-tie fly that opens the doors to a boxful of variations and ideas. My main reason to include this fly, aside from covering the requisite streamer category, is the hackling technique. The procedure used here is the same for the Elk Hair Caddis and Stimulator that follow. The best way to wrap the hackle is from front to back, reinforcing the hackle stem with wire. You could, indeed, tie a Bugger hackle in by its tip at the hook bend and wrap it forward over the chenille body, but the method we'll use here makes for a more durable fly. I am often asked why you couldn't just tie the hackle feather in by its butt end at the hook bend and follow the same path. If you tie the feather in by the wide end at the butt of the feather, you will get a fly that has big long hackle at the back and shorter, stiffer hackle at its front and doesn't breathe well in the water.

WOOLLY BUGGER

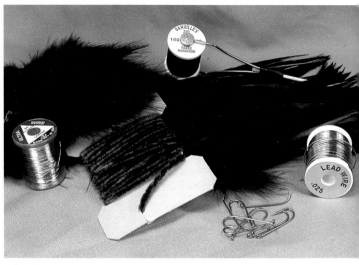

Woolly Bugger materials.

Hook:	#2–12 Tiemco 5262, 5263, or Daiichi 2220
Weight:	.025-inch-diameter lead wire
Thread:	Black 3/0 monocord
Tail:	Black marabou
Rib:	Copper Ultra Wire
Body:	Medium olive chenille
Flash (optional):	Black Holographic Flashabou
Hackle:	Black rooster saddle

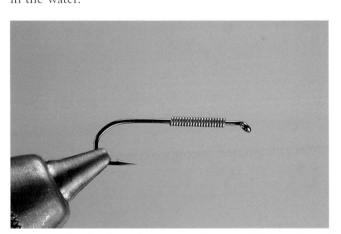

1. Place the hook in the vise and break off 10 inches of lead wire from the spool. Grasp one end of the wire in your material hand and hold it against the shank's midpoint. Grab the other end of the wire and wrap the lead around the hook 20 or so turns toward the hook eye. Of course, you can make fewer turns for a lighter weight fly or more for a heavier fly. Be sure to stop the lead wraps about ⅕ of a hook shank back from the eye so you still have plenty of room to finish off the fly. Break the ends of the wire off with your thumbnail and fold any stubs down flat with the tips of your scissors.

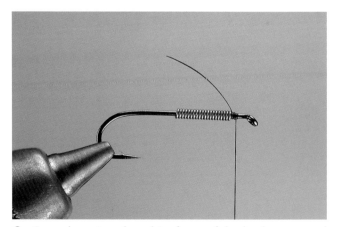

2. Start the tying thread in front of the lead wraps and build a small thread dam against the front edge of the lead.

PROPORTIONS AT A GLANCE

RIB:
5 or 6 turns

HACKLE:
Fibers should equal the
length of two hook gaps

TAIL:
One shank-length long

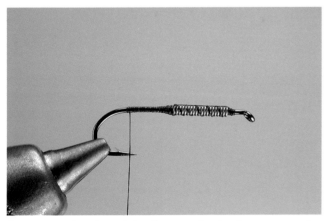

3. Wrap the thread back over the lead wraps to the hook bend. Once you reach the back edge of the lead, wrap another small thread dam to build a transition from the shank to the lead wraps. Continue back with the thread to the bend, forming a smooth thread base.

4. Select a nice fluffy marabou feather and pinch the feather into a single clump. Measure this clump against the hook so it is one shank-length long. Pinch the feather in your material hand just behind the hook eye and bring the base of the feather back to the hook bend.

5. Pinch the base of the marabou feather directly above the hook barb and make two loose wraps over the base of the feather. Tighten these turns to anchor the feather down at the hook bend. Make sure the tail is now centered on top of the hook shank.

6. Check that the tail is one shank-length long.

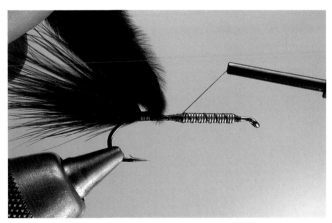

7. Lift the butt end of the marabou feather up and back with your material hand and bring the thread forward over the hook shank to just behind the front edge of the lead wraps.

8. Lay the marabou feather on the shank again and bind the front end down with several tight turns of thread.

9. Clip the remaining marabou as close to the hook as you can in front of your thread wraps. The marabou butts form an underbody for the Bugger, creating a bit of bulk and smoothing off the underbody shape at the same time.

10. Tightly spiral-wrap the thread back to just in front of the hook point.

11. Tie in a length of copper wire at the hook point using the right-angle technique and wrap back over the wire to the base of the tail. Leave a bit of wire sticking out to the front so you can be sure to anchor the wire down tightly.

12. Wrap forward over the stub end of the wire to secure it to the shank. Return the thread to the hook bend.

13. Clip an 8-inch-long piece of chenille from the card and peel a few fibers from one end, exposing the core. Tie the core to the hook with a pinch wrap at the base of the tail. This eliminates the lump that would result if you just tied the thick chenille to the shank.

14. Spiral-wrap the thread forward to the back edge of the index point.

15. Wrap the chenille forward much like you did with the wire on the Brassie, tilting the chenille back a bit as you wrap. This results in a much denser chenille body that both looks better and is more durable than a loose spiral-wrap.

16. Tie the chenille off at the back edge of the hook eye by holding it in your thread hand and crossing the thread over it with a few tight turns in your material hand.

17. Clip the excess chenille as close to the hook shank as you can.

18. Select and pull a soft rooster saddle feather from the skin. Measure the feather against the hook gap to check that it is from 1½ to 2 hook gaps wide. Saddle feathers tend to be more tapered than neck feathers and will generally be much wider at their bases than they are at their tips. On a Bugger, this taper creates a slightly larger head that tapers down toward the bend, mimicking the natural taper of many real critters like small fish and leeches. Prepare this feather by cutting the fluff from the base, leaving just soft, wide hackle fibers. Strip a few of the fibers from the base of the feather, exposing the stem for about an eye length or two. Strip the inside of the feather just a bit more to prevent trapping the fibers on the first turn. By inside, I mean the inside of the turn or far side of the feather. This side is what will touch the body on that first turn and stripping these fibers will leave a nice clean base for the feather to perch on with that first turn.

19. Tie the prepared feather in by the stripped stem just behind the hook eye and wrap back over it to the front of the body. Anchor the feather tightly, and be sure the inside/concave of the feather is facing the body of the fly.

20. Make two turns with the hackle feather at the front edge of the chenille body to create a collar at the front of the fly. These turns should butt next to each other.

21. Palmer the feather back to the hook bend with five or six even spiraling turns. Palmering simply means to spiral-wrap a feather through a body. It is just like you did with the wire on the Black Beauty, except that you are going from front to back and wrapping a feather this time instead of wire. Once you reach the hook bend, hold the feather tip in your material hand to prepare for the next step.

22. Grab the wire and bring it up over the tip of the hackle feather, binding it down tightly to the chenille body. Once you have made this first complete turn, let go of the tip of the feather but hang onto the wire.

23. Spiral-wrap the wire forward through the hackle over the chenille body. The trick to wrapping the wire through the hackle without trapping the fibers is to wrap like there are no hackle fibers in the way. Just evenly spiral the wire forward through the hackle with the same amount of turns as you wrapped the hackle. You want the wire to travel at an opposite angle than the hackle, forming an X with the hackle stem as it travels forward. If you bind a few fibers down along the way, you can go back later and pick them out, but try to miss as many as you can.

24. Continue wrapping the wire to the back edge of the index point.

25. Grasp the end of the wire in your thread hand and make two tight turns of thread over it at the point where it intersects the hook shank to anchor it down.

26. Break off the excess wire and build a small, smooth thread head to cover the stub. Whip-finish and clip the thread and then add a shot of Gloss Coat to the thread head.

PATTERN VARIATIONS

BEADHEAD AUTUMN SPLENDOR

Hook:	#2–12 Tiemco 300
Bead:	Copper-colored tungsten bead or cone (weight with lead wire if desired)
Thread:	Brown 3/0 monocord
Tail:	Brown marabou and copper Krystal Flash
Rib:	Copper Ultra Wire (small)
Body:	Brown chenille (medium)
Legs:	Yellow rubber legs (medium)
Hackle:	Grizzly dyed orange saddle hackle

Note: This fly comes from Tim Heng in the Roaring Fork Valley and is a great attractor fly in any water conditions.

VANILLA ICE VARIATION

Hook:	#2–6 Tiemco 300
Thread:	Tan 3/0 monocord
Cone:	Gold-colored tungsten, weighted with lead wire on shank
Tail:	Cream marabou with gold Krystal Flash
Body:	UV Light-yellow Ice Dub
Legs:	Natural Latex-colored rubber legs (medium), mottled with permanent marker
Hackle:	Gold UV Krystal Hackle

Note: The Vanilla Ice comes from my good friend Dennis Collier. Dennis loves to fish streamers, and his creations are amazingly effective. I added the synthetic Krystal Hackle and rubber legs to this pattern to toughen it up and add a bit of color. The unusual color bands on the legs imitate the spotted lateral line on a small brown trout when this fly is wet.

BLACK LEAD-EYED BUGGER

Hook:	#2–6 Tiemco 5263
Thread:	Black 3/0 monocord
Eyes:	Plated lead eyes (medium)
Tail:	Two black marabou feathers flanked by red, blue, and green Krystal Flash
Rib (optional):	Black Ultra Wire (small)
Body:	Black opal Ice Chenille
Head:	Black chenille (fine), wrapped around lead eyes
Hackle:	Black schlappen

Note: The Lead-Eyed Bugger is one of my favorite streamers. The lead eyes add a lot of weight at the front of the fly and keep it down in the water column as I rapidly strip it back to me. I often attach a smaller streamer on a dropper behind the Lead-Eyed Bugger, letting the heavy Woolly Bugger pull the back fly down along with it.

CHAPTER 15

Hair Selection

Selecting the right hair for a fly is one of the hallmarks of an accomplished fly tier. After years of tying with all sorts of hair, you will start to develop a sense of how different types react on the hook when you apply thread tension. Unfortunately, developing this sense can take an awful long time, and since you bought this book hoping that I would shed some light on topics like this, here goes.

For our purposes here, I will talk about hair from deer, elk, and moose, and calf body hair. Caribou and antelope both have useable hair for fly tying, but I think the only ones who find this stuff useful are the caribou and antelope. These hairs tend to be soft and have mostly broken tips, rendering them useless for wings and collars. While these soft hairs do spin nicely, I find nice thick deer hair to be much better for spinning. A little more skill may be involved in spinning deer rather than antelope and caribou, but the result is more durable and certainly looks cleaner to my eye.

HAIR AND TIP CHARACTERISTICS
While deer, elk, and moose hairs float well, they are not hollow like a drinking straw. Instead, they are cellular in nature, more like a piece of cork inside of a drinking straw. The differences in texture between different types of hairs results from a combination of the hair's diameter

Hair bugs like this are just one of the many ways to use up a deer hide.

Not all hair is created equal. Choose the right hair for the job.

and wall thickness, sometimes referred to as the hardness of the hair. The outside wall thickness determines how much the hair can be compressed with the thread and the degree to which it flares on the hook. Thicker walls prevent the hair from being completely compressed under thread pressure or just don't compress as much as thinner-walled hairs. Thicker walls also make the finished fly more durable.

The larger the inside diameter, or more air space you have in the center of the hair, the better it will float. Too much inside diameter, or air space, and the hair flares wildly. Thick hair (large outside diameter) with thin walls and lots of inside diameter like deer rump and body hair is great for spinning but hard to tame into a decent looking wing on a fly like an Elk Hair Caddis. Hairs with a thick wall and little inside diameter, like moose and elk hock, flare very little or not at all and are great for tailing dry flies because they are manageable and form a straight, stiff tail that supports the heavy hook bend without deforming.

When selecting hair for any fly with hair tips used as a wing or tail, choose hair with quickly tapering, short tips. These short-tipped hairs are more hollow (have a bigger inside diameter) toward their tips, providing air space and adding buoyancy to the finished fly. Long tips

are typically dark-colored and solid, adding no floatation to the fly and making the hair harder to compress. Broken hair tips are absolutely unacceptable in my book, and I go to great lengths to avoid them. I always carefully remove any broken tips I see in a stacked bunch of hair before tying it to the hook.

All hair is good for something, but it may or may not be just right for what you have in mind. When you buy a new chunk of hair and sit down to tie with it, take stock of its attributes and perceived applications. When you find a piece that works wonderfully for this or that, write it on the back of the hide with a permanent marker. I have a whole box of hair labeled with things like "Stimi," "EHC" (Elk Hair Caddis), "Humpies," and "spinning hair." This labeling system keeps me from having to go through that trial and error each time I sit down to tie a new fly. Also, it's not a bad idea to leave a little hair left on the patch when you are running down to the end. Bring the remaining chunk of hair with you when you go to the fly shop to buy a new piece to compare the old with the new to match up the color and textures. Eventually, you will be able to select hair by looking it over and feeling it in your fingers, but until you have worked with a variety of different textures and consistencies, trial and error will be your best friend.

TYPES OF HAIR
Elk Hair

Elk hair is perhaps the most useable of all hairs for fly tying. Whether from a bull, cow, or yearling elk, this versatile hair has a beautiful range of colors. I use elk in every application that I can, because it is so commonly available and generally durable and of good quality. There are textural and quality differences between the hair from a bull, cow, or yearling elk, and I will try to explain them here.

Natural Bull Elk

Natural bull elk hair is lighter in color and slightly longer than cow or yearling elk hair. While this hair is hollow and buoyant, the wall thickness near the tips prevents this hair from flaring much. This thick wall makes the hair durable, and it is my hair of choice for many downwing patterns like the Elk Hair Caddis. This is a hard hair, particularly near the tips, but as you get closer to the butt ends of the hair it gains inside diameter and flares well along its base. Its longer length limits it to larger-than-average flies. A good piece of bull elk hair should have beautiful tips that taper to short, abrupt points. When stacked, the dark tips form a striking band of color on wings. Bull elk hair has a slightly smaller outside diameter than cow elk hair but a thicker outside diameter than yearling elk.

Natural Cow Elk

A good piece of cow elk hair is a fly-tying staple. Cow elk hair is slightly darker and shorter than bull elk hair but also slightly bigger in outside diameter. The texture and color of a good piece of cow elk hair is similar to that of deer body hair, but the wall of the cow elk hair is

Bull elk hair tips. Note the small degree of flare.

Bull elk hair tied in near the butts. Note how much more this hair flares when tied in closer to the butt ends.

Bull elk hair.

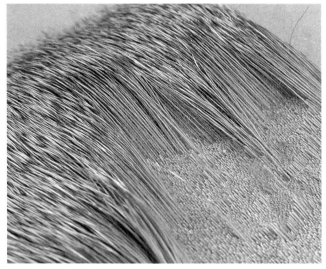

Natural cow elk.

Natural cow elk tips.

generally much thicker. Cow elk can be used on patterns like the Elk Hair Caddis, Stimulator, and the Humpy and produces tough, durable flies with a darker tone than if you tied them with yearling elk hair. The overall diameter of the hair is bigger than both the bull and yearling hair, and I find this hair a bit large to use on smaller flies. Like the bull elk hair, a good piece of cow elk has tips that taper quickly to sharp points. Short tips make wings that end all in the same place and create a stark edge rather than longer wispy tips that result in a wing that just sort of fizzles out near the tips. Cow elk hair flares more than bull elk hair.

Yearling Elk

I have fallen in love with yearling elk hair. Yearling elk epitomizes what I search for in a piece of hair to use for wings on flies of all sizes. The soft texture coupled with the quickly tapered tips makes this hair great for nearly all winging applications. The somewhat thinner wall thickness and thinner overall diameter makes this hair easy to compress on the hook, yet it is still thick enough to keep the hair from flaring out of bounds when I apply thread tension. Yearling elk hair is longer than cow elk and often as long as bull, making it useable for a range of fly sizes. The tips of a good piece of yearling elk hair taper quickly to a point just as a good piece of cow or bull hair will, forming clean color bands along the tips of hair wings. I use yearling elk on patterns like the Humpy and Stimulator, as its thin wall and diameter allows me to anchor it to the hook and completely compress it with heavy thread tension. Hair that compresses completely on the shank creates far less bulk than hairs with thicker walls. A great piece of yearling elk hair inspires me with its hidden potential, and I have been known to hoard the good stuff to excess. I am a bad man.

Elk and Moose Hock

Elk and moose hock come from the animals' legs and is a fine hair with sharp tips and very little inside diameter. This solid texture prevents the hair from flaring and makes it great for tailing dry flies. The hard texture of this hair makes it easy to use and durable and resistant to bending and breaking. I have even used this hair for tailing on nymphs, particularly on patterns that have sparse two- or three-fiber tails. Moose hock has a slightly bigger outside diameter than elk hock and is generally much darker (dark brown to jet black) in color. Near the top of the moose's leg, you can find patches of hock hair that have silvery tips, which makes great tails on little flies. Elk hock is generally a bit more mottled than moose and has a chocolate-brown color with tan tips. These are both beautiful hairs and are the only hair I use to tail dry flies like the Humpy and Royal Wulff.

Yearling elk hair.

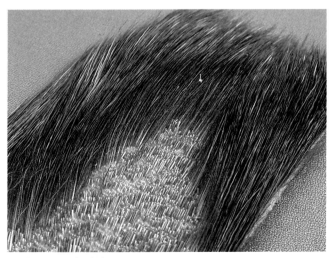

Light moose hock hair.

Dark moose hock hair.

Elk hock hair.

Moose Body Hair

There was a time when moose body hair was all the rage for dry fly tails on patterns like Wulffs and Humpys. I have replaced moose body hair with moose hock for my tailing applications and expect most other good tiers have also. Moose body hair is much longer than moose hock and is considerably bigger in diameter. Moose body hair is at best a pretty even mix of white and black hairs, and at worst consists of hair that is white from the base up to about the halfway point where it then turns black. The butt ends of moose body hair are thick and spin like deer hair. These days, I most commonly see moose body used in steelhead dry flies because of its large diameter, mottled coloration, and ease of procurement. My biggest issue with moose body hair is that the tips are often ragged and split, making them useless as tails on the perfect flies I strive for. Aside from the less-than-adequate tips, the larger overall diameter of this hair causes it to flare more than I like, even when I use just the very tips of the hair.

Deer Body Hair

Deer body hair is long and has mottled tips, a thin wall, and a large inside diameter. Deer body hair can come from the body of a whitetail or mule deer, and there are significant differences in the color of the hair from either species. Mule deer hair tends to lean more toward a mousy gray brown color with dark mottled tips, while whitetail hair is more of a creamy tan shade with lighter tips. I've always read directions in other books that say to use hair from along the back for this use, and hair from along the flanks for that use and wondered how many people really go out and buy an entire deer hide? Generally, you're faced with a wall of hair at the local fly shop,

Moose hock hair lashed to the hook. Note the small degree of flare resulting from the hardness of the hair.

Moose body hair.

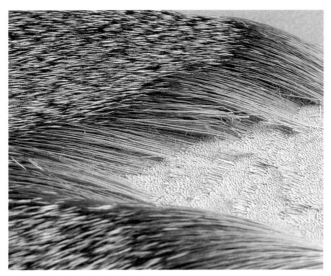

Deer body hair (mule deer).

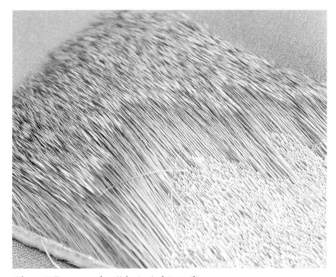

Short "Comparadun" hair (whitetail).

all cut into tidy little rectangles with no indication of which body part they formerly occupied. Knowing what to look for in these little chunks will serve you much better than learning the entire anatomy of the deer.

We will use deer body hair for the Comparadun wing and the body on the Goddard Caddis. For the Goddard Caddis, you want the hair to spin, so look for deer hair with long butt ends with large diameters and thin walls. Picking out a piece of hair with larger diameter butts is easy enough, but trying to determine wall thickness requires a little trick. Press your thumbnail into the hair at its base and note how much the hair flares under pressure. Hair that buckles up wildly is what you want; hair that merely stands up a little probably has walls that are too thick for a fly like this. The condition of the tips of the hair is of little consequence, as you will be cutting them off before tying the hair to the hook. I typically select this hair to have all of the above characteristics as well as nicely mottled tips. The tips can come into play on larger flies with spun deer hair heads and collars, so you may as well try to kill both birds with one piece of hair. The large butt diameter of this hair contributes to the floatation of the finished fly, while the thin wall makes the hair easier to compress, flare, and spin around the hook.

Conversely, the tips of the hair you'll use for the Comparadun need to be quickly tapered to a sharp point and have a short overall length with slightly larger diameter butts. This hair is often sold as Comparadun Hair and usually comes from a whitetail deer, although it is sometimes from coastal deer that resemble mule deer hair more than that of a whitetail. This short deer body hair needs to have quickly tapered tips to form the wing

Mule deer body hair attached to hook. Note the tips and degree of flare.

Short "Comparadun" whitetail deer hair attached to hook. Note the larger degree of flare and short tips.

on the Comparadun so there is still some hollowness to the hair at the tips. Hair with long wispy tips may be useable for larger-sized flies, but on smaller #18s or #20s, where the proportionate wing length becomes much shorter, these wispy tips provide no floatation and do not flare as well as hair with more diameter. You want the butt ends of the Comparadun hair to be larger diameter so they flare on the shank when you tie them down, spreading the tips in a nice arc across the top of the shank, which helps the fly float.

Deer Belly Hair

Deer belly hair comes from a whitetail deer and is a bright white color in its natural state. This white hair takes dyes extremely well, which produces vibrant, colorful hair. The tips of deer belly hair are generally pretty ragged, but this is of little concern as this hair is typically used for spinning large bass bugs and similar flies. This hair is large diameter with a thin wall (but not as thin as deer body hair) and has a somewhat waxy texture. Deer belly hair is coarser and slightly stiffer than deer body hair but spins beautifully and creates durable hair bodies. Its larger diameter makes it a bit harder to work with than body hair, but the somewhat thicker wall also makes this hair more durable. I find this hair a bit coarse to work with on smaller trout flies, but love it for my bigger hair-

Deer belly hair is thicker than body hair and can be dyed bright colors.

bodied bass flies. Incidentally, dyeing the hair can change its characteristics, but this usually stems from a subpar dye job that uses too much heat. Quality hair dyed by companies like Nature's Spirit is a pleasure to use.

Calf Body Hair

A good piece of calf body hair will be one of your best finds. Calf body hair is fine and often somewhat wavy. The most useable calf hair is dense and straight, making it much easier to clean and stack than its wavy counterparts. Tiers come into the shop all the time complaining

Spinning, flaring, and stacking hair creates spots, stripes, and bands on hair bugs like this. Hair bugs are fun to tie but can be time consuming.

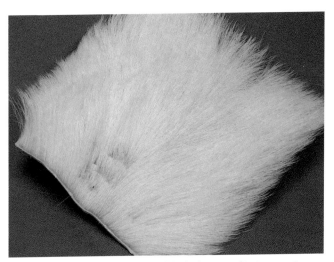

Look for reasonably straight calf body hair to eliminate tying headaches.

about the overall quality of calf body hair, and for the most part I have to agree with them. Most commercially available calf hair is extremely short, wavy, and sparse, rendering it perhaps the most frustrating of all materials to work with. A bad piece of calf body hair is enough to make you give up on the hair and look for an alternative.

So, what to do? Keep looking. There is some good hair out there. In my shop, I typically order calf hair two dozen pieces at a time. Out of those twenty-four patches of hair, a little more than half is useable, and the remainder is typically garbage and goes back to the supplier. Most shops just put them all on the peg and leave it up to you to know what to look for. The inherent process of elimination leaves these weak links on the peg for eternity, and the shop owner doesn't order any more because, well, the peg is full. What's left for you is the garbage. Ask your favorite shop's fly-tying guru to order a new batch of hair and perhaps even bribe him into letting you high-grade through the patches when they arrive. Tying gurus are easily bought off with shiny bits of flash and pretty materials, not unlike crows or raccoons.

Once you have a new batch of calf hair in front of you, look for densely packed hair with few bare spots or sparse areas. You'll want hair that is as straight as possible, although if a small portion of the patch is wavy and the rest is straight, it is still a viable candidate. Calf hair is generally short, but select the longest hair that you can find. If you can find a patch with hair that is three-quarters of an inch or longer, you are doing pretty well. Check for nicely tapered and intact tips; broken tips on calf hair ruin the overall effect you want on flies like Royal Wulffs and other hairwings. When you find good calf hair, grab several pieces so you'll have them when you need them.

CHAPTER 16

Elk Hair Caddis

MAIN FOCUS

Wrapping a rib through hackle • Selecting, cleaning, stacking, and transferring elk hair
Forming a caddis-shaped body • Sizing dry fly hackle • Palmering hackle

The Elk Hair Caddis brings us smoothly into the wonderful world of dry flies. Proportion is more important with dry flies than with nymphs because the proportions of a dry fly can affect the way it sits on the water's surface. The body taper and diameter, the hackle size and density, and the length and density of the wing are all things to keep in mind on this fly.

I try to make the body no thicker than one-third the gap width and tapered from back to front. This makes for a more slender pattern and shows a more realistic silhouette to the fish. Hackle that is too large or dense makes the fly appear bigger than it really is. Hackle serves two functions on this fly: flotation and the appearance of legs. Caddis only have six legs, so it

The Elk Hair Caddis, invented by Al Troth, is a great all-purpose caddis pattern.

PROPORTIONS AT A GLANCE

WING:
Extend to rear edge
of hook bend

RIB:
6 or 7 evenly spaced
turns to two eye lengths
behind hook eye

BODY:
Dubbed forward to two eye
lengths behind hook eye

HACKLE:
1 ½ hook gaps wide

doesn't take many turns to fulfill this requirement. More importantly, hackle serves as outriggers to support the fly on the water's surface. Six to eight evenly spaced (palmered) turns of hackle create more than enough surface area while still letting the body shape and color show through. I size the hackle (over the dubbed body) so it is equal to 1¼ to 1½ gap widths. If it is too large, the fly looks bigger; too short, and the fly may float on its side.

Flies intended for calm, flat water over selective fish suffice with less hair than the same size fly meant for heavy pocketwater. For heavier water I use as much hair as I can securely attach to the hook (be sure to thoroughly clean all the underfur and short hairs out of the clump before stacking it). As a rule of thumb, the right amount of hair when compressed is about equal to the body diameter. For wing length, anywhere between 1 and 1¼ shank-lengths seems about right to me. If I make the wing any longer, the fly appears too big.

I always use a wire rib on this fly, which adds durability and allows me to wrap the hackle from the front of the hook to the back. Tying the hackle in this manner slightly tapers the length of the hackle fibers from longer at the front to shorter at the back, giving the fly a more

realistic attitude on the water. Some tiers use fine monofilament for this ribbing, but the wire holds its shape better and is a bit easier for me to work with.

I fish the Elk Hair Caddis a few different ways. Dead-drifting under bankside vegetation can have great results. It seems as though trout can't resist a bug that is trying to get away, and sometimes skittering the fly really rings the dinner bell. One reason caddis adults are such a staple menu item during the summer is that trout see so many of them. Caddis fly off to the bushes along the stream bank after hatching and live there for some time, essentially becoming terrestrial insects. Breezes blow these bugs into the water, and trout can be on the lookout for them. There doesn't have to be an actual hatch in progress to clean up with a caddis. This pattern also creates a larger dimple in the surface film, perhaps attracting fish even when they are not looking up.

For flat water, I often omit the hackle and wire rib on this fly so it will ride lower on the water and create a more realistic silhouette. The X-Caddis, developed by Craig Mathews of West Yellowstone, Montana, is a great flatwater version of this fly. The Elk Hair Caddis shown here was invented by Al Troth, the same man who brought us the American Pheasant Tail Nymph.

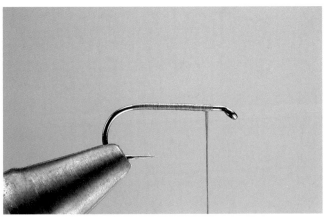

1. Start the thread about an eye length back from the hook eye (index point), and wrap a smooth thread base back to the bend. Return the thread behind the index point.

ELK HAIR CADDIS

Elk Hair Caddis materials.

Hook:	#10–22 Tiemco 100 or 100SP-BL
Thread:	Tan 6/0 Danville down to #16; 8/0 Uni-Thread for smaller sizes
Rib:	Gold, silver, or copper Lagartun wire (fine or extra fine)
Body:	Tan or olive Super Fine, or color to match the natural.
Hackle:	Brown genetic rooster neck
Wing:	Natural cow, bull, or yearling elk body hair

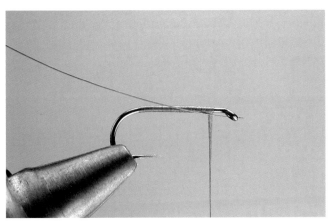

2. Tie in a length of fine wire using the right-angle technique.

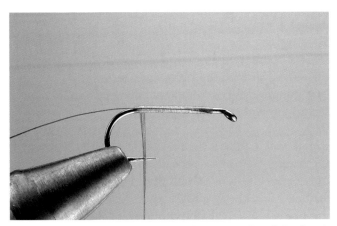

3. Try to keep the wire along the near side of the hook as you wrap back over it to the hook bend.

4. Bring the thread back to the midpoint on the shank and dub it with a thin strand of dubbing. Use the bare thread between the dubbing and the hook to work back to the bend so the first turn of dubbing is right at the hook bend.

22. Put the tip of your index finger under the clump of stacked hair and pinch your thumb down on top of the hair. Pull the hair from the stacker, but do not let the hair slide in your fingertips. Make a conscious effort to grip the hair without it moving in your fingertips. Make sure to put the top of the stacker back into its base. The tubes have a strange tendency to roll away if laid on their side, and rest assured, they will roll as far away from you as they can. Don't ask how I know, just put the stacker back together every time.

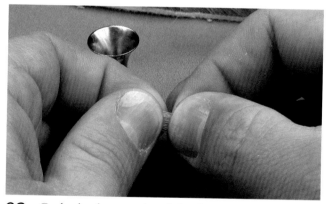

23. Grab the butt ends of the hair with the thumb and forefinger of your right hand and butt the ends of your fingers against each other to keep the hair bundled together.

24. Release the hair from your left hand, and make sure the hair tips are still even. If they're not, put the hair back in the stacker and try again.

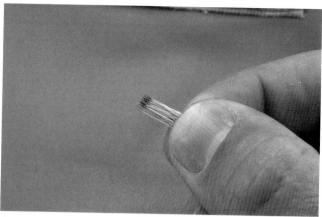

25. To get the hair tips facing the right direction to place on the fly, you need to transfer this nicely stacked and bundled clump of hair from one hand to the other without messing it up. If you are tying traditionally, and wrapping the thread with your right hand with the hook eye facing to the right, you are in good shape, but if you have listened to reason, see the sidebar.

26. Hold the butt ends of the clump of hair in your thread hand and lay them up against the top of the hook shank. Measure the tips so they extend back to the outside edge of the hook bend. Be sure the hair is parallel to the hook shank as you measure this length. If the hair is tilted up, it will throw off the measurement. Once the tips of the hair are at the outside of the hook bend, visually mark where the back edge of the hook eye meets your fingertips and grasp the tips of the hair with your material hand at that point. Butt the tips of your thumbs together and transfer the hair to the other hand so the tips of the hair are in the fingertips of your material hand and exactly one hook-length long.

SWITCHING HANDS

Whether you tie right or left handed, sometimes you need to switch hands with the hair, such as when tying a Comparadun.

1. Turn the tips of the hair so they stick straight up in your right hand.

2. Grasp the hair between your left thumb and forefinger right above the fingertips of your right hand.

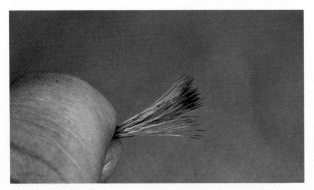

3. Let go of the hair tips with your right hand and turn the butt ends of the hair to your left by rotating your left hand down a bit so the tips of the hair are now facing to the right.

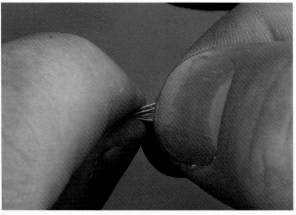

4. Re-grasp the tips of the hair in your right hand. This transfer is mostly to re-group the hair into a nice bundle rather than a flattened sheet of hair. The bundle is much more conducive to being attached to the hook and makes for much easier measuring.

5. Now you have the stacked tips of the hair inside the fingertips of your right hand. Pinch the butt ends once again to hold the hair in your left hand with the tips facing to the right.

This all sounds complicated but is really not that hard, as you are just switching hands with the hair. Just open and close your fingertips each time so the hairs don't slide in your fingertips.

27. Cut the butt ends of the hair just in front of your fingertips straight across (perpendicular to the hairs). Make one clean cut with your sharpest straight-bladed scissors. Place this pre-measured, pre-cut clump of hair flat on top of the hook shank. Your thread should be slightly in front of the dubbed body and hackle and slightly twisted. I like to spin the bobbin and twist the thread, because twisted thread bites into the hair better on these initial wraps. If your thread has been hanging while you cut, cleaned, and stacked the hair, chances are it has unwound and flattened out considerably. Spin the bobbin a bit to twist the thread into a cord. You don't want it in a super-tight twist, just enough to bundle the thread strands into a single hard rope.

28. Bring the thread up and over the butt ends of the hair just in front of your fingertips. These wraps should be snugged down to the hair but not much tighter than that. Try to avoid trapping any hackle fibers as you bring the thread around the hook. I know it appears that I have trapped one here near the front of the body but that would be an amateurish mistake, and I just don't let that happen, so think again Mr. Smarty-Smart.

29. Tighten the two thread wraps around the base of the hair clump by steadily and firmly pulling the thread directly toward you on the near side of the hook shank. Do not let go of the tips of the hair as you tighten the thread or anytime while wrapping the thread in this step. Draw those first two wraps tight by pulling toward you. Make several more tight turns of thread going toward the hook bend over the base of the hair, forming a smooth band of thread about an eye-length wide. Again, do *not* let go of the tips of the hair as you do this.

Once you feel as though you have secured the hair in place, you may let go of the tips. Pull the thread toward you firmly to check if the hair has been compressed and anchored to the hook. If you pull on the thread and the wing flips to the far side of the hook, you didn't get the job done. Twist the hair back up, make a few more tight turns, and try this test again. If the wing still doesn't stay in place, unwind the thread wraps and try again. I really try to anchor the hair with a minimum number of thread turns to keep from making the head of the fly too heavy and bulky. Concentrate on crushing the outer wall of the hairs as you tighten the thread, compressing the hair tight to the hook. Too many thread wraps can prevent you from getting enough pressure to compress the hair, and to that end I try to get the job done with no more than seven or eight turns of thread.

I am using natural bull elk hair on this fly as it is durable and has good wall thickness for this technique. This hair is hard and the thicker wall keeps it from flaring all over the place or being cut by the thread. Small diameter thread (8/0 Uni-Thread or UTC 50-denier GSP, for instance) can slice through soft hair like yearling elk or deer. A slow steady pull to tighten these threads rather than a firm yank most often solves this problem, and I find this hair-cutting phenomenon to be a technique issue rather than a thread issue. You can tie Elk Hair Caddis with cow or yearling elk hair and get great results as well, although these hairs will flare considerably more than the bull elk used here.

30. After all that, check to make sure the wing length is still right to the back edge of the hook bend. If it shifted, you can either live with it and resolve to do better on the next one or say a few choice words and start the winging process over. If you give up now, you'll never get it, so you know what I am going to suggest.

31. Whip-finish over the band of thread just behind the butt ends of the elk hair and clip the thread. Add a drop of Gloss Coat all the way around the thread collar, being careful not to soak the entire fly with cement.

32. The finished Elk Hair Caddis.

PATTERN VARIATION

X CADDIS

Hook:	#14–20 Tiemco 100SP-BL
Thread:	Brown 8/0 Uni-Thread
Shuck:	Amber Z-lon
Body:	Hare's mask dubbing
Underwing:	Amber Z-lon
Wing:	Natural deer hair

Stimulator

MAIN FOCUS

More of the same steps from the Elk Hair Caddis in different order.

The Stimulator enjoys the reputation of being one of the most popular dry flies in the Rockies. Fly shops sell them by the hundreds of dozens, and it is no wonder. Developed by Randall Kauffmann, owner of Kauffmann's Streamborne in Oregon, the Stimi is a great floater, highly visible, and sports a wide, fish-attracting profile. A good match for an adult stonefly, it mimics caddis and terrestrial insects just as well. Overall,

this fly just yells "Food!" to the fish, and I always have some in my box. At first glance, the Stimulator looks complicated, but it is made up of all the same components and steps as the Elk Hair Caddis.

Though the Stimulator is a relatively simple fly, there are a few tricks I can offer to help you master it. I build a small ball of thread at the hook bend to imitate an egg sac and add a bright "hot spot," which is sort of

The Stimi is a great floater, highly visible, and sports a wide, fish attracting profile. A good match for an adult stonefly, it mimics caddis and terrestrial insects just as well.

160

You can tie Stimulators in many different colors and sizes.

JAY NICHOLS PHOTO

my signature on this fly. The nub of thread also helps to flare the tail to better support the hook bend. I prefer using yearling elk hair for the wing and tail of this fly. The smaller diameter and thinner wall makes this hair easy to work with, and it compresses much more easily than regular cow- or bull-elk hair. The yearling elk hair also sports beautiful tip coloration and makes for a particularly handsome fly.

Using the butt ends of the tail hair as an underbody adds flotation, helps to build up the body of the fly, and allows the use of less dubbing for the abdomen. Wrapping the thread forward through the wing butts permits you to bind the hair more securely and with less bulk than more traditional methods, and tapers the thorax at the same time. The technique used in this step is a great advancement and has made all the difference in the overall look of my Stimulators.

I like to fish the Stimulator with a deaddrift with an occasional skitter. I also like to use it as an indicator with

a beadhead fly on a dropper below it. The combination of the attractor dry with a juicy tidbit hanging below often proves to be too much for hungry trout to resist. A Beadhead Prince, Copper John, or Beadhead Hare's Ear is a good choice, although I sometimes need to get a little more hatch specific and add another dropper below the beadhead fly. This rig opens a world of opportunity and combinations.

We'll tie a yellow Stimulator, but you can tie these in all the colors of the rainbow. Tan, olive, orange, and lime green are all good bets, and an all-black version has caught plenty of fish for me over the years. I typically use the hot-orange dubbing on the thorax of the fly, brown hackle on the abdomen, and grizzly hackle on the thorax, no matter what color, except for the all-black fly. These are my personal guidelines for the fly, but I hate following someone else's rules, so I guess I can't expect you to either. Grab your hair, hackle, and dubbing and go crazy.

Stimulators are great indicator flies—fish a Copper John or other nymph below them.

PROPORTIONS AT A GLANCE

WING:
Tips extend to base of tail

THORAX HACKLE:
Tied in at the base of the wing (60 percent point), 1 to 1 ½ hook gaps wide

TAIL:
One hook gap width long

THORAX :
From 60 percent point to index point

RIB:
6 or 7 evenly spaced turns

ABDOMEN:
From base of tail to the 60 percent point

BODY HACKLE:
1 to 1 ½ hook gaps wide

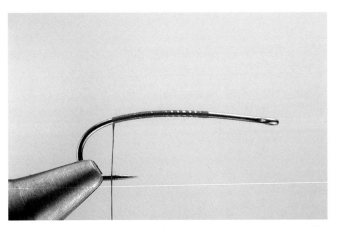

1. Attach the thread at the 60 percent point on the shank and wrap a thread base back to the hook bend.

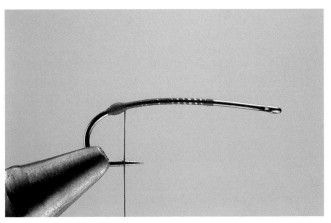

2. Build a small nub of thread at the hook bend, starting directly above the back of the hook barb. The nub, which may represent an egg sac or merely provide an attractive hot spot, helps flare the tail. Keep your bobbin close to the hook as you work the thread into a football-shaped bump. You may need to spin the thread to twist it into a cord to keep it from spreading down the hook bend. The front edge of this nub should be just in front of the hook barb. Leave the thread hanging at the front of the nub.

3. Clean and stack a small clump of elk hair like you did for the Elk Hair Caddis. Measure its length so it is equal to the hook gap.

STIMULATOR

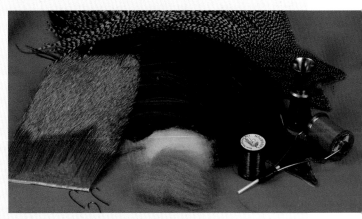

Stimulator materials.

Hook:	#6–18 Tiemco 2312 or 5212
Thread:	Fluorescent fire orange 70-denier Ultra Thread
Tail:	Natural yearling elk hair
Rib:	Copper Lagartun wire (fine or small)
Abdomen:	Yellow Antron Bright Dubbing
Body Hackle:	Brown rooster neck hackle
Wing:	Natural cow elk body hair
Thorax hackle:	Grizzly rooster neck hackle
Thorax:	Fluorescent fire orange Antron Bright Dubbing

Note: The Tiemco 200R is the standard hook for this fly, but I think the gap is a bit narrow, particularly in smaller sizes, so I use the Tiemco 2312 or 5212 instead.

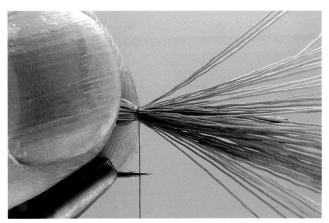

4. Lay the pre-measured hair clump in at the hook bend just in front of the thread nub and angle the butts slightly toward your near side. Wrap two turns of thread over the hair at the bend and snug them down to the hair. Do not let go of the tips.

5. Pull the thread toward you to anchor the hair, and then wrap a narrow band of thread to secure the clump to the shank. This is exactly the same process you followed to tie in the wing on the Elk Hair Caddis, but you are tying in the clump at the hook bend instead of at the head.

6. Lift the butt ends of the tail hair up and back and work the thread forward to midshank.

7. Pull the butt ends of the hair forward and down along the hook shank so the hair encompasses the hook.

8. Bring the thread around the hair two times just in front of the 50 percent point, but don't pull the thread tight yet. Making two loose turns will keep the hair from rolling around the shank when you do cinch it down in the next step.

9. Hold onto the butt ends while you pull the thread toward you to anchor the hair. This step will help create a hair underbody on the shank, adding flotation and diameter to the body.

10. Clip the butt ends of the hair as close to the shank as you can. The butt ends of the hair will stick forward to the 60 percent point on the shank, which is why you tied the hair down at the halfway point. If you had tied it down at the 60 percent point, the butt ends would then stick out to the 70 percent point, which is too far.

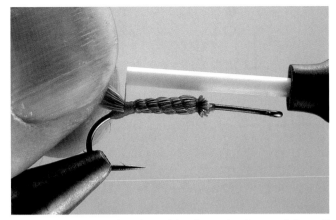

11. Spiral-wrap the thread back to the base of the tail over the elk-hair underbody. Keep these wraps spaced out and don't cinch them down tight into the hair. You want to keep the hollowness of the hair intact. Lift the tail up with your material hand and wrap the thread tightly back over the base of the hair to shove the base of the tail up against the thread nub at the bend. Keep your bobbin tube close to the shank as you wrap so you can place each wrap behind its predecessor.

12. This spreads the tail out laterally and makes the tail wider. This wide tail supports the heavy hook bend better than a narrow bunch.

13. Tie in a length of copper wire at the hook bend with the right-angle technique.

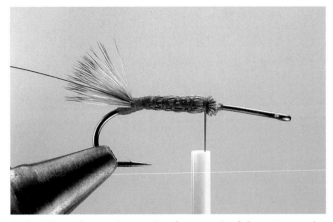

14. Wrap forward over the front end of the wire to the front edge of the underbody.

15. Dub the thread with Antron dubbing, and wrap it from the base of the tail up to the 60 percent point on the shank, forming a slightly tapered abdomen.

16. Measure a rooster neck or saddle hackle feather against the hook over the dubbed body so the hackle fibers are a shade longer than the hook gap is wide. This fly has so much hackle on it, I usually undersize the hackle a bit so it doesn't sit so high off the water. If you are fishing particularly heavy or rough water, you may want a hackle feather with barbs closer to 1 ½ times the hook gap. Strip the fibers from the base as you did on the Elk Hair Caddis.

17. Wrap the thread from the front edge of the abdomen up to the hook eye and back again. This forms a solid thread base for tying in the hackle and thorax.

18. Tie the hackle feather in by the bare stem at the front edge of the dubbed body. Wrap forward over the stem and back again to the dubbing. Like on the Woolly Bugger, leave a bit of that bare stem beyond the tie-in point so the first half turn or so is bare quill and the inside (concave part) of the feather is facing the hook shank.

19. Palmer the hackle feather back from the front edge of the body to the base of the tail with six or seven turns. For some reason, I always get seven turns, no matter how hard I try to vary it. When you get to the back of the hook, hold the feather in your material hand above the hook.

20. Grab the wire and bring it up and over the tip of the hackle feather. Once you have made this first turn, you can let go of the hackle tip and continue on with the wire rib.

21. Continue spiraling the wire forward through the hackle just as you did on both the Elk Hair Caddis and the Woolly Bugger. Tie the wire off with a few tight turns of thread at the front edge of the body.

22. Break off the wire and clip the tip of the hackle feather.

23. Cut, clean, and stack a bunch of yearling elk hair. There is some room for interpretation on the wing length for this fly. A wing that extends to anywhere between the base and the end of the tail is appropriate. On larger flies, I tend to make the wing longer, and on smaller flies I make it shorter, for no particular reason at all. On this fly we are going to shoot for midway up the tail. Measure the hair from the front edge of the body to the middle of the tail clump, and make sure you are holding the hair parallel to the hook shank.

24. Grasp the tips of the hair in your material hand and hold them down as close to the hook as you can. Make two loose turns over the hair at the front edge of the abdomen, without letting go of the tips. Pull the wraps down so they are snugged up to the hair, but not so tight that the hair begins to flare.

25. Draw the bobbin firmly toward you to compress and flare the hair as much as you can with these first two turns. You probably won't get all the hair compressed with just these two turns—and chances are you'll break your thread a time or two until you get the feel for it—but you want to crease the hair as much as you can.

26. Spiral the thread forward through the butt ends of the hair with several firm, closely spaced wraps. You want the thread to travel a bit between turns, and you want to pull tight as you make these wraps. The hair should flare out wildly as you wrap and be distributed all the way around the hook by the thread. Continue wrapping forward through the butt ends until you reach the back edge of the index point. Do not let go of the tips of the hair during this process.

27. The butt ends should splay all the way around the hook and be firmly anchored to the shank. The thread is hanging just behind the index point inside the mess of butt ends.

28. Removing the excess butt ends is going to require at least two cuts. The first cut should be from the top of the hook, so grab as much of the hair on the top of the hook as you can and bring your scissor tips in tight to the base of the hair. Pull up on the hair and push down on the scissors to cut as close to the hook as you can. I laterally tilt the scissors slightly so the hair is cut closer to the hook near the hook eye and a bit farther out near the base of the wing.

29. After the first cut, the butts should look similar to this.

30. Lift the thread and drape it over your thread hand so it is out of the way while you make this second cut on the bottom of the shank. Pull the hair on the bottom of the hook down and bring the tips of the scissors in tight along the bottom of the hook. Clip the excess butt ends as close to the shank as you can. If, perchance, you somehow cut your thread, it is no big deal. The thread is anchored through the butt ends of the hair and won't go anywhere, so just continue cutting the butt ends and then go back and restart the thread over what's left. But don't re-attach the thread until you have finished clipping the hair. There is no sense in risking it twice in a row. File this little lesson away for later.

31. You should now have a slightly tapered clump of butt ends on the front end of the hook. Note that the butt ends stop at the back edge of the index point, preserving head space for later.

32. Wrap over what is left of the butt ends of the wing, smoothing them out slightly. You don't need to bind every one of them down, but you do want to manage them a bit with a layer or two of thread. Work the thread back up to the base of the wing.

33. Turn the fly in your vise so you can see the bottom of the fly. Check the space between the base of the wing and the front of the dubbing on the abdomen. There is probably a small space left there. Wrap back over the base of the wing to cinch the wing up tight to the front of the abdomen.

34. Hold the wing in place in a single bunch so it doesn't spread around the hook as you wrap the thread here. Wrap back over the base of the wing, placing each succeeding wrap of thread behind the last, pushing the base of the wing back to the front of the dubbing. Keep the thread short and the bobbin tube close to the hook and wrap tightly back over the elk hair to bump the wing back in place.

35. This whole winging process results in an evenly distributed wing base that allows you to dub the thorax smoothly without an unsightly bump.

36. Prepare and size a grizzly feather with barbs at least as long or slightly longer than the brown feather's (absolutely not shorter). Tie this feather in by the stripped quill at the base of the wing with the inside of the feather facing the hook shank. Wrap forward over the quill to anchor the feather securely in place.

37. Dub the thread and start wrapping the dubbing at the back edge of the index point.

38. Wrap the dubbing back up the tapered butts to the base of the wing. When you reach the base of the wing, hold the wing clump together and wrap a turn of dubbing around the hook, overlapping the base of the hair and taming the wing fibers into a nice clean clump.

39. Wrap the remaining dubbing forward to the back edge of the index point, ending with bare thread behind the hook eye. The thorax should be the same diameter as (or slightly thicker than) the abdomen.

40. Palmer the grizzly hackle forward through the thorax with seven or eight turns. I like heavier hackle on the front of this fly to help the fly skitter. Tie the hackle feather off at the index point by pulling straight up on the feather at the hook eye and making two turns over it at the index point.

41. Clip the excess hackle tip as close as you can. Wrap a small but prominent head and whip-finish the thread.

42. Clip the thread and add a shot of head cement.

PATTERN VARIATIONS

FOAMULATOR

Hook:	#8–14 Tiemco 5212
Thread:	Fluorescent fire orange 70-denier Ultra Thread
Butt:	Fluorescent fire orange Antron Bright Dubbing
Tail:	Natural yearling elk hair
Shellback:	Orange 2mm Fly Foam
Rib:	Lagartun copper wire (fine)
Abdomen:	Light orange Antron Dubbing
Body hackle:	Brown rooster neck or saddle
Wing:	Natural yearling elk hair
Indicator:	Pink McFlylon
Legs:	Round rubber legs (medium), marked with black Sharpie marker
Thorax:	Fluorescent fire orange Antron Bright Dubbing
Thorax hackle:	Grizzly rooster neck or saddle

Note: The Foamulator is an extra buoyant version of the Stimulator and a great fly for using in a dry-dropper rig.

STIMULATOR (INDICATOR)

Hook:	#8–14 Tiemco 5212
Thread:	Fluorescent fire orange 70-denier Ultra Thread
Butt:	Fluorescent fire orange 70-denier Ultra Thread
Tail:	Bleached yearling elk hair
Rib:	Lagartun copper wire (fine)
Abdomen:	Ginger Antron Dubbing
Body hackle:	Brown rooster neck or saddle
Wing:	Bleached yearling elk hair
Thorax:	Yellow Antron Dubbing
Thorax hackle:	Grizzly rooster neck or saddle

Note: Bleached yearling elk for the wing and tail make a slightly more visible pattern. Tie this fly in colors to match the stoneflies, caddis, and hoppers in your area.

GREEN DRAKE STIMULATOR

Hook:	#6–12 Tiemco 5212
Thread:	Olive 6/0 Danville
Tail:	Natural dark gray deer hair
Rib:	Lagartun copper wire (fine)
Abdomen:	Olive Super Fine
Body hackle:	Grizzly dyed olive rooster neck or saddle
Wing:	Natural dark gray deer hair, tied long and upright
Thorax:	Olive Super Fine
Thorax hackle:	Grizzly dyed olive rooster neck or saddle

Note: This pattern has proven to be a killer. I make the wing a bit sparser than the usual Stimulator and prop it more upright. While not an exact match, this fly is a great floater and is just the ticket for banging the banks from a boat.

OLIVE STIMULATOR

Hook:	#8–14 Tiemco 5212
Thread:	Fluorescent green 70-denier Ultra Thread
Butt:	Fluorescent green 70-denier Ultra Thread
Tail:	Bleached yearling elk hair
Rib:	Lagartun copper wire (fine)
Abdomen:	Olive Antron Dubbing
Body Hackle:	Brown rooster neck or saddle
Underwing:	Pearl Flashabou
Wing:	Bleached yearling elk hair
Thorax hackle:	Grizzly rooster neck or saddle
Thorax:	Olive Antron Dubbing

RUBBER-LEGGED STIMI

Hook:	#8–14 Tiemco 5212
Thread:	Fluorescent fire orange 70-denier Ultra Thread
Butt:	Fluorescent fire orange 70-denier Ultra Thread
Tail:	Natural yearling elk hair
Rib:	Lagartun copper wire (fine)
Abdomen:	Yellow Antron Dubbing
Body hackle:	Brown rooster neck or saddle
Wing:	Natural yearling elk hair
Legs:	Orange round rubber legs (medium), marked with Sharpie marker
Thorax:	Orange Antron Dubbing
Thorax hackle:	Grizzly rooster neck or saddle

Note: Adding rubber legs is a great fish attracting option on the Stimi. After the wing is anchored in place, tie in the grizzly hackle just like usual. Now, tie a single strand of rubber leg in along each side of the thorax then dub from the hook eye back to the base of the wing and back again. Palmer the grizzly hackle forward over the thorax.

PURPLE AND BLUE STIMULATOR

Hook:	#8–14 Tiemco 5212
Thread:	Fluorescent fire orange 70-denier Ultra Thread
Butt:	Fluorescent fire orange 70-denier Ultra Thread
Tail:	Natural yearling elk hair
Rib:	Lagartun copper wire (fine)
Abdomen:	Navy blue Spirit River Atlantic Salmon Microdub
Body hackle:	Brown rooster neck or saddle
Wing:	Natural yearling elk hair
Thorax:	Purple Spirit River Atlantic Salmon Microdub
Thorax hackle:	Grizzly rooster neck or saddle

PEACOCK STIMULATOR

Hook:	#8–14 Tiemco 5212
Thread:	Red 70-denier Ultra Thread
Butt:	Tying thread
Tail:	Natural yearling elk hair
Rib:	Lagartun copper wire (fine)
Abdomen:	Peacock herl
Body hackle:	Brown rooster neck or saddle
Wing:	Natural yearling elk hair
Thorax:	Peacock herl
Thorax hackle:	Grizzly rooster neck or saddle

Note: A great general attractor pattern with a dark coloration that mimics many terrestrials.

ROYAL STIMULATOR

Hook:	#8–14 Tiemco 5212
Thread:	Red 70-denier Ultra Thread
Butt:	Red 70-denier Ultra Thread
Tail:	Natural yearling elk hair
Rib:	Lagartun copper wire (fine)
Abdomen:	Peacock herl and red floss, equal thirds
Body hackle:	Brown rooster neck or saddle
Wing:	Natural yearling elk hair
Overwing:	White calf body hair
Thorax:	Orange Antron dubbing
Thorax hackle:	Grizzly rooster neck or saddle

CHAPTER 18

Adams

MAIN FOCUS

*Mixed hackle fiber tails • Matching hen hackle tip wings
Wrapping a hackle collar with two feathers*

Like the Hare's Ear and Comparadun, the Adams is more than just a fly pattern. It is what I refer to as a pattern fly, a fly that can be morphed into a new pattern by altering the materials or colors. Given this definition, hundreds of patterns are simply variations of an Adams, at least in how they are tied. Changing the color of the materials converts an Adams into a plethora of other flies. An Adams with a gray hackle-fiber tail, gray hen-hackle-tip wings, olive dubbed body, and a gray hackle collar is a traditional Blue-Winged Olive. Change these components to pale yellow or ginger and you have a Pale Morning Dun. By following the basic design, you can mix and match the color combinations for a wide array of patterns.

Developed originally as a caddis imitation by Len Halladay in Michigan, the Adams has become the iconic American fly. Learning the techniques to tie it lays the foundation for many other patterns.

PROPORTIONS AT A GLANCE

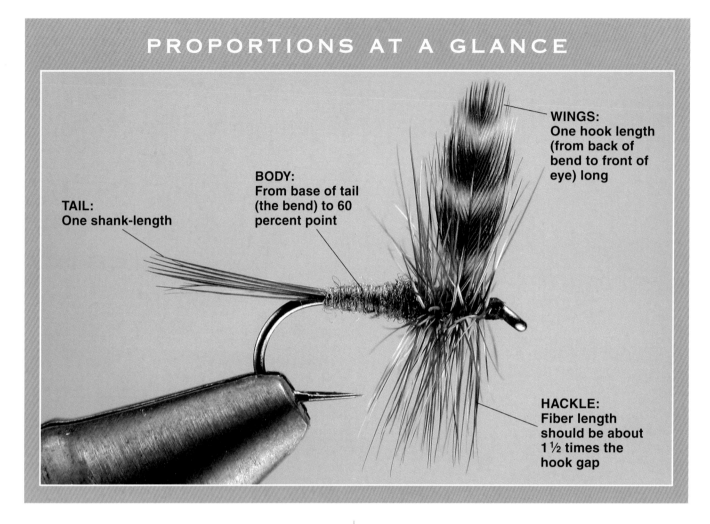

TAIL:
One shank-length

BODY:
From base of tail
(the bend) to 60
percent point

WINGS:
One hook length
(from back of
bend to front of
eye) long

HACKLE:
Fiber length
should be about
1½ times the
hook gap

The Adams is a great pocketwater fly. It floats well and is relatively easy to see. It can imitate a huge range of insects from the ubiquitous *Baetis* to Green Drakes, and in small sizes, even midges. Much like the Hare's Ear, the Adams is a reasonable facsimile of a variety of common insects. This great catch-all pattern should be in everyone's fly box. The mixed brown and grizzly hackle is buggy, and I have adapted that combination on most of my flies that I tie with a collar-style hackle. I fish the parachute version of the Adams nearly every time I am out during the summer months and highly recommend this fly on a daily basis in the shop.

The Adams teaches a plethora of techniques from a mixed hackle-fiber tail to upright hen-hackle-tip wings to wrapping a double-feather collar. To mix things up, I often use dubbing in colors other than the original gray. Purple, black, and tan are all favorites, but these are only limited by your dubbing supply. The Adams can also be tied with a hair tail, which is generally my preference as it seems to resist bending and becoming misshapen as you fish the fly. I have tied the fly here with the hackle

fiber tail to show the technique more than anything, and I cover the hair-tail technique later in the Royal Wulff chapter.

The wings on an Adams are made from hen neck hackles and should not be made from rooster neck hackle tips. Yes, I know you already own an expensive rooster neck that seems to have a ton of perfectly fine feathers for this use, but if you look a bit more closely you'll see that they aren't the same. Rooster hackle tips are much narrower than the soft webby hen neck feathers and don't create the same wide wing profile as the hen feathers. The narrow rooster hackle tips just disappear into the hackle collar and make all the work of mounting the wings a waste. And, not just any hen neck will supply adequate feathers for an Adams. I prefer generic barnyard hen necks over genetically raised hens. The genetic hen feathers, as a side effect of rooster production, tend to have more and more of the rooster feather characteristics these days and are just as narrow and pointy as their male counterparts. The generic hen necks are a bit harder to find but make for a better winging experience overall.

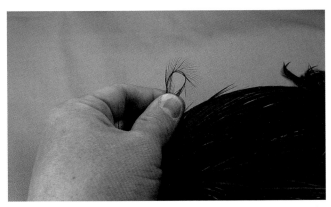

1. Pull two spade hackles from a dry-fly rooster neck. The spade hackles are located along the edges of the neck at the widest point. Spade hackles have long stiff hackle fibers with little web. In the old days, these feathers were actually shaped like a spade shovel, but with genetic breeding, these feathers are a little slimmer than they used to be.

2. Pull one brown spade feather from the brown neck and one from the grizzly neck.

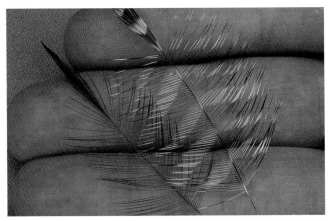

3. Clip the fluff from the base of each spade feather and preen the fibers so they stand out from the stem of the feather. If you pinch the feather near the tip and draw the fibers against the grain through your fingertips, they will stand out nicely and be much easier to work with.

ADAMS

Adams materials.

Hook:	#10–24 Tiemco 100 or 100SP-BL
Thread:	Black 6/0 Uni-Thread down to #14; black 8/0 on #16 and smaller
Tail:	Mixed brown and grizzly spade hackle fibers
Wings:	Grizzly hen hackle tips
Body:	Gray Super Fine
Hackle:	One brown and one grizzly rooster neck hackle feather

Note: You can substitute gray beaver or muskrat fur dubbing for the body and moose hock for the tail.

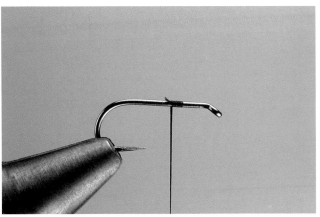

4. Attach the thread at the 75 percent point and wrap a smooth thread base back to the bend.

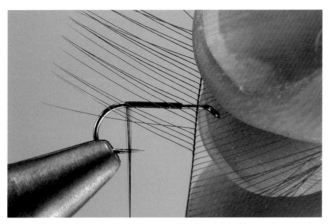

5. Peel about six brown spade hackle fibers from the feather, taking care to keep the fiber tips even.

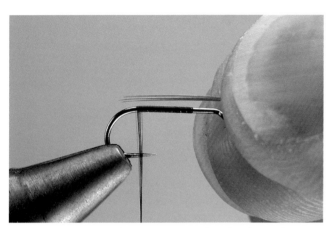

6. Measure these fibers against the shank so they are equal to one shank-length long, and tie them in at the hook bend with a single temporary turn of thread.

7. Peel another six fibers from the grizzly spade feather and measure this clump against the first brown clump so it, too, is a shank-length long.

8. Grasp the tips of both clumps in your material hand, making sure to keep them even.

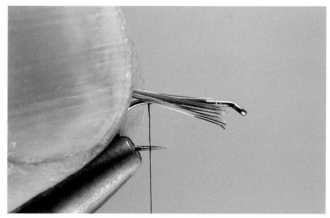

9. Remove the thread turn holding the brown fibers in place and let the two bundles intermix in your fingertips. The first turn of thread was just there to hold the brown fibers while we peeled and measured the grizzly fibers.

10. Tie the mixed clump of spade hackle fibers in at the hook bend so they are one shank-length long.

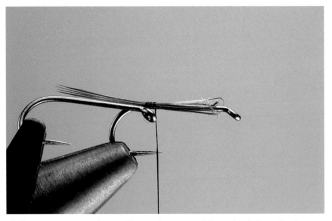

11. Measure the tail against an identical hook (same size and style) held in hackle pliers to assure it is one shank-length long. If it isn't, unwrap the thread holding the fibers in place and re-position the fibers. Do not try to pull them to length, because you will just make the tips uneven and ugly. No one likes an ugly tail.

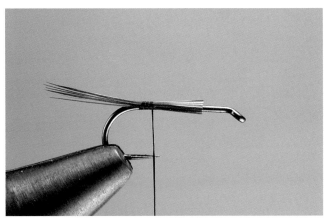

12. Clip the butt ends of the tail even with the 75 percent point on the shank.

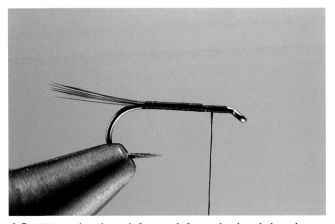

13. Wrap the thread forward from the hook bend over the butt ends of the tail and all the way up to the hook eye. Bring the thread back to the 87.5 percent point. That's right, I'm splitting hairs here, but what you are shooting for is to have the thread in the middle of the front quarter of the hook shank. Do the math.

14. Select two hen neck feathers from the cape. They should be the same size and shape and have rounded tips that are about as wide as the hook gap. The best way to pluck the feathers from the hide is to first select the two targeted feathers (they are usually going to be right on top of one another) and grasp them by their bases. Pull the bases of the feathers, not the tips, away from the hide to pull them out so you don't break the tips off in your fingers.

15. Oppose these two hen feathers so they are outside to outside like the biot tails on the Prince Nymph and Copper John. Even the tips so the feathers are the same length.

16. Measure the two feathers against the shank. Conventional wisdom says that they should be one shank-length long, but exactly one shank-length looks too short to me. I tie the Adams with wings that are just a touch, maybe an eye length, longer than a shank. To accommodate for a little tying-in space on the feather, measure the feathers so they are equal to the entire hook length, from the outside of the hook bend to the front edge of the hook eye.

17. Clip the feathers off at the back of the hook bend while holding the tips between the thumb and forefinger of your thread hand.

18. You should have the tips of the feathers between your fingertips at this point with the butt ends sticking out just slightly. Place these pre-measured feathers on top of the hook with the butt ends extending just past the middle of the front quarter of the hook shank.

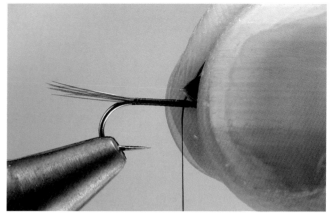

19. Now you are going to execute a reverse pinch wrap, which is exactly the same as a regular pinch wrap, but you will be wrapping the thread with your material hand while you hold the wings in place with your thread hand. Bring the bobbin up from the bottom of the hook and push the thread back between your fingers by pushing the bobbin tube forward toward the hook eye. You want the thread to come up between your thumb and the outside edge of the near wing. Now bring the thread loosely over the top of the wing butts and down again between your index finger and the far side of the far wing. Let the thread hang on the far side of the hook for a moment. The loop of thread should be pinched in your fingertips along with, and surrounding, the butt ends of the wing feathers. Draw the thread straight down to snug the pinch wrap down inside your fingertips, trapping the feather butts against the top of the shank. Make another reverse pinch wrap before you let go of the feather tips.

20. You should now have the two feather tips tied in by their butt ends squarely on top of the hook.

21. Before you go on, measure the wings against an identical hook to make sure they are the right length. They should be a shank-length plus about an eye-length. If they are not, pinch the tips in your thread hand and unwind the thread turns holding them. Reposition the wing to the correct length and repeat the above steps.

22. Wrap the thread back over the base of the wings with a few flat, smooth turns of thread. You just want to anchor the wing on the hook without creating bulk.

23. If you did this right, the wings should look like this now when viewed from the top.

24. To stand the wings up, close the thumb and forefinger of your material hand below the hook eye from the rear of the hook. With your fingertips closed, slide your fingers up and over the hook shank, trapping the wing tips between your fingers as you go. Lift the wings up and back. Bring the thread to the front edge of the wings and build a small thread wedge against the base of the wings. It shouldn't take many wraps, but they do need to be placed right up against the base of the wing. This thread dam will hold the wings upright. I find it easiest to place these wraps with the bobbin tube close to the hook shank and use a short length of working thread.

25. The wings should now be at a 90-degree angle to the hook shank and be tied in at the middle of the front quarter of the hook shank.

26. Many tiers like to make figure-eight wraps of thread between the wings to help separate them. Because the feathers have a nice natural curve to them and will separate nearly perfectly on their own, I think this is a wasted step. If your wings are stuck together from pinching them in the previous processes, just push your index finger into them to divide them.

27. Wrap the thread to the midpoint on the shank.

28. Apply a thin layer of dubbing to the tying thread. Use the bare thread between the end of the dubbing and the hook shank to work the dubbing back to the hook bend. The first turn of dubbed thread should be right at the base of the tail. Work the dubbing forward on the shank in a single, even layer.

29. Continue that single layer of dubbing up to the 75 percent point. A good rule of thumb for where to stop the front edge of the body is to make sure the distance from the back edge of the hook eye to the wing is the same as the distance from the wing to the front edge of the body.

30. Work the dubbing back over the front end of the body to taper the abdomen. End with bare thread at the front edge of the dubbing, and let the thread hang there.

31. Select and size a brown and a grizzly rooster neck feather. Make sure the barb length on the two feathers is about 1 ½ times the hook gap.

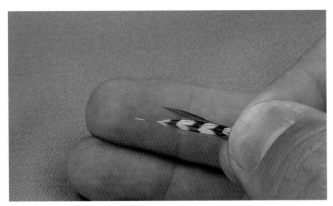

32. Strip the bases of both feathers so the bare stems are equal to about half a shank-length, and lay them one on top of the other with the inside of the top feather facing the outside of the bottom feather.

33. These two hackle feathers should be "spooned" together. It makes no difference which feather is on top.

34. Tie the bare quill of the feathers in at the front edge of the dubbed body as a single unit. You want the inside of the feathers to be facing the hook shank, and there should be about a quarter shank or so of bare quill behind the hackle tie-down point. If you measured the bare stem section correctly, the butt ends of the quills should reach to just behind the hook eye as well. Tie the feathers in on the lower near side of the hook so the stems do not influence the wings and you have a clear path to wrap over the stems without having to work around the wings.

35. Grab both feathers and pull them up and over the top of the hook at the same time. I prefer to wrap double hackles at the same time rather than individually because I can pack the hackle wraps much tighter on the shank. No hackle fibers should splay out on the first half turn as the bare stems come over the shank. These wraps should be as tight as you can make them. The hook is slightly deflected from the pressure I am putting on the hackle feathers as I wrap them.

36. Bring the feathers under the hook and straight up again on the near side of the hook, splaying the hackles. As you continue wrapping the feather over the top of the hook, be sure the feather stems butt up to the first turn. Wrap this hackle collar much like you did the wire on the Brassie, tilting the feathers back slightly as you wrap to really pack the wraps tightly together with no spaces in between the turns.

37. Make another two wraps around the hook with the feathers coming right up to the back edge of the wings. Here you can really see the hook bend as I wrap the feathers. Make sure those wraps are tight. Notice also that the outsides of the feathers are facing the hook eye.

38. Preen the wings back out of the way as you did when we propped them up earlier. You may even need to preen some of the hackle back as well. Bring the hackle feathers up in front of the wings on this next turn as close to the front edge of the feathers as you can.

39. Make another two turns coming forward to the rear edge of the index point, for a total of six turns of hackle. Bring the feathers up above the shank and transfer them to your thread hand. Hold the feathers taut and slightly upward while you pick up the bobbin in your material hand and make two absolutely vertical wraps over them at the index point. Be sure the thread turns are straight up and down so you don't capture any stray hackle fibers as you tie the feathers down.

40. Grasp the tips of the hackle feathers as close to the hook as you can while still leaving space to get the scissor tips between your fingertips and the hook eye. Slide the very tips of your fine-tip scissors in around the base of the hackle tips and push the scissors down against the hook while you pull up on the hackle tips. Clip the feather tips as close as you can.

41. When done right, the leftover feather stubs should be minimal.

43. Finished fly.

42. Make a few tight turns of thread over the stubs to smooth off the head. Whip-finish and clip the thread.

44. Front view.

PATTERN VARIATIONS

GREEN DRAKE

Hook:	#10–12 Tiemco 5212
Thread:	Olive 6/0 Danville
Tail:	Moose hock
Wing:	Hen neck hackle tips dyed gray
Rib:	Brown Uni-Floss
Abdomen:	Olive-gray Super Fine
Hackle:	One brown and one grizzly dyed olive rooster hackle feather, mixed

BLUE-WINGED OLIVE

Hook:	#14–24 Tiemco 100
Thread:	Gray 8/0 Uni-Thread
Tail:	Gray spade hackle fibers
Wings:	Dyed gray hen neck hackle tips
Abdomen:	Olive-gray Super Fine
Hackle:	Gray rooster neck or saddle

BLUE DUN

Hook: #14–24 Tiemco 100
Thread: Gray 8/0 Uni-Thread
Tail: Gray spade hackle fibers
Wings: Dyed gray hen neck hackle tips
Abdomen: Gray Super Fine
Hackle: Gray rooster neck or saddle

PALE MORNING DUN

Hook: #14–24 Tiemco 100
Thread: Light cahill 8/0 Uni-Thread
Tail: Gray spade hackle fibers
Wings: Dyed gray hen neck hackle tips
Abdomen: Pale-yellow Super Fine
Hackle: Gray rooster neck or saddle

ADAMS IRRESISTIBLE

Hook: #14–20 Tiemco 100 SP-BL
Thread: Black 8/0 Uni-Thread
Tail: Moose hock
Wings: Grizzly hen neck hackle tips
Abdomen: Spun and trimmed deer hair
Hackle: Brown and grizzly rooster neck or saddle,
mixed

Note: The stouter wire hook holds up to the thread tension required to spin the hair on the thread body. Spinning deer hair is covered in the Goddard Caddis chapter.

CHAPTER 19

Rusty Spinner

MAIN FOCUS

Mounting and splitting a three-fiber tail • Wrapping goose biots
Mounting and cross-wrapping a pair of spinner wings

L‌ike the Adams, the Rusty Spinner is more of a pattern fly than a specific fly pattern, although the Trusty Rusty, as it is sometimes known, is a great fly. This fly, and spinner patterns in general, imitate the true adult phase of a mayfly after it has mated and laid its eggs. Once the deed is done, mayfly spinners fall to the water and die, becoming easy meals for trout. These dead and dying bugs can't fly off and are typically present in large numbers, so the trout simply take up feeding stations along good current lines and pick the bugs off one by one. The most difficult part of fishing a spinner fall is timing the cast so the fly intersects the fish at the right moment. These feeding trout often develop a timed rhythm to their rises and will eat a bug every three or four seconds as long as they are coming down the river. Laying a perfect cast in front of them that doesn't

Once you master the basic Rusty Spinner pattern, you can mix and match colors and sizes to imitate any spinner on your local waters.

PROPORTIONS AT A GLANCE

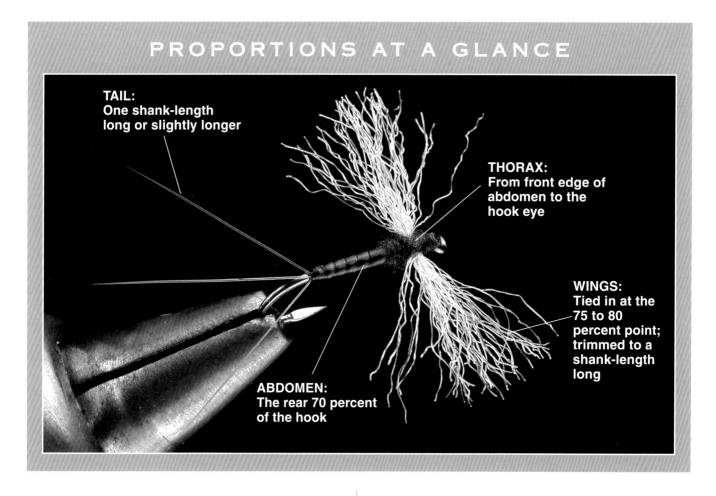

TAIL:
One shank-length
long or slightly longer

THORAX:
From front edge of
abdomen to the
hook eye

WINGS:
Tied in at the
75 to 80
percent point;
trimmed to a
shank-length
long

ABDOMEN:
The rear 70 percent
of the hook

RUSTY SPINNER

Rusty Spinner materials.

Hook:	#12–24 Tiemco 100SP-BL, 100, or 101
Thread:	Rusty brown 70-denier Ultra Thread
Tails:	White or rusty brown Microfibetts
Abdomen:	Rusty brown goose biot
Wing:	White McFlylon
Thorax:	Rusty brown Super Fine

Note: Use smaller diameter threads for smaller patterns

coincide with their cadence results in a fly that is just never seen by the fish, so if you encounter a dense spinner fall, keep this little timing trick in mind: Your fly needs to be the next fly in line at the time when the fish is ready to rise again.

You can use the techniques shown here to tie mayfly spinners for any species, simply by altering the color of the materials and the hook size. Tricos, Pale Morning Dun, and Blue-Winged Olive spinners are but a few of the options possible. Since most of the common Colorado mayflies are a rusty brown color after they have molted into spinners, this color variation is typically all I need, but I carry olive and pale-yellow spinners in my vest as well. The tiny black and olive Trico spinners of late summer are an event unto themselves, and I have a whole separate box of spinners to imitate them.

On this fly you will be learning several new techniques: A three-fiber split tail created with a spare loop of thread, a smooth biot body, and spent wings. On these sparsely tied flies, the three-fiber split tail holds up the bend of the fly, where the hook can really use some support. You can also tie this fly with two fibers as we did on the RS2 and the trout probably won't care, but I will include the three-fiber technique here so you can add it to your repertoire.

The biot body is a matter of personal preference on a fly like this, but the beautifully ribbed variegation from the biot is hard to argue with. There are a few little idiosyncrasies to working with biots, and I hope to alleviate some of the questions that so commonly arise in regard to wrapping these odd little feathers. At any rate, the biot can be replaced with a slender thread body and be just as effective, but nobody will "ooh" and "ahh" when they see a box of thread-bodied flies.

To mount spent wings so they lie perpendicular to the shank and imitate the sprawled-out wings of the natural, you'll use X-wraps, a technique that provides a foundation for forming the post on the Parachute Blue-Winged Olive.

Biots are found along the leading edge of goose or turkey primary flight feathers. Only the first feather on each wing has long biots, and the biots get shorter and softer the farther you get from the front of the wing. I have been involved in several spirited debates about the proper way to tie in and wrap a biot body and would like to clear up a bit of the confusion surrounding these beautiful feather bodies.

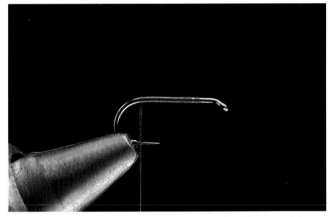

1. Cut 6 inches of thread from the bobbin and lay it aside. You'll need this piece of thread in a minute, so put it somewhere where you won't lose it. I clip the end into my hackle pliers so I know where it is and it won't blow away. Also, pull a strip of biots from the package and place them in a cup of warm water. You want to pre-soak the biots ahead of time to make them more pliable. If you are tying left-handed, select biots from the right wing of the goose and vice versa if you are tying right-handed. Start the thread an eye-length back from the hook eye and wrap a thread base back to the bend.

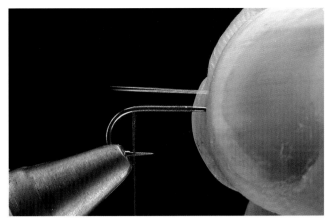

2. Select three tailing fibers from the bundle and clip them off. Even their tips and measure them against the hook so they are a shank-length long.

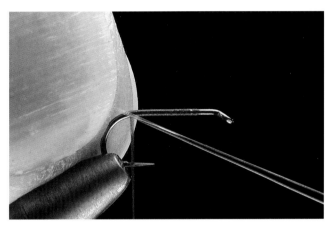

3. Transfer the tailing fibers to your material hand and lay them across the bend with the butt ends facing toward you and slightly down.

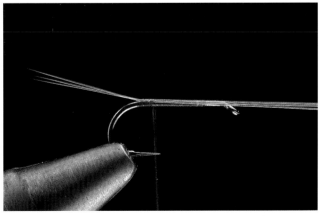

4. Bring the thread up and over the tailing fibers at the hook bend, binding them directly on top of the hook shank. They need to be squarely on top of the shank for the tail-splitting technique to work. Make a few turns going forward over the butt ends to anchor them in place.

5. Press your thumbnail up under the tails at their bases to flare and separate them.

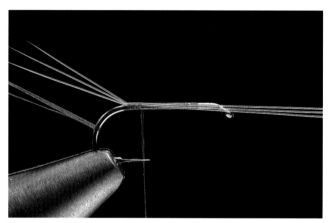

6. Grab the piece of thread you reserved earlier and remove it from the hackle pliers. Loop it around the hook bend by bringing it up from the bottom of the hook between the hanging bobbin and the vise.

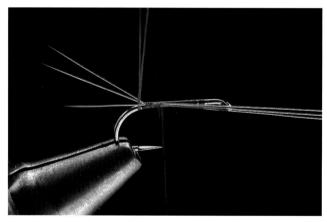

7. Draw the loop of thread up to the base of the tails with the strands of the loop straddling the center tail fiber. The strands should flare the outside tail fibers, leaving the center tail fiber in-line with the hook shank.

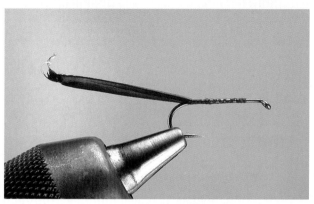

1. The picture above shows a biot from the right wing of a (dyed) Canada goose feather attached to the hook by its tip. To form a smooth biot body, I tie the biot in with the notch at its base facing down.

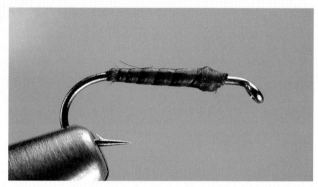

2. Tying the feather in this way allows me to wrap the feather with the stand-up edge leading the way down the hook, and to overlap it with the smooth back edge of the biot to create the smoothly segmented body shown on the right. If you were to tie it in with the notch up, you would get a body with fuzzy ribs. Another way of looking at it is that a stand-up edge that leads will be covered by the backside of the next turn, creating a smooth body. A stand up edge that follows will create the fuzzy rib.

Wrapping the biot with its natural curve (concave side toward the hook shank) will create a somewhat more streamlined body shape than if you wrap the biot against its natural curve, and it is less prone to buckling and breaking. The easiest way to determine the direction of the natural curve is to look at the biot

BIOT TUTORIAL

from its long edge to see if the curve of the feather matches the direction you will be wrapping it around the hook. If you are a right-handed tier, feathers from the left flight feather will curve in the direction you are wrapping; if you are a left-handed tier, you'll want feathers from the right flight feather.

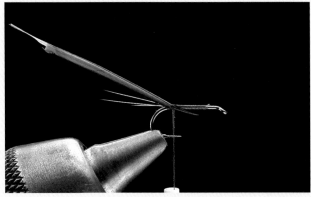

This photo shows the biot tied in for the Rusty Spinner. Note the curvature of the tip of the feather is cupped toward the hook shank, and that the stand-up edge of the biot is on the top. Attaching the biot and wrapping it in this manner will create a smoothly tapered body.

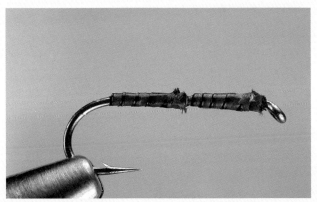

3. On the back of the hook I have wrapped a biot *against* its natural curve to form a smooth body. On the front of the hook, I have wrapped a biot *with* its natural curve, again, to form a smooth body. The biot on the front of the hook presents a better taper, and the segments fit more tightly together.

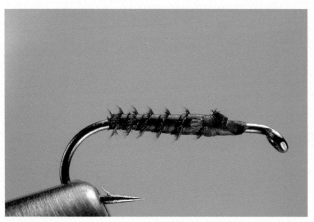

4. If I attach a biot with the notch facing up and wrap it forward *with* its natural curve (concave side toward the hook shank), the stand up edge follows the smooth edge up the shank, forming a fuzzy rib. Still a very nice looking segmented body, but a totally different effect.

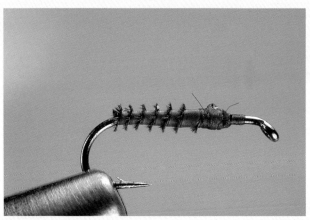

6. The results of a biot tied in with the notch facing up and wrapped *against* its natural curve. The spiraling rib formed with this technique stands up more prominently.

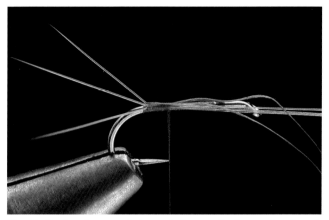

8. Pull the loop of thread forward along the hook shank and tie it down with a few flat turns of thread. You may need to tug on one end of the thread loop or the other to fine-tune the tail angles.

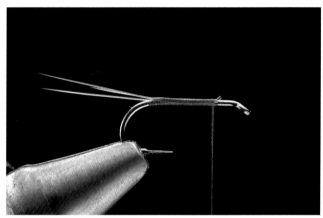

9. Once the tails are properly positioned and splayed out evenly, wrap the tying thread forward over the thread loop and the butt ends of the tails up to the starting point and clip the excess.

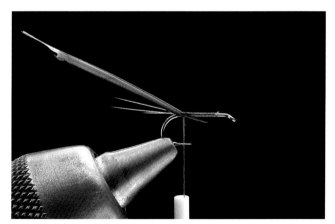

10. Return the tying thread to the hook bend with a smooth, even thread layer.

11. Select a dyed goose biot from the stem of the feather. I prefer to wrap the biots to form a smooth (rather than ribbed) body on spinner patterns as it more closely matches the real insect's shape and texture. Right-handers should look for feathers from the left wing so that you can wrap in with the natural curve. Because I tie left-handed, I select a biot from the right wing. Wrapping biots with the natural curve makes it much easier to lay the wraps flat along the shank versus wrapping them against this curve, which makes the biot harder to work with and more prone to buckling and breaking.

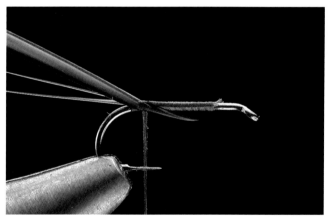

12. Tie in the biot on its edge at the hook bend by the tip with the notch at the base of the feather facing down. You want the tip of the feather to extend up to just past the halfway point on the shank so it becomes part of the underbody. If you look closely at this photo, or even your own biot, you will see the stand-up edge is going to be on the top, leading edge of the feather as you wrap, allowing the smooth, darker edge to follow and overlap the front edge.

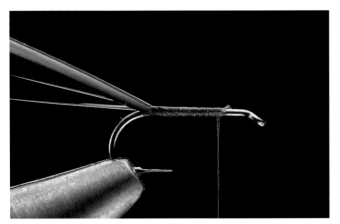

13. Wrap the thread forward over the tip of the biot, smoothing it down along the hook shank. Be sure to keep the shank as smooth as possible as you wrap forward and try to keep the underbody relatively level as you go. The increasing thickness of the biot forms a slight taper as you wrap, and you don't want to create any unnecessary bulk along the way on an imitation of such a slender insect.

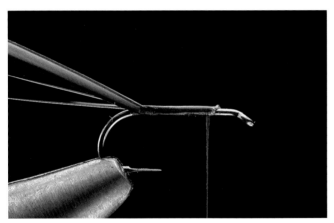

14. Smear a drop of Gloss Coat along the thread base on the shank to help toughen the biot body.

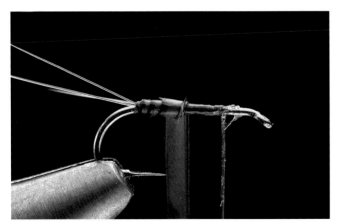

15. With hackle pliers, grasp the butt end of the feather in-line with its length, not at a right angle. Wrap the biot so the ribbed edge leads each turn.

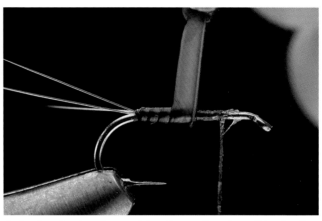

16. Look closely at this photo for the ribbed edge along the front of the third turn. You can see where the next turn will overlap the front edge of the third wrap and cover that ribbed edge, creating a smooth colored rib rather than the fuzzy stand-up rib provided by the front edge of the feather.

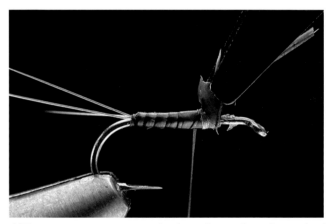

17. Continue wrapping the biot forward to the end of the thread base, overlapping the turns as you go.

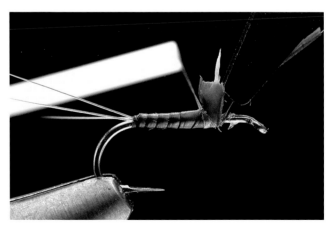

18. Tie the biot off with two firm wraps of thread at the end of the thread base.

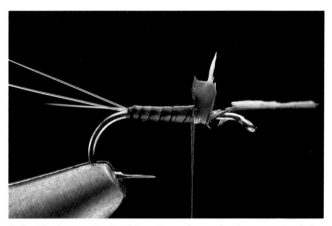

19. Release the hackle pliers from the butt end of the biot.

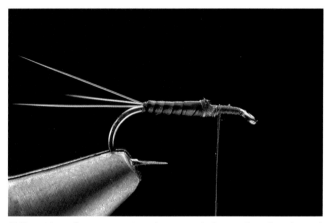

20. Clip the remaining butt end from the shank and wrap the thread forward over the shank all the way up to the hook eye. Wrap the thread back to the 80 percent point on the shank, just in front of the leading edge of the biot body, to create a thread base for the wing in the next few steps.

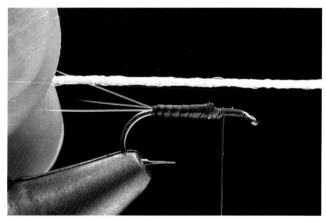

21. Brush out a 3-inch strand of McFlylon with a wire brush to separate the fibers. For a size 16 fly, you want to separate about half a strand and roll it into a cord by twisting the ends in opposite directions. As a rule of thumb, the diameter of this cord should be about equal to the body diameter.

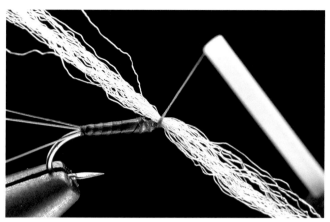

22. Hold the end of the McFlylon in your material hand and lay it across the hook at an angle just in front of the biot abdomen. Catch the center of the McFlylon with a thread wrap coming from the near side of the back of the wing clump to the far side of the front of the wing. Make another turn in the same path and leave the thread hanging on the far side in front of the wing.

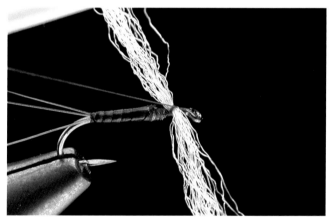

23. Bring the thread under the hook and up on the near side in front of the wing, but do not come over the top of the shank. Angle the second half of this turn from the near side of the shank in front of the wing to the far side in back of the wing, crossing over the first two wraps in an X shape. Make another turn in the same path to complete tying down the wing.

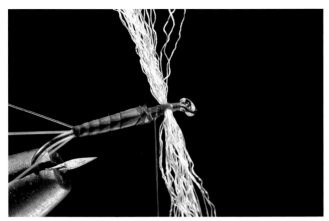

24. The McFlylon should now be at a right angle to the hook shank and sticking out to the sides of the fly like airplane wings. Grab either end of the McFlylon wing and tweak them a bit to make sure they are not higher on one side than the other. You want the wings lying flat across the top of the hook shank. You may make another few X-wraps to really anchor the wing down tightly, particularly if you are tying a larger fly. End with the thread hanging behind the wings.

25. Close-up of X-wraps anchoring wing in place.

26. Dub the thread and begin wrapping the dubbing at the front edge of the biot abdomen.

27. Wrap the dubbing up to the back edge of the wings, forming the beginning of a thorax slightly thicker than the abdomen.

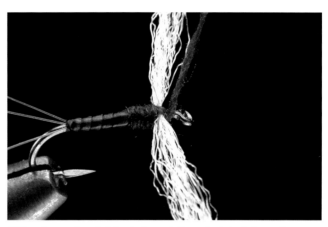

28. Cross the dubbed thread from behind the wings on the far side of the hook and bring it up on the near side of the hook in front of the wings. Keep this turn against the front edge of the wings. To cover the thread wraps from the winging, follow the same path with the dubbed thread.

29. Cross this wrap over the top of the wing from the near side of the front of the wing to the far side behind the wing.

30. Bring this wrap of thread down behind the wings . . .

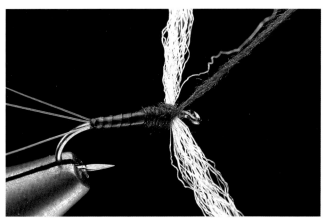

31. and up again on the near side, angling toward the front of the hook between the wings.

32. Bring the dubbed thread to the front of the wings by coming across the top of the shank between them. Pull the wings back out of the way in your material hand.

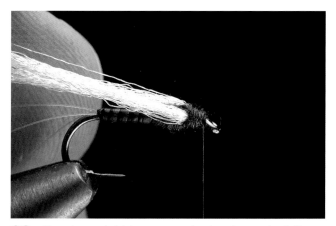

33. Continue dubbing up to the hook eye, building a descending taper from the base of the wings down to the hook eye.

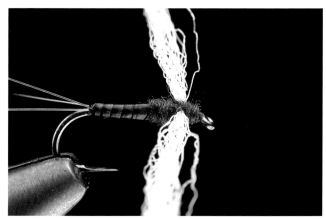

34. Whip-finish and clip the thread behind the hook eye.

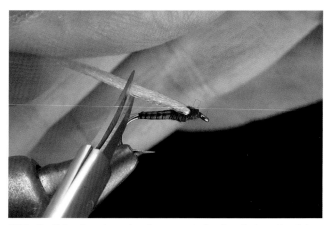

35. Pull both wings back toward the hook bend, taking care to keep them even so you cut them to the same length. Trim both wings at the same time at the inside edge of the hook bend.

36. Fluff the wings and reposition them out to the sides of the hook if need be.

37. Quarter top view.

38. Underside view.

TRICO SPINNER

Hook:	#18–26 Tiemco 101
Thread:	10/0 Gudebrod
Tails:	White Microfibetts
Wing:	White McFlylon
Abdomen:	Black tying thread
Thorax:	Black Super Fine

Note: The biot is not necessary on this pattern as the ribbing on a black biot is not apparent enough to bother with.

CHAPTER 20

Parachute Blue-Winged Olive (BWO)

MAIN FOCUS

Spade hackle fiber tail • More practice with smooth goose biot bodies
Mounting and posting a single parachute-style wing post • Working with parachute posts

Aparachute-style fly is characterized by the way the hackle is wrapped horizontally around the wing post rather than vertically around the hook shank. This method of wrapping the hackle lets the body of the fly sit lower in and on the surface film of the water and gives a more realistic impression to the fish. Not only does the upright wing post give the fish the

wing silhouette they are hoping for, it also makes the fly much easier for you to find and follow on the water. Most of the mayfly patterns I fish these days are tied with parachute hackles.

When anglers say that they can't see their fly, what they generally mean is that they are having trouble finding their fly. If you can see your fly one out of a hundred

Parachute-style flies are popular because you can create flies that ride low in the water like many naturals that are also easy to see.

198

casts, you are fully capable of seeing the fly. You should have a pretty good idea of where your fly is going to land on each cast. If you don't, it's probably due more to your wacky casting than it is your meager vision. The fly is out there and still visible as can be, it's just not where you are looking for it. Do not confuse poor vision with poor casting. To see your flies better, work on your casting.

While I will show the Parachute Blue-Winged Olive (BWO) here, you can alter the colors and sizes of this fly to match any adult mayfly. Twist up this same pattern in a light creamy yellow and you'll have a perfect Pale Morning Dun imitation, a tannish rust color yields a Red Quill, a great big gray-olive colored parachute makes a great Green Drake, a gray body with brown and grizzly tail and parachute hackle collar gives you a Parachute Adams, and so on.

The tail of any parachute-style fly can be tied with a bundle of hackle fibers (as shown here) or a two- or three-fiber split tail like on the RS2 and Rusty Spinner. I have noticed no difference in the way the flies float, although I do lean toward the hackle-fiber tails when fishing from the boat because they provide a little bit better support than the split tails. I prefer the split-tailed flies when wade fishing over selective fish that have a bit more time to eyeball my offering, if for no other reason than that I know the split tail is accurate, and I can eliminate that variable from any question of why the fish wouldn't eat it. Sometimes I just like having that in my head.

There are several different materials available to use for the wing. My material of choice these days is McFlylon, a synthetic material made from polypropylene. McFlylon is readily available in a variety of colors, and I believe it is the best parachute wing material I have found thus far for the following reasons:

McFlylon floats all by itself. Materials like Antron and Z-lon soak up a bit of water and don't float as well.

McFlylon has a sheen to it that makes the fly show up on the water much better than conventional polypropylene yarn.

McFlylon holds its shape and doesn't ball up while being fished. Standard poly yarn and Antron both have a tendency to "knit" up on the hook when you fish them, crumpling down into an unattractive knot on the top of the fly.

McFlylon is a synthetic fiber that comes in a wide range of colors and is ideal for parachute posts.

PROPORTIONS AT A GLANCE

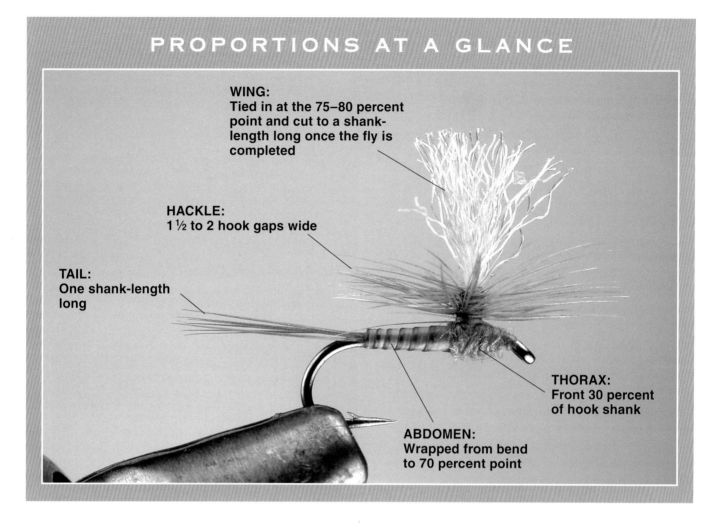

WING:
Tied in at the 75–80 percent point and cut to a shank-length long once the fly is completed

HACKLE:
1 ½ to 2 hook gaps wide

TAIL:
One shank-length long

THORAX:
Front 30 percent of hook shank

ABDOMEN:
Wrapped from bend to 70 percent point

Using a synthetic wing material like McFlylon allows us to mount the wings on the hook using the spinner wing to upright method (yes, I just named the technique), which creates almost no bulk on the hook shank. Contrast this with bulky wing materials like calf body hair or turkey T-base feathers, and you'll quickly see why the McFlylon has an edge. While calf-body hair and turkey are super visible, tying them down creates a huge lump on the hook shank that is completely out of place on a slender little pattern like a Parachute Adams or Blue-Winged Olive. This lump also makes it hard to form a smooth lifelike taper under the body.

McFlylon comes in a variety of visible colors—gray, white, and hot pink are standards in my fly box. I use gray wings when I want the most accurate match to the naturals, white when I want visibility under most conditions, and hot pink for weird light or along foam lines where the white winged flies just blend in. The only other wing color I carry in my box is black, which is perfect for fishing in the evening when the sun is at a flat angle across the water and turns the surface to a sheet of silver. The afternoon glare on the water can negate the color and visibility of nearly any wing color. Everything that was dark under the high sun is now glaring white, and your previously visible fly now disappears when it touches down. A black wing will show up like no tomorrow in this flat light.

We are going to use a biot abdomen on this fly as well, though you can also use a dubbed body. I really like the natural taper and color variation of smooth biot bodies, and find that they float longer than conventional dubbed-body flies. The solid biot body doesn't soak up enough water to affect the flotation of the fly, while dubbing gets slimed when a fish eats the bug and is much harder to dry out and bring back to life. I even tie my Parachute Adams with a natural gray Canada goose biot body, and use dyed goose biots for every other parachute pattern I tie.

On a final note, I always dub the thorax of the fly to match either the abdomen color or the thorax color of the real insect. Some folks get all excited about matching the natural's exact abdomen color, then go and leave bare thread for the thorax. If you are going to go to all the trouble to tie this fly, spend the extra five seconds to dub the thorax so the fly looks like it's finished.

1. Before you begin tying, take an entire length of goose biots from the package and place them in a shallow bowl of warm water. Start the thread at the 75 percent point and wrap a smooth thread base back to the bend.

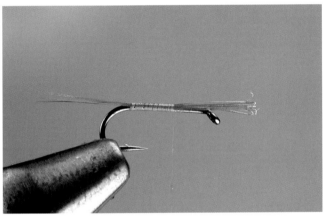

2. Peel a clump of about a dozen spade hackle fibers from a spade hackle on the outer edges of a dry fly neck. Make sure these fibers are aligned at their tips. Measure the hackle fibers against the shank so they are equal to one shank-length. Tie the hackle fibers in at the bend so the tips extend one shank-length beyond the hook bend. Wrap forward over the butt ends of the fibers to just past the halfway point on the shank.

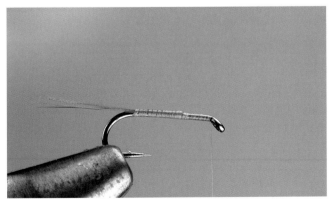

3. Clip the remaining butt ends from the hackle fibers flush with the hook shank. Continue wrapping the thread forward up to the hook eye, making a smooth thread base.

PARACHUTE BLUE-WINGED OLIVE (BWO)

Parachute Blue-Winged Olive materials.

Hook:	#16–24 Tiemco 100
Thread:	Gray 10/0 Gudebrod, Gordon Griffiths 14/0, or Giorgio Bennechi 12/0
Tail:	Blue dun (gray) spade hackle fibers
Wing:	White or gray McFlylon
Hackle:	Blue dun (gray) rooster neck or saddle feather
Abdomen:	Olive-gray goose biot
Thorax:	Olive-gray Super Fine

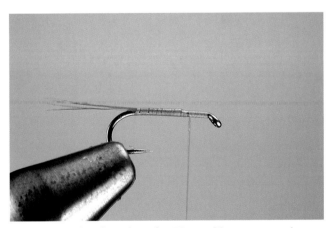

4. Return the thread to the 75- to 80-percent point on the shank.

25. We'll switch views here to a parachute hackle tied on a bare hook shank. Grab the tip of the hackle feather in your rotary hackle pliers and pull the feather around the post and out over the hook eye. You want the hackle to go around the post in a clockwise direction for left-handed tying and counterclockwise for right-handed tying. Bend the feather over backward so the inside of the feather faces up as you wrap down the post.

26. Make the first turn of hackle at the extreme top edge of the thread post.

27. Make the next turn of hackle directly under the first, butting the wraps tightly together just as you would on a conventional hackle collar.

28. Continue wrapping the feather from the top of the post to the bottom for a total of three to six turns.

29. Your hackle should look like this.

30. Pull the hackle pliers down on the near side of the hook. Pick up the thread and make a clockwise turn around the base of the wing post, between the last wrap of hackle and the dubbed thorax. Make another tight clockwise turn to cinch everything down if you are left-handed and a counterclockwise turn if you are right-handed.

31. It is imperative that these wraps don't catch any hackle fibers, so take care to keep them tight to the base of the post. The hackle and the thread tying it off need to wrap in the same direction so the thread wraps tighten the hackle around the post, rather than what they would be doing if the thread was going the opposite direction of the feather.

32. The tie-off procedure on this fly seems a bit tricky but is really pretty simple, so stay with me here. Your thread is coming from the backside of the wing post and out over the hook eye on the underside of the hackle.

33. Here is what step 32 should look like on your fly.

34. Bring the thread forward to the hook eye and down on the far side of the eye. Bring the thread up on the near side of the hook along the bottom of the shank at the index point.

35. Bring the thread up from the far side of the hook right behind the hook eye, catching the thread against the shank and bringing it back to its normal direction of travel, which is around the hook. Make another wrap of thread around the shank behind the hook eye.

36. Whip-finish the thread by setting up the whip-finisher and working the knot in around the hook shank but under the hackle fibers. Pull the knot up from the bottom of the hook to prevent catching any hackle fibers in the loop. Clip the thread and the remaining hackle tip at this point. To clip the hackle, bring the tips of your scissors in from the bottom of the fly and snip the hackle feather as close to the post as you can without cutting any of the hackle that you wrapped.

CHAPTER 21

X Comparadun

MAIN FOCUS

Working with hair • Mounting and flaring a hair wing

I have made a slight change to this popular pattern. Rather than tying the wing on first and trying to smoothly bury the thick butt ends of the wing in the underbody of the fly, I have taken a page from Art Sheck's Spun-Dun and given this fly a new twist. I now mount the wings on my Comparaduns after the body is dubbed and clip their stub ends down flush to the hook. This tying method eliminates the bulk of the wing butts under the body, allows for a slender fly, and provides an extra bit of flotation from the exposed hair butts. Additionally, this new method of winging makes it much easier to fan the wing into a perfect 180 degree arc, creating a nice wing silhouette.

I include this pattern here as a precursor to the hair-wing flies to come. The simply flared hair wing will transition smoothly into the upright, divided hair wings

The Comparadun is popular because it floats well and doesn't require expensive hackles. I have modified the traditional pattern by tying in the wing after the body is dubbed.

My method of winging the fly eliminates the bulk behind the wing on the original.

on the Humpy and Royal Wulff. Changing the size of the hook, the dubbing color, and shade of the deer-hair wing on the Comparadun makes it possible to match nearly any mayfly species.

I split the tail with a figure-eight wrap of thread to illustrate yet another tailing technique. If you substitute a short hank of Antron or Z-lon to form a trailing shuck on this fly, you can call it a Sparkle Dun Variation instead. This pattern is a great all-around adult mayfly imitation and is a favorite of many tiers because of its simple tying steps and cheaply and easily obtained materials. This pattern can be tied in colors and sizes to match any mayfly species known to man without breaking the bank, because there is no expensive hackle required on this fly.

I use UTC 50-denier Gel Spun Polyethylene (GSP) thread to tie this fly, as its small diameter creates little bulk on the hook and this coupled with its slippery nature binds the wing in place with minimal bulk. 8/0 Uni-Thread will suffice if GSP is not available, but I recommend that you at least give the GSP a try.

Finding the correct hair for Comparaduns can be tough. You want hair with short, abruptly tapered tips that still have some thickness. If you tie this fly in small sizes with hair that has fine wispy tips, the hair left on the hook has little hollowness and buoyancy in it. You want hair with some diameter at the tips that is soft enough to flare easily and is the right shade of gray/brown to mimic mayfly wings.

CALLIBAETIS COMPARADUN

X Comparadun materials.

Hook: #10–24 Tiemco 100SP-BL, 100, or 101
Thread: Brown 50-denier GSP
Tails: Tan Microfibetts or tailing fibers
Abdomen: Callibaetis Super Fine
Wing: Deer hair with fine tips
Thorax: Callibaetis Super Fine

Note: Change thread, body, and tail colors to match natural.

PROPORTIONS AT A GLANCE

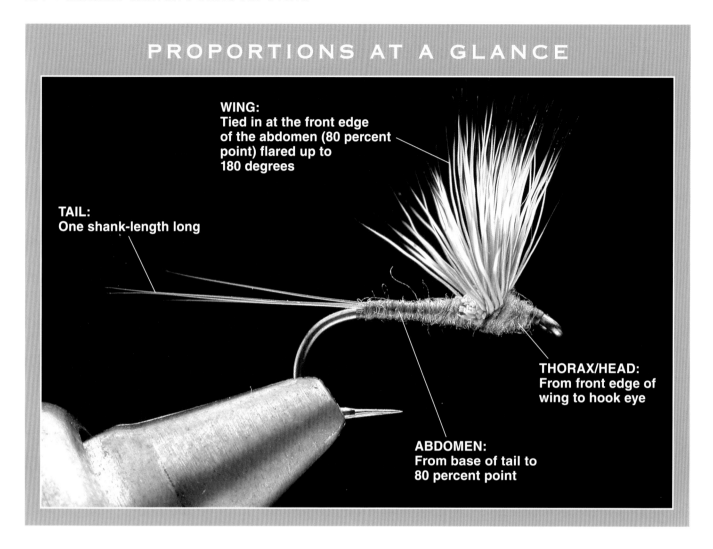

WING:
Tied in at the front edge
of the abdomen (80 percent
point) flared up to
180 degrees

TAIL:
One shank-length long

THORAX/HEAD:
From front edge of
wing to hook eye

ABDOMEN:
From base of tail to
80 percent point

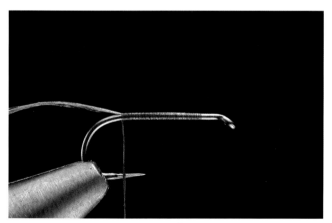

1. Attach the thread about 1 ½ eye-lengths behind the hook eye, leaving a long tag end. Wrap back over the tag, keeping it on top of the shank, to the hook bend.

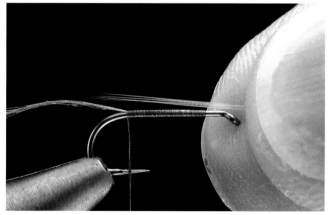

2. Select and clip four tailing fibers from the bundle. Make sure the tips are even, and measure the tails against the hook so they are a full shank-length long.

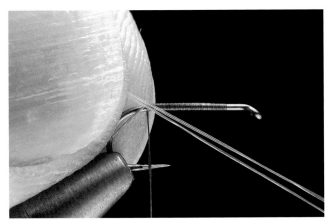

3. Transfer the measured tails to your material hand and place their bases at the hook bend with the butt ends angled toward you and slightly down.

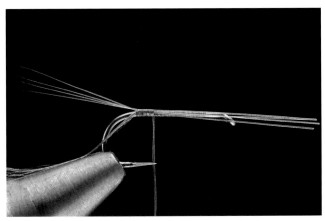

4. Bring the thread up and over the tailing fibers, pinning them on top of the shank at the bend with two turns of thread.

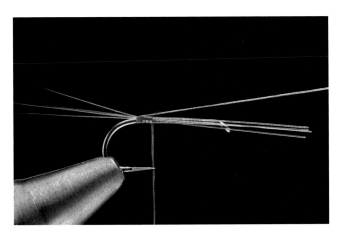

5. Bring the tag end of the thread that was hanging off the bend up between the tail fibers, with two fibers on each side of the tag. Pull the tag end taut to separate the tails into two equal bunches.

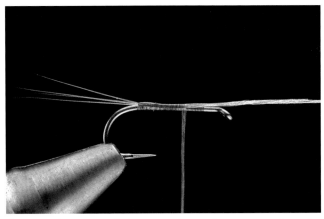

6. Tie the tag end down and continue wrapping the tying thread forward over the butt ends of the tail and the tag end up to the 80 percent point.

7. You should have a nicely split tail. If the tailing fibers are stubborn and not splitting easily, pull them into position. These fibers are made of plastic and are strong, so go ahead and push and pull to get them where they need to be.

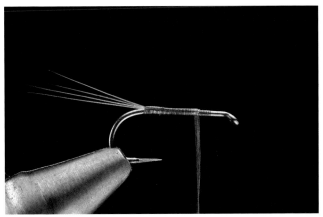

8. Clip the tag end of the thread and the butt ends of the tail flush to the hook shank.

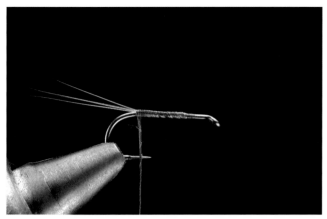

9. Dub the thread with a fine strand of dubbing and use the bare thread between the dubbing and the hook shank to work back to the hook bend. Ideally, you will be splitting and separating the tail with a finely dubbed strand of thread, but if you have bare thread still left over when you get to the bend, it will work as well.

10. To begin separating the tails, take the thread from the underside of the hook shank and up between the two tail clumps. As you work the thread around the tails in the next few steps, try to keep the thread loose and only pull it taut once you have completed the turns. Obtaining this light touch takes a bit of practice, so keep at it.

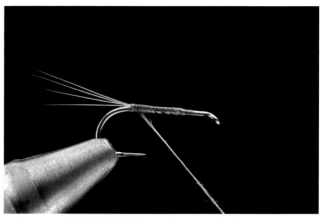

11. Bring the thread above the hook and down again on the far side of the shank with the thread in front of the tails.

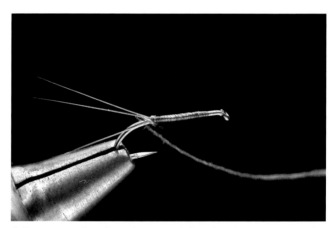

12. Bring the thread around the shank and up on the near side of the hook. Bring this wrap of thread loosely down between the near tail bunch and the far one. Essentially, you are making a figure-eight wrap of thread around the shank and the tail bunches. Draw the tying thread sharply forward so the thread turn pushes against the far tail clump.

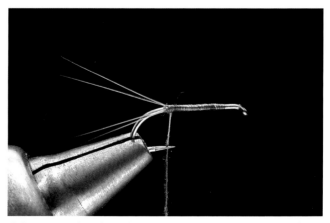

13. Bring the thread up and over the hook at the front edge of the tails to lock everything in place.

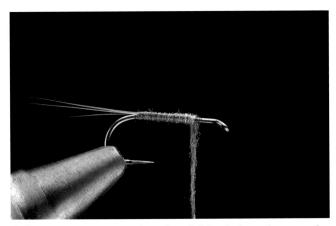

14. Continue wrapping the dubbed thread up to the 80 percent point on the shank.

15. Wrap the dubbing back over the front half of the abdomen to create a tapered body and end with bare thread at the front edge of the body.

16. Wrap a smooth thread base up to the hook eye and back again to the front edge of the body.

17. Cut, clean, and stack a bunch of fine-tipped deer hair. Measure the tips of this clump against the hook so they are a shank-length long.

18. Move the butt ends of the shank-length forward to the front of the abdomen, so the tips extend one shank-length past the tie-in point.

19. Make two taut, but not tight, turns of thread over the hair. Make sure these two wraps of thread are on top of one another and right at the front edge of the abdomen.

20. Pull the tying thread toward you to flare the hair while holding the butt ends of the hair in place along the top of the shank.

21. Make two more tight turns of thread over the first two wraps, and then let go of the butt ends.

22. Lift the butt ends of the hair up above the hook and come in with the tips of your scissors. Pull up on the hair and push down against the shank with the sides of the scissor blades to trim the butt ends as close as possible. You may need to go back in and clean up some loose ends, but try to get as much of the hair as you can with this first cut.

23. The trimmed butt ends should look something like this.

24. Reach under the hook shank and close your thumb and forefinger of your material hand together at the base of the wing.

25. Lift your closed fingers up above the hook, dragging the wing fibers up and back as you go.

26. Bring the thread to the front of the wing and build a small thread dam against the front edge. You don't need to build a lot of bulk with the thread, as you will be propping the wing up with the dubbing in the next step. You just want to hold the wing in position momentarily.

29. As you approach the base of the wing, smash the dubbing wraps as tight as you can to the base of the wing, forming a dubbing dam to hold the wing upright. Put each wrap of dubbing behind the last to wedge it right up to the wing.

27. Dub the thread once again and begin wrapping this dubbing at the back edge of the hook eye.

30. Wrap the remaining dubbing forward to the back of the hook eye and end with bare thread at the index point.

28. Hold the wing back as you did before and wrap the dubbing right up to the base of the hair.

31. Whip-finish and clip the thread at the hook eye.

32. Back view of flared wing.

34. Quarter front view.

33. Preen the wing so it forms a 180-degree arc, or at least a 167-degree arc.

35. Bottom view.

PATTERN VARIATIONS

MELON SPARKLE DUN

Hook:	#14–22 Tiemco 100
Thread:	Brown 50-denier GSP
Shuck:	Brown Z-lon
Abdomen:	Cinnamon Caddis Super Fine
Wing:	Natural deer hair
Thorax/Head:	Cinnamon Caddis Super Fine

PMD COMPARADUN

Hook:	#14–18 Tiemco 100
Thread:	Yellow 50-denier GSP
Tails:	Pale yellow Microfibetts
Abdomen:	Pale yellow Super Fine
Wing:	Light deer body hair
Thorax/Head:	Pale yellow Super Fine

Note: Also works well for eastern Sulphurs (use Sulphur orange dubbing)

BLUE-WINGED OLIVE COMPARADUN

Hook:	#14–18 Tiemco 100
Thread:	Olive 50-denier GSP
Tails:	Gray Microfibetts
Abdomen:	Olive-gray Super Fine
Wing:	Deer body hair
Thorax/Head:	Olive-gray Super Fine

MAHOGANY COMPARADUN

Hook:	#14–18 Tiemco 100
Thread:	Brown 50-denier GSP
Tails:	Gray Microfibetts
Abdomen:	Mahogany Super Fine
Wing:	Deer body hair
Thorax/Head:	Mahogany Super Fine

GREEN DRAKE SPARKLE DUN

Hook:	#10–14 Tiemco 5212
Thread:	Brown 50-denier GSP
Shuck:	Brown Z-lon
Rib:	Brown Uni Floss
Abdomen:	Olive-gray Super Fine
Wing:	Dark deer body hair
Thorax/Head:	Olive-gray Super Fine

CHAPTER 22

Royal Wulff

MAIN FOCUS

Working with calf body hair • Forming upright, divided hair wings
Forming a three-part body with a floss band

The Royal Wulff has become the standard attractor dry in the years since its inception by the legendary Lee Wulff. Hair wings and tail, a multi-colored body, and a heavily hackled collar make this a buoyant, highly visible fast-water fly. I have no idea what makes this fly so attractive to the fish, but perhaps Lee Wulff had the right idea when he suggested that this fly imitates a piece of strawberry shortcake. The Royal Wulff is part of the Wulff series of flies characterized by buoyant hair wings and tails. Like so many other flies, you can change the body materials and colors and change the hackle colors to suit your taste. For instance, if you use a moose-hock tail, white calf-body wings, gray dubbing for the body, and mixed brown and grizzly hackle, you have an Adams Wulff.

As complicated as this fly seems, the only thing we haven't covered in the previous patterns is tying in the red floss sash in the center of the fly. The hair wings are

I have no idea what makes the Royal Wulff so attractive to fish, but perhaps Lee Wulff had the right idea when he suggested that this fly imitates a piece of strawberry shortcake.

Wulff-style flies have hair wings and tails and are more buoyant than most conventional dry flies.

mounted like the hair on the Comparadun, divided like the wings on the Rusty Spinner, and posted like the wings on the Parachute Blue-Winged Olive. The moose hair tail is mounted like the tail on the Adams. The ribbing is exactly as it is on nearly all the other flies you have tied thus far, the peacock sections of the body are built in the same manner as the thorax on the Pheasant Tail (alright, maybe just slightly different—with a twist, if you will), and the hackle collar is mounted and wrapped like the hackle collar on the Adams. You never realized you knew so much until you got here.

Calf body hair is a bit different to work with than the deer and elk hair you have used thus far. Calf hair is not hollow like deer and elk hair and won't flare when you apply thread pressure. This trait makes this hair easier to work with than deer and elk, but the overall short length and fineness of the calf hair present other issues. The biggest issue when working with calf body hair is finding some that is straight and long enough to work with easily. Be sure to clean the short hairs out of the clump of hair before stacking it. Often, I clean the hair

first by holding it close to the tips, pulling any short hairs out, and blowing on the butt ends to clear out any remaining short fibers. I then place the hair in the stacker and tamp it several times, and when I take the hair out, I check to be sure the short hairs are all gone. Sometimes I repeat this process a few times to guarantee the short hairs are gone, but the trouble is well worth it. If those short hairs are left in, the hair is hard to anchor to the hook. Dividing and posting the wings becomes much harder as well because the fibers in them aren't all the same length.

I don't use calf-tail hair for the wings on my Wulffs because the curly hair is much harder to stack evenly and results in wings with tapered and ragged tips. The waviness of calf-tail hair can add to the overall buoyancy of the fly, however, as the air space created by the waves in the hair helps keep the fly dry and afloat. I simply find the effort involved in finding and preparing good calf-tail hair to be more work than necessary. Calf body hair makes clean, straight beautiful wings, and is overall a much easier material to work with.

PROPORTIONS AT A GLANCE

WINGS: Tied in at 75 percent point, one shank-length long

BODY: Equal thirds of peacock, red floss, and peacock on the rear 60 percent of the hook

TAIL: One shank-length long

HACKLE: From front of body to rear edge of index point, covering the front 40 percent of the hook shank

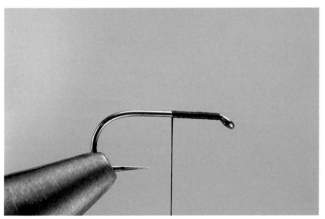

1. Start the thread just behind the hook eye and wrap a single-layer thread base back to the midpoint on the shank. On this fly you have to break the bare index point rule, but by now you should know to avoid crowding the eye.

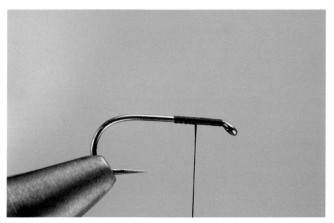

2. Return the thread to the 75 percent point on the shank, at the middle of the thread base.

3. Cut, clean, and stack a clump of calf body hair. Make double sure to clean all the short underfur from the clump and perhaps give it a few more raps in the hair stacker to even the tips. Stack the calf hair and measure the clump against the hook so it is one shank-length long.

4. Move the butt ends of the calf hair clump up to the 75 percent point so the tips extend past the tie-in (75 percent) point about one shank-length. Tie the calf hair down on top of the hook by making two soft turns around the hair, and then tighten these wraps by pulling the thread toward you. The calf hair won't flare like the deer and elk hair, but you still want to hold onto the butt ends to keep it from rolling.

ROYAL WULFF

Royal Wulff materials.

Hook:	#8–20 Tiemco 100 or 100SP-BL
Thread:	Black 6/0 Danville or 8/0 Uni-Thread
Tail:	Moose hock
Wings:	White calf body hair
Rib:	Lagartun copper wire (fine)
Body:	⅓ peacock herl from the eye, ⅓ red floss, ⅓ peacock from the eye
Hackle:	Two brown rooster neck or saddle feathers

5. Hold the butt ends of the hair on top of the shank and wrap the thread back toward the bend, forming a short band of thread and anchoring the hair in place. This band of thread works just like the band on the Elk Hair Caddis and travels toward the bend rather than toward the hook eye.

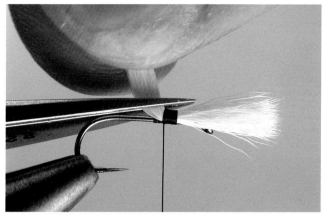

6. Lift the butt ends of the hair and bring the tips of your scissors in from the rear of the hook to clip them off at an angle. The cut and the scissor blades are almost parallel to the shank, but the curve that the lifted hair produces will result in nicely tapered butt ends. If you are tying right-handed, this maneuver is going to seem a bit odd because you will need to make the cut with your left hand. You can make the cut from the top of the clump down toward the shank, but that requires some extra snips to really smooth it off. You've tied all the other flies in this book so far, and are becoming a good tier, so buck up and try making this cut with your left hand; it's not as hard as it looks.

7. The butt ends should now be tapered down to the shank.

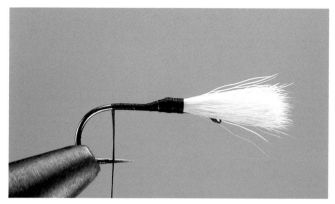

8. Continue wrapping the thread back over the butt ends to the hook bend, forming a smooth thread base.

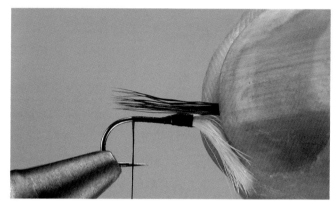

9. Cut, clean, and stack a modest amount of moose hock hair. Moose hock (leg hair) is a hard hair that floats well and doesn't flare. I prefer hock to moose body because the tips are generally much more intact and the hair reacts much better to thread tension. Measure this clump of hair against the hook or the wing, if you trust your one shank-length measurement from earlier, so it is equal to one shank-length.

10. Transfer the moose hock to your material hand and place the butt ends of the measured clump against the shank at the bend so the tips extend beyond the hook bend one shank-length. Angle the butt ends of the hair so the hook shank blocks the fibers from rolling over the hook—exactly as you have on nearly all the other tails used in this book.

11. Make a few wraps of thread over the butt ends of the tail, coming forward from the hook bend to anchor the hair on top of the shank. Flatten (untwist) the thread so it doesn't bite too hard into the hair and flare it. Flat thread will anchor the tail in place without pinching it. Be sure the hair is centered on top of the hook shank and that it hasn't rolled to the far side of the hook.

12. Continue wrapping the flattened thread forward to just behind the tapered butt ends of the wing.

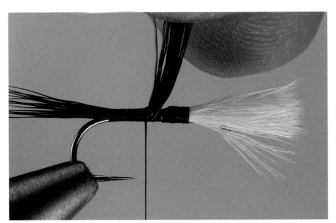

13. Lift the butt ends of the tail. You are going to cut them so they match up with the butt ends of the wing and form a smooth underbody on the shank.

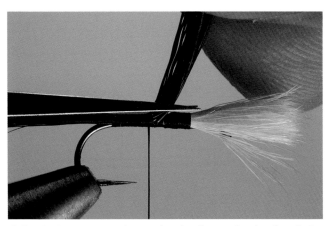

14. Bring your scissor tips in from the back of the hook, in-line with the shank, and clip the butt ends of the moose hair straight.

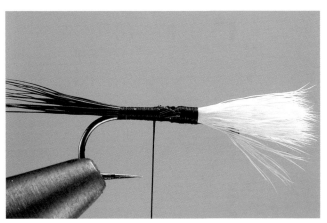

15. The resultant butt ends should mate up exactly with the opposite angle of the wing butts.

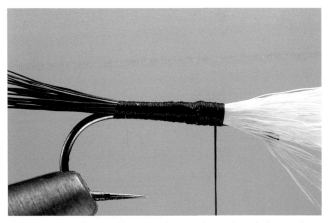

16. Wrap forward over the stub ends of the tailing butts to smooth the underbody up to the back of the wing. You don't want any lumps, bumps, or spaces in the underbody, just a smooth, relatively level layer of thread. If you leave a space between the butt ends of the wing and tail, you'll never be able to smooth out the gap.

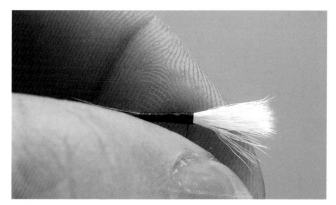

17. Reach under the wing at the front of the hook with your material hand and pinch your thumb and index finger together below the shank.

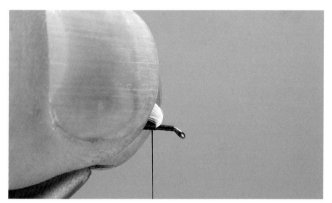

18. Lift your closed fingers up above the hook, trapping the calf hair wing inside your fingers and drawing it back along the shank on top of the hook.

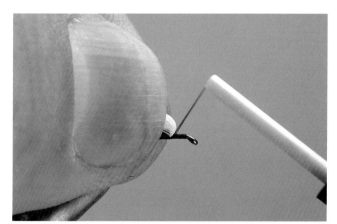

19. Start building a thread dam at the front edge of the wing as you did on the Adams. This thread dam will be more pronounced than what you did on the Adams, as the hair wing is stiffer than the hen hackle tips. You will need to work the thread back and forth, building a smooth taper up to the base of the wing rather than piling the wraps at the base of the hair. When you get back to the base of the wing, place one wrap behind the other to smash the thread wraps tight against the front edge of the hair to prop the hair upright on the shank.

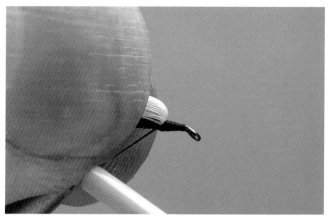

20. To really pack the thread wraps tight to the base of the wing, push the end of the bobbin tube behind the wing as you come under the hook, forcing the thread wraps as far back against the wing as possible.

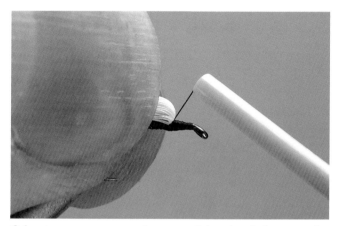

21. As you come to the top of the shank, be sure the thread wraps are snugged as close to the front of the wing as you can get them.

22. The calf hair should now be upright and at a right angle to the hook shank.

23. Grasp the hair in your thread hand and make a thread wrap from the front of the wing to the back, right up against the back edge of the hair.

24. This wrap helps gather the hair on top of the shank.

25. Tilt the vise jaws so the hook is quartering toward you and you can see the back side of the wing bunch.

26. Divide the hair into two equal bunches with your fingertips. I find I can more easily tell when I have equal bunches by holding them in my fingertips, rather than trying to eyeball the amounts. Grasp the far half of the wing in your material hand down near the base of the hair.

27. Hold the far wing out to the far side of the hook and make four or five tight turns of thread diagonally from the back of the wing on the near side of the hook to the front of the wing on the far side of the hook. These wraps should all be on top of each other and be neatly stacked at the base of the wing clump.

28. Bring the thread under the hook and back up again behind the wings, encircling the hook to anchor the dividing wraps.

29. Grasp the near wing near its base and make several more turns through the center of the wing clumps, this time from the front of the wing on the near side of the hook to the back of the wing on the far side of the hook, forming an X when paired with the first set of wraps. These wraps will divide the wings into two equal bunches and should not create a lot of bulk.

30. Wrap around the shank behind the wings to lock the previous wraps.

31. You might as well have gravity working for you, so tilt the jaws of the vise once again, this time so the far wing is pointing straight up. Post the base of the far wing by wrapping the thread counterclockwise, if tying right-handed, (clockwise, if tying left-handed) around the base of the hair, forming a short post to gather the hair into a single bunch.

32. Wrap from the base of the wing post, up about an eye-length or so, and back down to the base. You don't need to make these post wraps as tall as you did on the Parachute Blue-Winged Olive (BWO), but you do want the wing to end up in a nice even bundle. Posting these hair wings is a fair bit harder than the yarn post on the BWO, but stay with it and develop a technique that works for you. I freehand the post wraps, but only after many years of practice. You may find it easier to hold the wing in one hand and work the thread between your fingertips and the base of the wing to prevent the thread from sliding over the top of the post.

33. Make a single locking wrap around the shank before posting the other wing.

34. Post the near wing, starting at the base and working up the bottom of the wing.

35. Work the thread back down the wing post to the bottom and take a lock wrap around the shank.

36. Position the wings so they are perpendicular to the shank. If your thread posts are tight, you ought to be able to position the wings anywhere your heart desires, but they really should be upright as shown here.

37. Add a drop of Gloss Coat to the thread base, coating the wing posts and the thread underbody.

38. Tie in a length of fine wire at the 60 percent point using the right-angle technique.

39. Wrap back over the wire to the hook bend, keeping the wire along the side of the shank.

40. Peel six or eight peacock herls from the eye of the quill, like you used for the thorax on the Pheasant Tail Nymph. Smaller herl is less bushy and more proportioned to the size of the fly than the bushier herls near the base of the feather. Clip the tips square and tie them in at the base of the tail.

41. Wrap forward over the tips of the peacock herls to just in front of the hook point. Divide the rear 60 percent of the hook shank into thirds, allowing 20 percent of the shank for both sections of peacock herl and red floss.

42. Roll the peacock herl in your fingertips to bundle the herl into a cord, which prevents it from spreading out as you wrap it forward.

43. Wrap the bundled herl forward to the hook point, forming a small ball of peacock just in front of the tail. Tie the herl off with a two tight wraps of thread at the hook point and clip the excess. With longer herl from farther down the quill, you could, in theory, leave the butt ends on the hook and wrap forward over them from the 20 percent point up to the 40 percent point and use the butt ends for the second bunch of herl. But, the smaller herl used here is just too short to form two bunches of peacock without the woody butt ends ruining it. I prefer the velvetlike texture of the smaller herl, so I just deal with tying two separate bunches in.

44. Wrap the thread forward to the 60 percent point on the shank.

47. Wrap forward again over this first layer to the 60 percent point.

45. Tie down the end of a piece of red single-strand floss at the 60 percent point and let the thread hang. If all you have is four-strand floss, separate and use only one of the strands. All four strands create far too much bulk and are a nightmare to work with.

48. Tie it off with two wraps of thread. Clip the excess floss. This method of wrapping the floss forms a double-layer floss body, which is smoother and eliminates the bare spot at the rear of the hook that would have resulted from tying the floss down all the way to the front of the peacock.

46. Wrap the strand of red floss from the back edge of the 60 percent point back to the front edge of the first bunch of peacock herl.

49. Peel another small bunch of peacock herl from the eyed quill, clip the tips square, and tie them in at the 60 percent point, just as you did with the first bunch.

50. Wrap back over the tips of the peacock herl to the 40 percent point on the shank.

51. Roll the herl into a bundle and wrap a second small ball of herl at the front of the floss body. This section of herl should start at the 40 percent point on the shank and extend up to the 60 percent point. Tie the herl off and clip the excess.

52. You should now have three relatively equal body sections: 20 percent peacock herl, 20 percent red floss, and 20 percent peacock herl.

53. Spiral-wrap the wire from the hook bend to the front of the second bunch of peacock with evenly spaced turns. Wrap the wire through all of the peacock and over the floss as if they weren't there. This wire reinforces the herl and the floss and is somewhat optional, but I find the improved durability to be worth the extra step. Tie the wire off at the 60 percent point.

54. Clip the excess.

55. Select, size, and prepare two brown rooster (neck or saddle) hackle feathers. Strip the butt ends of the feathers so the bare portion of the quill is half a shank-length long. Stack the feathers inside to outside so they are spooned like the feathers on the Adams. Lay the butt ends of the hackles in at the front edge of the last peacock herl bunch, but be sure that there is at least half a turn of bare stem behind the front edge of the peacock. The tips of the hackle stems should reach to the back edge of the hook eye.

56. Tie the hackles in at the front of the peacock with the insides of the feathers facing the hook shank. The bare stem before the fibers assures a clean wrap on the first turn of hackle.

57. Wrap forward over the butt ends of the feathers to the back edge of the wing.

58. Bring the thread to the front of the wing and continue wrapping forward over the butt ends of the hackles up to the hook eye.

59. Wrap the thread from the hook eye back to the front of the wing.

60. Wrap back again to the hook eye to smooth out the thread base and build a better transition from the shank to the larger wing butts behind the wing. You will never get it all the way even, but you can make it a bit closer.

61. Wrap both hackles in tight concentric turns from the front edge of the peacock herl to the back edge of the wing.

62. Preen the wings back out of the way and continue wrapping the hackle forward with the next turn right in front of the wing.

63. Make another two or three turns with the hackle feathers up to the back edge of the index point. You should have an equal number of wraps behind the wings and in front, plus or minus one turn.

64. Pull both hackle fibers up above the hook eye and tie them off with two firm wraps of thread.

65. Clip the excess hackle tips as close to the hook as you can, build a smooth thread head over the stubs, and whip-finish the thread. Clip the thread as well, unless you like casting the fly with the bobbin attached.

PATTERN VARIATIONS

H & L VARIANT

Hook:	#8–20 Tiemco 100SP-BL
Thread:	Black 8/0 Uni-Thread
Wings:	White calf body hair
Tail:	White calf body hair
Abdomen:	Stripped peacock quill
Thorax:	Peacock herl
Hackle:	Brown rooster neck or saddle

IRRESISTIBLE WULFF

Hook:	#8–16 Tiemco 100SP-BL
Thread:	Brown 50-denier GSP
Tail:	Elk hock
Wings:	Natural yearling elk hair
Body:	Spun and trimmed deer hair
Hackle:	Mixed brown and grizzly rooster neck or saddle

GTH VARIANT

Hook:	#8–20 Tiemco 100SP-BL
Thread:	White 8/0 Uni-Thread
Tag:	Opal Mirage Tinsel
Wings:	White calf body hair
Tail:	White calf body hair
Abdomen:	Fluorescent green 70-denier Ultra Thread
Thorax:	Black peacock Ice Dub
Hackle:	Mixed brown and grizzly rooster neck or saddle

ADAMS WULFF

Hook:	#8–18 Tiemco 100SP-BL
Thread:	Black 8/0 Uni-Thread
Tail:	Moose hock
Wings:	White calf body hair
Body:	Adams gray Super Fine
Hackle:	Mixed brown and grizzly rooster neck or saddle

AUSABLE WULFF

Hook: #8–18 Tiemco 100SP-BL
Thread: Rusty brown 8/0 Uni-Thread
Tail: Moose hock
Wings: White calf body hair
Body: Cinnamon Caddis Super Fine
Hackle: Mixed brown and grizzly rooster neck or saddle

BLONDE WULFF

Hook: #8–18 Tiemco 100SP-BL
Thread: Tan 8/0 Uni-Thread
Tail: Elk hock
Wings: White calf body hair
Body: Pale yellow Super Fine
Hackle: Ginger rooster neck or saddle

CHAPTER 23

Humpy

MAIN FOCUS

Working with hair • Testing your skills with proportions

I have spent years behind the vise and have tied all sorts of flies for all sorts of fish in all sorts of places, but the Humpy just may be my favorite. Though many consider it difficult to tie, the Humpy was one of the first dry flies I learned to tie. My cousin Danny showed me one when I was about nine years old or so, and I was enamored with the deer hair hump. It just looked so buggy.

The pattern Danny showed me was a Humpy in name only. The tail was deer hair, tied in at the bend and clipped to length; the hump and wings were formed in the conventional manner, by folding the deer hair over from the bend; and the hackle was oversized feathers from whatever you had handy. These were tied on "tiny" size 16 hooks, with hackles that were about size 8. Not to worry, as Dan had a plan. We just cut the wings and

The Humpy is a challenging fly to master, but the fact that it catches so many fish makes it a worthwhile pattern to learn.

The hair body and tail coupled with a heavy hackle collar make the Humpy a great floater, and you can alter the color of the thread underbody to match any bug.

hackle down to length, forming a sort of cube-shaped hackle collar at the front of the fly. The flies looked like little square bits of fluff that had been through a blender, but they still caught the little brookies and browns in the Front Range streams we fished.

I took to the Humpy from that day forward and have tied tons of them since then. The Humpy intrigues me because it is a complicated fly to tie and one most folks would just rather buy. Challenging flies like this are my favorites because they force me to pay attention.

Jack Dennis' *Western Trout Fly Tying Manual* taught many of us Westerners to tie, and the Humpy is a cornerstone of this book, though it was featured in both volume 2 and 3 with entirely different tying steps. I believe this to be because the Humpy has evolved over time, first using deer hair for all the parts, then elk, and finally adding the moose hair and even dubbed bodies. Well, as you know by now, I am not one to leave well enough alone, and I have come up with my own version

of the Humpy, cobbled together from a variety of different tiers' techniques. This new, dare I say improved, Humpy is much easier to tie than the conventional version and eliminates many of the previous "tricks" that made the fly much harder than it needed to be. Although my method eliminates the original version's proclivity for failure, this is still a complicated pattern. Proportions are ultra-important on this fly. If you tie the wings too far forward or back it will throw off the rest of the fly.

The Humpy is the second compilation fly in this book, chosen for the combination of techniques used in its construction. You will use moose hair for the tail like on the Royal Wulff. The hair wings will be mounted similarly to the wing on the Comparadun, then divided and posted as per the Wulff. The body hump will be formed by folding the butt ends of the wing hair forward over a thread underbody, and the hackle will be tied in and wrapped just like you did on both the Adams and the Royal Wulff.

PROPORTIONS AT A GLANCE

BODY HUMP:
Folded forward from
the hook bend to the
60 percent point

TAIL:
One shank-length long

UNDERBODY:
Thread built up to
about ⅓ as wide
as the hook gap

WINGS:
Tied in at the 75 percent
point; one shank-length
long

HACKLE COLLAR:
Tied in at front edge of
body (60 percent point)
and wrapped to hook eye

I tie hundreds of Humpies every winter to fill my box and enjoy every one of them. Fishing the Humpy reminds me of hot summer days with lots of caddis, stoneflies, and terrestrial insects on the water, floating down my favorite river, and picking pockets with my fly along the way. The visibility of the Humpy makes it a great fly for the angler, and the fish attracting profile lets it stand in for a variety of insect forms. The Humpy can match caddis, small stoneflies, mayflies, hoppers, beetles, and anything else the fish mistake it for. The hair body and tail coupled with a heavy hackle collar make it a great floater, and the color of the thread underbody can be altered to match any bug. Bright colors are great attractors, with fluorescent lime green topping my list of favorites. Yellow, tan, orange, and black follow on that list, with the ever-popular red Humpy falling dead last. I don't know why, and I don't need any letters extolling the virtues of red Humpies showing up in my mailbox. If you like red ones, tie 'em up and fish them all you want. Perhaps one day I will fall in love with the red version, but alas, only time will tell.

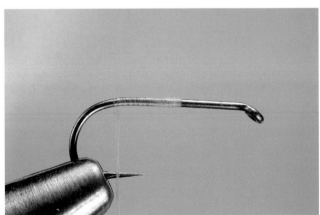

1. Start the thread at the midpoint on the shank and wrap a single-layer thread base back to the bend.

HUMPY

Humpy materials.

Hook:	#8–18 Tiemco 100SP-BL
Thread:	Fluorescent green 70-denier Ultra Thread
Tail:	Moose hock
Wings/Body Hump:	Natural yearling elk hair
Underbody:	Tying thread
Hackle:	Brown and grizzly rooster hackle

Note: Tan, yellow, black, and orange are all great choices. You could even try red.

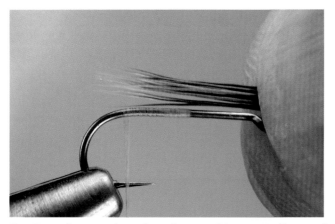

2. Cut, clean, and stack a clump of 15 to 20 fibers of moose hock hair. Measure this clump of hair so that it is one shank-length long.

3. Tie the moose hock in at the bend as you did with the tail on the Royal Wulff. Check your measurement with an identical hook to assure that the tail is one shank-length long.

4. Wrap forward over the butt ends of the moose hair to the midpoint on the shank and clip the butt ends.

5. Wrap the thread up to the hook eye, forming a smooth, single-layer thread base. Return the thread to the 75 percent point.

6. Cut, clean, and stack a generous clump of yearling elk hair. You are going to form two wings from this clump of hair, so the first few flies require a leap of faith to determine how much hair you'll need to form adequate wings. Clean the hair well and make sure the tips are absolutely even. Measure the tips of the hair so they are as long as the shank.

7. Place the base of this clump of elk hair at the 75 percent point so the tips extend forward one shank-length. Make two taut, but not tight, wraps around the hair as you did on the Comparadun. These wraps will just bundle the hair on top of the shank for the moment.

8. Pull the bobbin toward you to tighten the first two thread wraps and flare the hair on top of the shank. Do not let go of the butt ends. Cinch the thread down to compress the hair on the shank.

9. Form a band of thread to anchor the hair tips by wrapping back toward the hook bend while holding the butt ends of the hair in place with your material hand.

10. Do not allow the butt ends to be distributed around the hook shank or let the thread move forward from the 75 percent point, as this will move the wing forward and leave you with no room for hackle in front of the wings.

11. Separate half, or perhaps slightly more than half, of the butt ends of the hair at the back edge of the thread band. I try to make this half the top half of the hair in the butt ends. With your scissors, clip out the top half of this hair as close to the shank as you can. Clip some of the thicker butts. They are just too bulky to form a proportioned shell back on the fly.

12. Using an adequate amount of hair for the wings makes for a bulky tie down. Removing some of this hair lets us alter the body diameter a bit yet keep the fly proportioned and buoyant.

13. Hold the remaining butt ends of the hair taut and above the hook shank with your material hand and wrap back over them with wide, open spiral-wraps to the base of the tail, keeping the hair on top of the hook shank.

14. When you reach the hook bend, cinch the thread down tight over the butt ends of the hair and wrap a narrow band of thread to anchor them on top of the shank.

15. Return the thread to the back edge of the wing clump. Don't yet worry about smoothing off the thread base in between the bend and the wing.

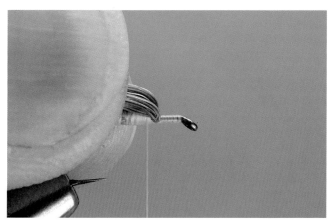

16. Close the thumb and forefinger of your material hand under the wing at the front of the hook shank. Lift your fingers up and back to sweep the wing fibers up and back along the hook shank, as you did on the calf body hair wings on the Royal Wulff. You will assemble the upright, divided hair wings using the exact same steps as you did on the Wulff, but it will be easier to do since elk hair is much more manageable than calf hair.

17. Bring the thread to the front edge of the wing and build a thread dam to prop the hair upright on the shank. Tuck the thread wraps in as tight to the front of the wing as possible.

18. The wing should look like this when you are through.

19. Turn the jaws of the vise so you can see the back-side of the wing. Use your fingers to divide the hair tips into two equal bunches. Wrap the thread to the back edge of the wing and let it hang there.

20. Make five or six wraps diagonally through the center of the two wing bunches, from the back of the wing on the near side of the shank to the front of the wing on the far side. Make sure these wraps are on top of each other and firmly anchored to the hook shank.

21. Before you make the second set of diagonal wraps, wrap the thread once around the hook shank behind the wings to prevent the tension from the previous wraps from influencing the wraps to come. Now, bring the thread under the shank from the back of the wings and up and over the hook at the front of the wings, crossing the wing base along the bottom of the hook. Make five or six more tight diagonal wraps from the front of the wings on the near side of the shank to the back of the wings on the far side and follow them up with an anchor wrap around the shank at the back edge of the wings. These are simple X-wraps, just like you did on the Royal Wulff and Rusty Spinner.

22. Post the base of the far wing by wrapping from the bottom of the hair up about an eye-length and back down again. This post wrap should bundle the hair into an even clump. Make an anchor wrap around the shank before going on to post the near wing.

23. Post the near wing in the same manner as you did above, including the finishing anchor wrap.

24. You should now have two nicely divided, upright hair wings. If your wings are out of position, maneuver them so they are at about a 45-degree angle to each other and at a 90-degree angle to the hook shank.

25. If your post wraps are firm and well-placed, you should be able to maneuver the wing into any position.

26. Wrap back over the elk-hair underbody, forming a smooth thread hump from the base of the tail to the 60 percent point on the shank. You may need to stop every now and again to unwind your thread so it lies flat as you wrap. You want a smooth layer of thread, and it may take several trips back and forth from the 60 percent point back to the bend to form this hump. The thread hump should equal approximately ⅓ the hook gap when measured from the top to the bottom. That is not to say that it should fill ⅓ of the gap, but rather ⅙, as the other half of that will be on top of the shank. Once you are happy with the diameter of the thread hump, leave the thread hanging at the 60 percent point.

27. Pull the butt ends of the elk hair forward over the top of the hook shank and up to the tips of the wings. Hold the butt ends of the elk in your thread hand and give them about a half twist to keep them bundled neatly together. This slight twist shouldn't make the hair into a cord, but just help to hold the hair in a single even bunch and prevent it from sliding down the far side of the hook shank when you bind it down in the next step.

28. Reach under the hook and spin the bobbin to twist the thread so it will bite into the hair better. Hold the elk hair taut above the hook and bring the thread up and over the hair, but do not let the thread pull the hair down to the shank. Make another turn over the hair at the 60 percent point, right on top of the first. Now, reach down and pull the bobbin straight down to pull the hair down on the top dead center of the hook shank. This maneuver is similar to what you did to anchor the front of the wing case on the Hare's Ear. If you don't hold the hair above the hook and just make a wrap or two over it, the thread torque will pull the butt ends of the hair to the far side of the hook.

29. Clip the remaining butt ends of the elk hair as close as you can to the shank.

30. Cover the remaining stub ends of the hump with thread, forming a smooth base for the hackle. Try to cover these butts with as few wraps of thread as possible to minimize bulk.

31. Select, size, and prepare one brown and one grizzly rooster feather. Strip the butt ends of both feathers so there is a half shank-length of bare stem. Place the feathers one on top of the other, with the inside of one touching the outside of the other, just like you did on the Adams. Tie these two feathers in at the same time at the front edge of the hair hump with the concave insides of the feathers facing in toward the hook shank. Be sure some bare stem protrudes behind the tie-in point to eliminate the chance of fibers pointing back on the first turn of hackle. Wrap forward over the butt ends of the feathers to the back edge of the wing.

32. Continue wrapping forward over the butt ends of the feathers up to the back of the hook eye. I have made a minimal number of turns here to help show the path of the thread. Notice that the butt ends of the feathers reach up to the back of the hook eye without any additional trimming. Measure twice, cut once.

33. Wrap the thread back over the stems of the feathers to the base of the wing, cross back under the shank, and continue back to the front edge of the hair hump. Move the thread forward again to the back of the hook eye, anchoring the feather stems and forming a smooth foundation for the hackle all at the same time.

34. Begin wrapping both feathers at the same time. The little bit of bare stem ensures the hackle fibers don't point back.

35. Make three more tight wraps of hackle forward from the back edge of the body to the back edge of the wings. Wrap the hackle as you would the wire on the Brassie, with concentric abutting turns to form a dense hackle collar.

36. Cross to the front of the wings on the underside of the hook shank. The last wrap behind the wings should be smack up against the back edge of the wings and the first wrap in front should be smack up against the front edge. Wrap both feathers two or three more turns to the hook eye and tie them off with two firm wraps of thread. Clip the excess hackle tips flush against the hook.

37. Build a smooth thread head to cover the stub ends of the hackle and whip-finish.

38. The finished fly.

PATTERN VARIATIONS

ORANGE HUMPY

Hook:	#8–18 Tiemco 100SP BL
Thread:	Orange 6/0 Danville
Tail:	Elk hock
Wings/Body Hump:	Natural yearling elk hair
Underbody:	Tying thread
Hackle:	Brown and grizzly rooster hackle

YELLOW HUMPY

Hook:	#8–18 Tiemco 100SP-BL
Thread:	Yellow 6/0 Danville
Tail:	Elk hock
Wings/Body Hump:	Natural yearling elk hair
Underbody:	Tying thread
Hackle:	Brown and grizzly rooster hackle

TAN HUMPY

Hook:	#8–18 Tiemco 100SP-BL
Thread:	Tan 6/0 Danville
Tail:	Elk hock
Wings/Body Hump:	Natural yearling elk hair
Underbody:	Tying thread
Hackle:	Brown and grizzly rooster hackle

RED HUMPY

Hook:	#8–18 Tiemco 100SP-BL
Thread:	Red 70-denier Ultra Thread
Tail:	Elk hock
Wings/Body Hump:	Natural yearling elk hair
Underbody:	Tying thread
Hackle:	Brown rooster hackle

ROYAL HUMPY

Hook:	#8–18 Tiemco 100SP-BL
Thread:	Red 70-denier Ultra Thread
Tail:	Moose hock
Wings:	White calf body hair
Body Hump:	Natural yearling elk hair
Underbody:	Tying thread
Hackle:	Brown and grizzly rooster hackle

CHAPTER 24

Goddard Caddis

MAIN FOCUS

Flaring, spinning, and trimming deer hair

The Goddard Caddis is one of my favorite old-timey flies and a great adult caddis imitation. The hair body keeps the fly afloat much longer than other more conventional patterns, which means it is one of the first patterns I tie on during a late evening river float. I hate having to change patterns or dry my flies after catching a few fish, especially when doing so means missing productive water while drifting down-river. The light color of the natural deer hair body makes this fly visible, and it is a great late evening fly. The hackle collar in front provides lift and allows me to skate it across the surface like the real bugs when they take off and lay eggs.

I remember tying this fly when I was a kid, and vividly recall the trials and tribulations associated with spinning deer hair. One of the biggest falsehoods in fly tying is the notion that you must have a bare hook shank in order to spin hair. To the contrary, I find that a bare

The Goddard Caddis is a superb adult caddis imitation. The deer hair body floats well and is easy to see.

PROPORTIONS AT A GLANCE

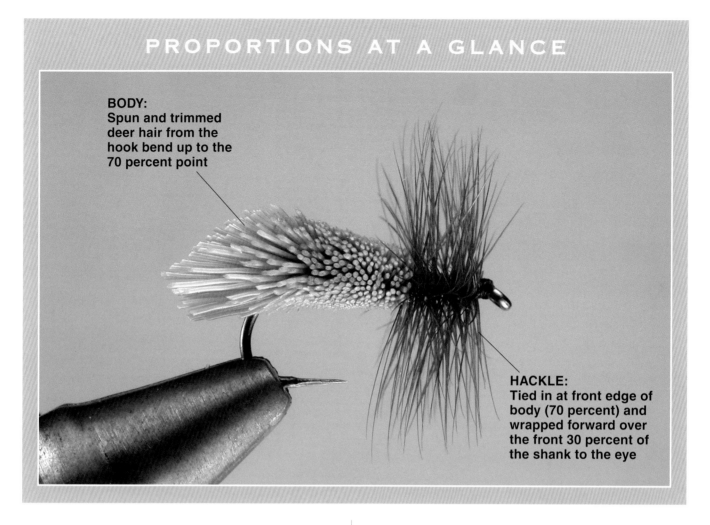

BODY:
Spun and trimmed deer hair from the hook bend up to the 70 percent point

HACKLE:
Tied in at front edge of body (70 percent) and wrapped forward over the front 30 percent of the shank to the eye

shank doesn't provide any texture for the thread and hair to adhere to, and while the hair does indeed spin easier on a bare shank, it also comes apart much easier. A thread base under the deer hair body provides a textured foundation for the hair and results in a more durable fly.

Another misconception is that you need to use the biggest, strongest thread you can to spin deer hair. When I tie spun and stacked deer-hair bass bugs, I reach for the Kevlar thread every time, but in the case of smaller trout flies like the Goddard Caddis and Irresistible, smaller thread creates less bulk, bites into the hair better, and allows me to trim the hair closer to the hook shank without risk of nicking the interior thread wraps. Because of the relatively small amounts of hair on these flies, the strength of the smaller thread coupled with a skillful touch is more than adequate to distribute the hair around the hook.

Hair selection on this fly (and all others) is of paramount importance. Deer hair comes in a variety of colors and textures. The exact color shade of hair is not terribly important, but texture is. You want straight deer

hair that has a large diameter at its butt ends for flotation and a thin wall that will allow the hair to compress easily under thread tension. Hair that has a thicker wall, such as the elk hair you used on the Elk Hair Caddis, is just too hard and thick to compress and flare on the hook. Soft, spongy deer hair from the rump or shoulders of the deer is perfect.

My biggest epiphany on this fly was the fact that I didn't need to spin the first bunch of hair at the back of the hook. When I followed others' directions, the hair would catch and bind on the hook point, preventing it from spinning evenly around the shank. I discovered that if I simply flared the back ends of the first bunch of hair and distributed the rest of it by spiraling the thread through to the front, I could get a dense, durable hair body with the proper shape.

This fly took me many years of practice. I hope that some of these tricks can alleviate any fear you may have about spinning and flaring deer hair. Remember, practice makes perfect, and walking away only assures that you will never learn it. Be strong.

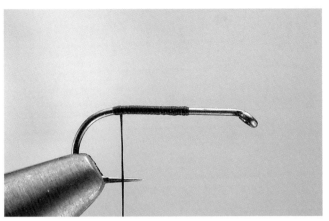

1. Start the thread just in front of the midpoint on the shank and wrap a tight concentric thread base back to the bend. Leave the thread hanging at the hook bend for the time being.

2. Cut a relatively large clump of hair from a patch of deer hair. One of the most common mistakes I see in spun and flared hair flies is using too little hair. It will take a few tries to determine the correct amount of hair, but essentially you are looking for the maximum amount of hair that you can compress on the shank without breaking the thread. The more hair you can pack onto the hook, the better the fly will float and the easier the fly will be to shape when you trim it later. The hardness and diameter of the hair, the size of the fly you are tying, and the strength of the thread you are using will all come into play in determining the amount of hair you use.

Clean all the underfur from the hair. You may want to use a bone comb (a steer-horn comb, that prevents static) to help remove the bulk of the underfur. Clean any short fibers from the bunch as well, leaving a bunch of hair that is all the same diameter and length. You will be trimming the natural tips of the hair off anyway, so cut them off down nearer to the base of the hair leaving only the larger diameter butt ends to work with. This shorter clump of hair will be easier to maneuver on the shank and spins better than the finer tip ends of the hair.

GODDARD CADDIS

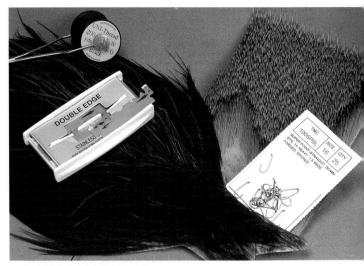

Goddard Caddis materials.

Hook:	#10–18 Tiemco 100SP-BL or 100
Thread:	Black 3/0 or 8/0 for the hair body;
	black 8/0 for the hackle portion
Body/wing:	Spun and flared natural deer body hair
Hackle:	Brown rooster neck or saddle

Note: I use 3/0 monocord for #8–12 Goddards, but I switch to 8/0 thread for the hackled portion even on these bigger flies. For flies from #14 down, I use 8/0 thread throughout.

3. Place this clump of hair on the top of the shank at the bend, with the front half of the hair extending past where the thread is hanging.

4. Make two taut wraps of thread over the hair, one on top of the other. I usually use just a bit of tension on the first wrap to crease the hair and form the groove where the next wrap will go. Do not let go of the butt ends of the hair.

5. While holding onto the butt ends of the hair with your material hand, start to tighten the two wraps of thread down by drawing the bobbin tube toward you and slightly back. The hair will flare as you put more tension on the thread.

6. Continue tightening the thread with steady pressure, all the while holding the butt ends firmly in place at the hook bend. You should feel the thread sink down into the hair and against the shank of the hook, compressing the hair. This first bunch of hair is not spun, but rather flared. This step is done essentially the same as tying in the wing on the Elk Hair Caddis, but with much softer hair that will flare more on the hook.

7. Work the thread tightly around the hook, moving forward in small increments, allowing the thread to distribute the front end of the hair clump around the shank. This is similar to what you did on the Stimulator wing.

8. Do not let go of the back end of the hair clump until the thread has reached the front of the bunch of hair.

9. The hair extending off the back of the shank is flared in place and the hair that extends from the hook bend forward has been distributed evenly around the shank.

10. Press your material hand thumb up against the hair at the hook bend, then pinch the thumb and forefinger of your thread hand against the front of the bunch. Hold the hair in place at the hook bend while you push back with your thread hand to compress the hair bunch on the hook. You'll need to hold the back end of the hair in place with your thumb to keep from pushing all the hair back and down the hook bend. Stroke the distributed hair on the front of the hook so it is perpendicular to the shank. The thread should be hanging at the front end of the hair bunch on the hook shank.

11. The hair should look like this.

12. Clip and clean another bunch of hair and trim the tips as you did with the first bunch. Lay this hair on top of the hook, using your thread hand to overlap the back half of this clump over the front half of the hair already on the hook. The middle of the new bunch of hair should be centered over the thread.

13. Place a turn of thread over this bunch of hair, using your material hand to situate the thread wrap. Cinch this wrap down just enough to crease the hair, forming a groove to guide the next few wraps.

14. Make two more wraps of thread, for a total of three turns, over the top of the first wrap. Draw the thread toward you to bite it down into the hair.

15. The hair should flare a bit with this added tension, but you don't want to pull so hard that you spin it just yet.

16. Grasp the back of the hook shank with your material hand to keep the hook from bending when you apply tension to the thread. Make sure you do not have any of the second bunch of hair in your fingertips as you do this, as you need this hair free to spin when you apply tension to the thread.

17. Draw the thread toward you and just slightly back with even tension, allowing the hair to roll and distribute around the hook shank. Do not yank the thread, just apply steady even pressure and you will see and feel the hair rolling around the shank. If you pay close attention, you will see that you draw the slack from one of those previous three turns of thread completely out of the fly. If you were to try this maneuver with just two turns of thread, the hair would start to spin and then corkscrew out from under the second thread wrap as you drew it tight. Three turns of thread is the key here.

18. You should now have an evenly distributed bundle of hair spun on the front of the shank. Note the spherical nature of this bunch of hair. This is a result of tying the hair down at its exact center, and while it looks impressive here, is really of little importance later. I tie the hair at the center so that when I see this sphere, I know when the hair has spun all the way around the hook.

19. Work the thread forward through the front half of this bunch of hair exactly as you did on the first bunch.

20. Stop the thread just in front of the halfway point on the hook.

21. Pack the two bunches of hair together, forcing the second bunch against the first.

22. Whip-finish and clip the thread. Take care not to bind down any of the hair as you do this.

23. You are about to trim the body/wing of the fly into a tent shape to mimic that of the natural caddis fly.

24. I typically hold the fly in my hand to trim but because that makes photographing the fly so much harder, I will show a general template of what I am shooting for here.

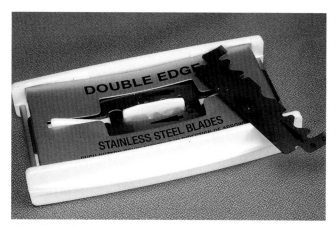

25. Double-edge shaving blades are astonishingly sharp, much more so than single-edge paint scraping blades. I break the blades in half lengthwise so I only have to worry about one side cutting me while I trim the fly. It probably wouldn't hurt to pick up a pack of Band-Aids at the store when you buy the razors to save yourself a trip later.

26. Start by holding the fly with the point of the hook up. Push the blade through the hair from the front of the hook toward the bend. Cut the bottom of the fly as close to the hook shank as you can, but be mindful of the thread on the inside. If you cut too deep, the hair will explode. It's better to first make a shallow cut to establish the parameters, then come back and trim the hair closer to the shank.

27. The trimmed underside of the fly.

28. Work your way around the fly, trimming from the front to the back of the hook.

29. This first round of trimming should result in an angular cone shape. One cut along the bottom, one along each side, and one along the top. Don't worry about the hair extending off the back of the hook yet.

30. Pinch the hair that extends off the back of the hook in your thread hand. Make a cut with your scissor blades, from the bottom of the hook, angled up toward the top to form the back edge of our triangle shape. Again, I am usually holding the fly in this step, but have placed it in the vise here.

31. The first cut of the back of the wing should look like this.

32. Cut across the bottom of the hair at the back of the fly to taper the hair to a point at the rear edge.

33. Round off the edges of the first round of cuts, smoothing the corners, trim the front of the body to a square edge, and smooth out the overall profile of the fly. By the end, you want a cone-shaped body with a tent-like profile.

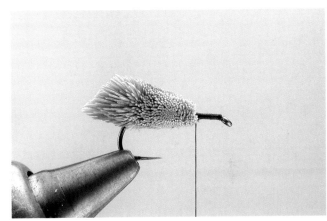

34. Once you are satisfied with the overall shape of the body, attach the tying thread at the hook eye and form a smooth thread base back to the front edge of the hair body.

35. Size, select, and prepare two brown rooster hackle feathers. Tie these feathers in by their butt ends at the front edge of the body.

36. Wrap forward over the stripped stems to the back of the hook eye.

37. Wrap both hackles forward at the same time (like you did on the Royal Wulff). Form a dense hackle collar with six to eight turns and tie the feathers off at the hook eye.

38. Clip the excess hackle tips flush, build a small thread head to cover the stubs, and whip-finish the thread.

39. The original pattern sports a pair of stripped hackle stem antennae protruding from the front of the hackle collar over the hook eye, and while they are undeniably sexy, they just get in the way when I tie the fly on my tippet and I usually end up cutting them off on the water anyway. Older and wiser, I skip the antennae altogether, and the fish haven't cared a bit. If you like the antennae, go ahead and tie them in, but when they tangle up in your clinch knot, don't cuss me out.

Index

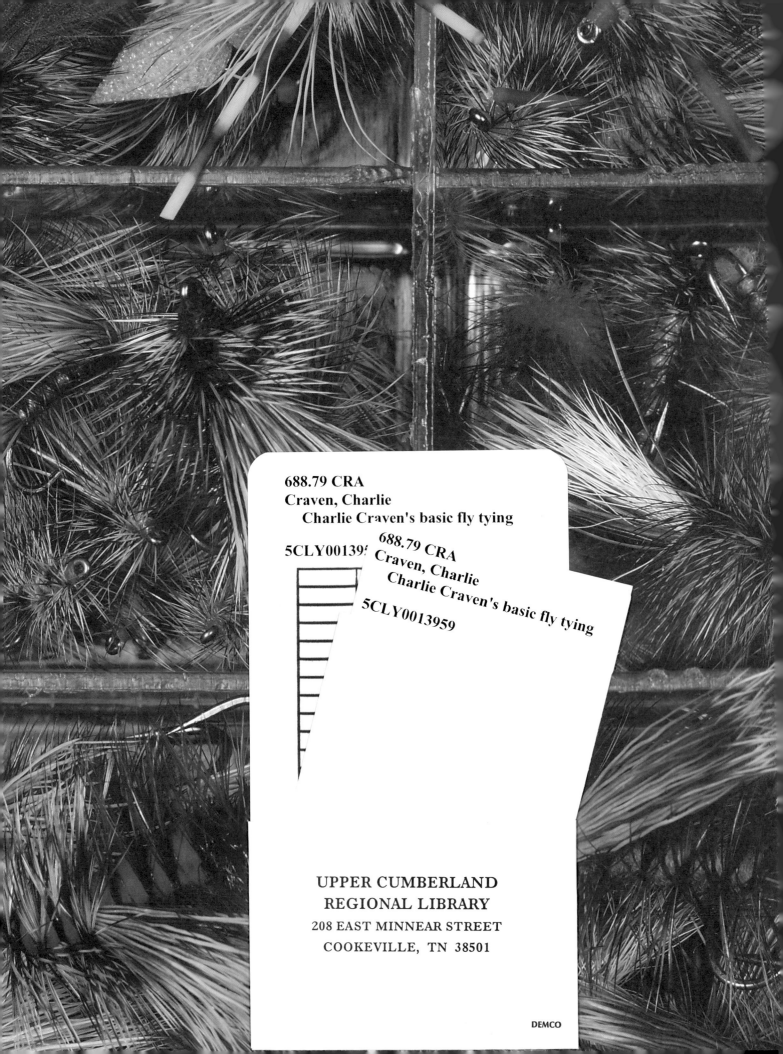